GENESIS
TO
ARMAGEDDON
AND
BEYOND

GENESIS
TO
ARMAGEDDON
AND
BEYOND

The Origin, History, Eternal Purpose, and Final Fate,

of Man, God and the Universe

KEITH GINO BARR

VOICE OF REVIVAL PUBLICATIONS
PONTIAC, MI

GENESIS TO ARMAGEDDON AND BEYOND
BY REV. KEITH GINO BARR

COPYRIGHT © 1990
by Keith Gino Barr
P.O. Box 431022
Pontiac, MI 48343

Scripture references are from the King James Version, unless otherwise noted.

ISBN: 0-9622727-4-4

Library of Congress Catalog Card Number: 90-90436

Printed in the United States of America.

Whereby, when ye read, ye may understand my knowledge in the mystery of Christ

How that by revelation he made known unto me the mystery...

Which in other ages was not made known unto the sons of men, as it is now revealed unto his holy apostles and prophets by the Spirit;

That the Gentiles should be fellow-heirs and of the same body, and partakers of his promise in Christ by the gospel:

whereof I was made a minister, according to the gift of the grace of God given unto me by the effectual working of his power.

Unto me, who am less than the least of all saints, is this grace given, that I should preach among the Gentiles the unsearchable riches of Christ;

And to make all men see what is the fellowship of the mystery, which from the beginning of the world hath been hid in God, who created all things by Jesus Christ:

To the intent that now unto the principalities and powers in heavenly places might be known by the church the manifold wisdom of God,

According to the eternal purpose which he purposed in Christ Jesus our Lord:

Ephesians 3:3-11

TABLE OF CONTENTS

PREFACE

Recently there was quite an uproar over a major motion picture about Jesus. It caused quite a stir among saints and sinners alike. It reminded me of something that has become very plain to me in my 17 years in the ministry. It is a sad fact, even though millions know the story of Jesus Christ, most only know part of the story.

They have watched such movies as King of Kings, Ben Hur, Ten Commandments, the Bible and Jesus of Nazareth. They have heard of how Jesus died on the cross for our sins but if you would ask them why this was necessary, they can't answer. They do not understand His sacrifice or why Jesus is the only way. The general public is very ignorant concerning the Eternal Christ and God's simple plan of salvation. They don't know why there is a Satan, a hell, sin and death or why they were created in the first place. One day soon, Jesus will return to earth and most people don't know why He came the first time. To make matters worse, here was another movie painting an inaccurate picture of Jesus, adding to the public's confusion.

As I reflected upon this appalling fact, I decided to do something about it. I fell to my knees and began to pray. I prayed "Lord, the world does not know the whole story of salvation. Even though it is in the Bible and many preachers and Bible scholars understand most of your plan, the general public does not. They don't really understand who Jesus is and what You are trying to do through Him.

I said "Lord why don't you move on someone to write a book that clearly tells the whole story. A book that will answer all of man's greatest questions, and settle the issues of evolution, reincarnation and other false teachings that challenge the Bible. Let someone write a book that will convey the God of Creation in all of His majesty, splendid glory, intellect, wisdom and power. If they could experience Your glory, they would know that all earthly pleasures pale beside it. Let someone write about Your glory and let it be so real, the reader will want to experience it himself."

"If the book depicted the power of Christ and the glory of the angels it would be like Star Wars and Superman meet the King of Kings. It would not show God, the Father, as some kindly, old grandfather who is mystified by technological things. Rather it would show an all-powerful, all-knowing God in His prime who designs such complex things as atoms, DNA and the universe itself.

It could and should be the most captivating story of all, that one day could be made into a movie. Unfortunately for us, movies are the greatest means of reaching the masses. If made exciting enough, it would reach hundreds of millions, telling the world all about Your glorious plan of salvation. Please move on someone to do this."

To my surprise His spirit spoke to me saying, "You do it."

I was astonished.

I said, "What?"

He repeated, "You do it."

A tidal wave of doubt and fear swept over me threatening to forever drown any hope of this book being completed in a sea of insecurity and unbelief. I felt as if I was a three year old child who had just been given the task to perform some herculean labor. I felt so inadequate and unworthy, as I considered the monumental task which had been set before me. I questioned whether I had the adequate writing skills to do such a job. Then I remembered the old saying, "Whom God calls, He qualifies." If He told me to do it, either I am already qualified or He will qualify me in the process. My doubt gave way to hope and my fear gave way to faith as I realized God does not make mistakes. Somehow, He was going to make this happen.

My years in ministry had taught me how to make any story exciting. In college I was nicknamed *the Storyteller*. It was my job, and I had become an expert in making people interested in a subject (religion) they were not interested in. I knew I could tell the story to make it irresistible reading. I resolved, "Perhaps I had some of the necessary skills after all." I agreed to do it if He would give me guidance and explain to me the things which I did not understand or that were still a mystery to man.

As I prayerfully set out to be obedient, my eighteen years in the ministry, that required constant studying the Bible along with my love affair with science proved invaluable in the writing of this book. However, it still required countless hours of studying new material to finish this book. As I gathered the information, I was presented with a new problem. Should I write it as fiction or non-fiction?

Since my aim was to tell the complete story and convince people of its truth using newly discovered scientific information, common sense, and the Biblical record, I resented my work being labeled fiction. Yet, there were so many things I wanted to discuss which the scriptures only provide scant information. Things such as what actually happened in the Satan's rebellion, who said what, and how they felt were not mentioned.

One possibility was to use certain theoretical stories to help the reader envision what may have happened. These are my theories based on Scripture and by no means would I claim them to be remotely infallible. The theoretical representations are my attempts to reconcile the Biblical record with scientific facts. Fiction would allow me the liberty to tell the story in the most exciting way, but I did not want the reader after he finished to say, "Nice story, but it was merely fiction."

After all, my goal is to inform them of God's divine plan and convince them of the truth of it. This would be done by presenting some of the "infallible proofs" God has provided for modern man. Like most Christians, I assumed that when scientists contradicted the Bible, it was because their information was incomplete. (Archaeologists had previously made similar mistakes.) Even recently scientists have made terrible mistakes based on inaccurate information.

As recently as the 1960's, they swore that the human body had several obsolete organs which they claimed were leftover throwbacks from evolution. These included tonsils, pituitary gland, thalamus and others. They later discovered all of these organs served very important functions.

Astronomers made similar mistakes. Many taught that the planet Venus was completely covered with an ocean of boiling water. This gave it thick cloud formations and made its surface impossible to view from the earth. Later when this view was challenged, bitter debates raged among the worlds leading astronomers, most of whom vehemently swore that Venus, our sister planet, was covered with water. New devices and techniques were created that *proved* Venus was covered with water. The debate was finally settled when a NASA probe visited Venus. It was much hotter than originally expected. Instead of surface temperature of 215°F it was over 800°F. Venus had no world covering oceans, no seas or lakes were ever discovered.

The mistakes of scientists who believe in evolution have been even more pronounced. They readily admit that if God created everything they have no idea how He did it. Therefore, all the studies are based on the assumption that He did not, and all data is interpreted in a manner to reinforce their biased beliefs. They try to ridicule and intimidate anyone who challenges their point of view. As I set out to study this subject, I was surprised at the amount of material that was written that challenges evolution.

Like most people, I had mistakenly assumed there was little or no scientific evidence for creation. I assumed since everything was created supernaturally that it did not involve a natural process and left little or no evidence. To my surprise I discovered the bulk of the evidence is on the side of creation. There was so much scientific information that it was difficult to decide what not to include.

Volumes of material have been written that give modern man all the proof he could ever ask for to convince him of the Bible's veracity. There is a huge debate going on privately among scientists who are becoming increasingly disenchanted with evolution.

Darwin hoped that one day there would be proof for his theory of evolution. Yet, after 100 years not one shred of evidence exist to prove his theory. He knew the fossils did not prove evolution but he hoped that one day evidence would be found that proves it. Although hundreds of thousands of fossils exist, not one transitional fossil exist that would prove evolution.

For example, if animal cells evolved from plant cells, where are the transitionary plant-animal fossil? If birds evolved from lizards, where are the lizard-bird fossils. Evolutionist claim that evolution took place gradually over millions of years. If this were true, there should be as many transitional fossils as there are regular fossils. Instead of hundreds of thousands of transitional fossils, there are none. How can this be? Because evolution is not true. These missing transitional fossils or missing links provide some of the best proof against evolution. The more they look for transitional fossils, they more frustrated they become.

In the more than 100 debates between evolutionists and creationists in recent years, creation scientists have won every one. Well known evolutionist such as Stephen Jay Gould, and Isaac Asimov were stating that since the creationist scientists had won all of the more than 100 debates, the evolutionist should not debate them.

I am deeply indebted to authors such as Henry Morris, John Whitcomb, Scott Huse, Josh Mcdowell and other creation scientists for their work in this field. I also used something far more important than scientific facts. It is said that the experience of one man has far more weight than 30 facts presented by another man. Although this book is not about my life, there are a few personal experiences and observations that were so important, I felt they had to be included in this book. These are things that **I** experienced that **I know were true.** These experiences should not be discarded as fiction.

This information could only be presented in a nonfiction format. Yet, I felt that a totally nonfiction work would not be interesting enough for the already uninterested general public. This was truly "The Greatest Story Ever Told" and deserves to be told in a form that befits its majesty. So what did I do? I merged the two forms.

I used the facts to convince readers of the Bible's truth and what Christian writers call the "sanctified imagination" to help tell the story. This brings it under the heading of Biblical fiction. All the Bible movies are Biblical fiction.

While I have tried to remain as close to the Biblical record and my understanding of the record as possible, the reader is encouraged to read the Bible for himself. Because of space limitations, it is not possible to cover every Biblical story in this book. I am sure, if the reader approaches this book objectively, he or she will be as convinced as I am, that the Bible is indeed true. While I know that this book will be a blessing to many, I do not claim it is infallible. This book is written to shed light and increase understanding of the only infallible book, the Holy Bible, the word of God.

INTRODUCTION

There are certain questions that have plagued mankind for countless generations. Questions that to some, seem to have no answers. Questions that every man, regardless of race, creed or color has asked at some point in his life. Have you ever been troubled about life's great questions and wondered "*Why*? What is the purpose of everything? Does life have meaning? There is great evil in the world. What is the purpose of evil? Why must I die? What really happens to me when I die? When I die is that really the end, or is there something more? Exactly what is death? Is there a hereafter? Will Earth endure forever or will it end in flames? Is all life a series of random occurrences or is there some grand design and cosmic scheme to all of existence? If there is a cosmic scheme, where do I fit in? Is there anyone we can ask who can give us the answers to our questions? Is there anyplace we can go to find such answers?

There is a place where you can find the answers that you seek. There is only one person who can answer these questions. He has already provided the answers! His name is Jehovah. He is God. In His Book it speaks of His grand design, and eternal purpose. The Bible says eye has not seen, ear has not heard, neither has it entered into the heart of man the things that God has prepared for them who love Him. But God has revealed them unto us by His Spirit.

There is a small voice deep inside the spirit of every man. If he listens, he can hear it. It will not speak in the region of a vain mind, but within the spirit. If you become still and listen intently, the "voice" will speak to you and say, "Yes it is true. There is a God and He is the Creator, the Giver of all Life."

Coupled with this is a hunger, a need, a desire to unite with Him. Somehow this "still small voice" lets us know that uniting with God is the purest, most righteous thing that one can do. Somehow it seems so right to find the pathway to God. You may ask, "But how?" The path can seem so confusing. How can one know what to believe? For such important questions, certainly God would provide irrefutable answers. Did He record answers to these questions with directions for the pathway to righteousness? Is there a record?

WOULD GOD LEAVE A RECORD?

There are some people who will say that they believe in a Supreme Being who was the Creator, but they do not believe that He cares about sin. Neither do they believe that He is behind any established religion. They believe that He just made everything and deserted it. Like an uncaring mother abandoning her child He, the embodiment of love, orphaned the universe. Nothing could be more illogical.

If He is good and He created us, then He must desire for us to be good as well. Yet, there are times when God seems indifferent to man. Why is this so? Any fool can see that good is better for everyone than evil. If there was no evil in the world, what a wonderful place this would be.

An intelligent, compassionate, moral, just God would have left something, a record for us that would answer all these questions and more. This record would tell us the purpose of all things. It would have to meet certain criteria.

1. It would be an ancient book or collection of books that would span from the beginning of creation to the end of time. Not only this but it would show and demonstrate Gods dealings with man from the beginning. A loving God would not wait thousands of years before He spoke or dealt with man but would start at his creation.

2. It would claim to be infallible and divinely inspired. It would either be written by God or some of His agents.

3. It would clearly demonstrate that these men were not ordinary men. It could prove through supernatural manifestations to the people of that day that these were men from God. If these men were sent from God, then certainly God would give them accompanying signs. If God sent them, they should either perform miracles or their prophecies should come to pass.

4. If it is to be a book of truth written by holy men inspired by God, it would not cover up or make excuses for their failure. It would tell the good, the bad and the ugly about these men if and when they failed.

5. If this book teaches that God is good, then it must explain the origin of evil. It must also show why a good and all-powerful God would allow it to continue.

6. It would be a book of love; reaching out to all mankind and showing the struggle of good vs. evil. It would extol good over evil; showing the rewards of both good and evil. Because it is written by

a good God, it would show that evil, pain, sorrow, sickness, and death would not endure forever. A good God would cause these things to come to an end.

7. If it is a book of good over evil, there would be much opposition by the forces of evil, who would hate it. They would try to blot out its existence and attempt to prevent others from reading it. Therefore, it would be the most loved and the most hated book of all.

8. Since it has the message for all mankind, it would be a widely known and read book. It would be available to all or most of mankind. It would be translated into most of the languages of the world, easily being one of the best sellers. (The Bible is the all-time best seller, outselling every book every year.)

9. We would not be expected to accept it just at face value, but it would be verifiable by several means.

1. Archaeologically accurate.
2. Historically accurate.
3. Scientifically accurate.
4. Workability.

Even though there would be much opposition to it by the forces of evil, an all-powerful God would have no trouble ensuring its survival and preserving its original content. Although this infallible message would be written by fallible men, it still would present no real problem. An all-powerful, all-knowing God would be able to preserve this book as it was originally written, and there would be no significant errors in His message even after centuries had passed. If necessary, He would use His power to intervene and take control to ensure the preservation of His message. Again, there would be proof of the preservation of His message.

The Bible is the only book that meets all these criteria. If God is a moral and just God, then He must desire for us to be moral as well. A moral caring God would provide us with moral direction. He would give us His "Truth." To believe that He would do otherwise defies all logic.

Pontius Pilate asked Jesus the question "what is truth." Jesus could not answer him then for it was necessary for Jesus to be crucified. One Day Pilate will get the answer to his question: When he stands before Jesus on Judgement Day. He will discover that Jesus is the "Truth." John 14:6, Jesus saith unto him, "I am the way, the truth, and the life: no man cometh unto the Father, but by me."

Every type of religion cannot be true. Especially when they say opposite things. There must be a record, a "Bible" that can intelligently show us the path to God. It is foolish and an exercise in arrogant vanity to believe that a wise, good, just, and powerful God would have created us and left us no record, no rules or no moral direction.

When you examine all the evidence you can see that The Bible is the only book that meets all these criteria. It is ridiculous to believe that a wise, good, just and powerful God, would have created us and left us no direction. No rules or guidance at all for us to live by. A loving God would not abandon His creation. We have the record and the record is true. To believe that He, a good God could care enough to make us and not leave a "Bible" that would meet these criteria, is the epitome of stupidity.

(For further reading on this subject, read my book "Would God Leave A Record?")

GENESIS TO ARMAGEDDON AND BEYOND

Chapter 1
IT IS TIME

For countless, countless ages, they have lived in harmony. During the eternity before creation, in all the cosmos, there are but three beings. Three entities who shall come to be known as, God, the Father, God the Son and God the Holy Spirit. Each one perfect. Each One, all powerful, all knowing and omnipresent. But...

IT IS TIME

For countless millenniums they have lived in total peace, in pure love. There is no strife, nor contention, no hatred, no bitterness nor evil. There is nothing in all of existence except themselves, but...

IT IS TIME

There is nothing in all of existence except this Holy Trinity. There is not one bird to sing, nor an angel with wings. In all of space and time could not be found one grain of sand; as strange as this may seem to the mind of man. Nor was there one ray of light or any creature for it to give sight. But now...

IT IS TIME ..

... FOR TIME.

IT IS...

...THE TIME FOR CREATION!!!

IN the beginning God created the heaven and the earth.
Genesis 1:1

Science teaches us that time, space and matter are so closely related that one cannot exist independent of the other. That is why although the Bible teaches that God is eternal and has always existed, time itself began only when God created the universe. This was not only the beginning of creation, but the beginning of time as well. So you see that even the first Scripture in the Bible is scientifically accurate. Thus, The Beginning.

IN the beginning God created the heaven and the earth.
Genesis 1:1

For untold eons the Trinity has been alone, but now it is time for new life to begin. God, the Father, God the Son, and God the Holy Spirit are in perfect agreement, as they prepare to begin the creation of all that will be. There will be suns, moons, stars, planets, angels, man, and woman. Their purposes and designs have been agreed upon before they begin.

From the very first chapter in the Bible it hints about the Trinity. The word God that is used here and more than two thousand other times in the Bible, is translated from the Hebrew word "Elohim." This is the plural form of the word god which is "Eloi." It is a plural word with a singular meaning. There are three separate equal entities which together comprise the one God. The Son will preform the task of creation under the direction of the Father.

Hebrews 1:1,2 God... Hath in these last days spoken unto us by his Son, whom he hath appointed heir of all things, by whom also he made the worlds;

The Holy Scriptures teach that the Son, who is also called the Word made everything.

John 1:1-3 In the beginning was the Word, and the Word was with God, and the Word was God. The same was in the beginning with God. All things were made by him; and without him was not anything made that was made.

The Bible also says in Ephesians 3:9

"...God, who created all things by Jesus Christ."
So powerful is He that He needs no device, no external force or much effort, to create all that will be. To create the matter of the entire universe, all He has to do is exercise His incalculable

power. The Godhead is the only One who can truly create matter or energy. Not since creation has anyone observed creation or destruction of matter. One of the laws of physics is that matter and energy can neither be created nor destroyed, but they can be changed from one form to another. All matter is made up of energy. Yet energy cannot be created. Where did it come from? It came from God.

The Father generates the necessary energy to form creation. Perhaps the energy was once a part of Him. If so, that would explain why He always has control over everything. Because it was once a part of Him, He always has control. Creation requires a tremendous amount of energy. We have come to define the relationship between matter and energy as $E = mc^2$. How does He release the energy and create matter? He unleashes these tremendous forces by speaking the word and commanding it to be so.

Psalms 33:6 By the word of the LORD were the heavens made; and all the host of them by the breath of his mouth.

As He prepares to begin, it is decided that such a magnificent event as creation must be witnessed; hence the first thing created are the holy angels.

Angels, Angels, Angels,

Indescribably beautiful, brilliant and awesome to behold are the angels. Most with human features, some with beastly features and all with powers that beggar human comprehension. God the Son creates them with different degrees of power which determine their rank. There are trillions and trillions of them. While the actual number of them is not known to man, it is as vast as the number of stars.

They all are created perfect. Each one given a different name. Gabriel, Michael and Lucifer are three of the hundreds and hundreds of trillions of angels. Each one is immortal. Each one perfect and given an indescribably beautiful voice. Each one gifted with a free will. Most will use their free will to serve the Trinity forever. Some will use their free will to go down the path of darkness.

Eventually, God will make creatures that will be able to live under the sea, under the ground, above ground and in the air. Many will especially suited for their environment. Angels will be the only creatures that will be able to go anywhere. They are the creatures that are most like God.

God had given each of the angels tremendous powers. They have all been blessed with the gift of flight. Only the seraphims have wings. The rest of them do not need wings to fly. And fly they can- faster than the swiftest bird, faster than a speeding airplane, faster than the speed of sound, faster still than the blazing comets, and faster than light itself. This is necessary, for they will fly across the universe on errands for the Father.

They can travel anywhere in the universe. Neither the poison methane and ammonia atmosphere of Jupiter nor the airless barren-ness of space can bother them, for they need not breathe. Neither do degrees of extreme temperatures faze them. They can endure extreme temperatures whether it is the extremely cold temperatures of space (-269° Fahrenheit) or the depths of the hottest star (Rev. 16:8).

They also can become so dense that nothing can hurt them or intangible so they can pass through anything. They have the ability to change their size and appearance. They can appear as mortal men or as bright as a star, but most of the time they are invisible to human eyes. They have supernatural strength.

They can also fire deadly beams of force from their hands (II Sam 24:15,16) or project an invisible shield of force to protect God's people. For most intents and purposes they are virtually invulnerable. They also have the ability to bend time and space. A sufficient number of them can destroy an entire planet.

One day God will command four angels to go to the four weather quadrants of the earth. Their mission is to completely stop the wind from blowing on the earth. This will send a worldwide famine to punish unrepentant men (Rev. 7:1). The heat from the sun and the rotation of the earth is what causes the wind. The amount of power necessary to counteract these forces is nigh incalculable.

With the tremendous forces they unleash, it is easy to under-stand why they are not flesh and blood. No human can do the things that they can do. No flesh and blood person can endure heaven or the rigors of space. That is why there will be a resurrection when the bodies will be changed. (I Corinthians 15). Even though at times they have disguised themselves as humans, they are not human. That is not their natural state.

Many of them are like Gabriel. Their skin is the color of beryl (yellowish-green) and their arms and legs are the color of fine brass.

(Dan 10:26)   Yellow-green is right in the middle of the visible electromagnetic spectrum.   Their eyes are red like fire.

Since their eyesight is totally different from ours, (our eyesight is quite limited) and they can see different frequencies along the electromagnetic spectrum, they may see themselves differently than they would appear to us.

Light is a form of electro-magnetic radiation.   The different forms of electro-magnetic waves are alternating electric current, long-wave radio waves, short-wave radio waves, infrared rays (heat), visible light, ultraviolet rays, x-rays, gamma rays and cosmic rays. Visible light only comprises 3% of the electro-magnetic spectrum. That means humans can only see 3% but the angels can see the full spectrum.

We do not know what the angels bodies are made of, but their bodies are of different material than ours.   Perhaps their arms and legs are different colors because they possibly generate their tremendous powers through their limbs.   Usually when a person saw them in their natural state the angels radiated so much power that the spirits of the people were overcome, and he/she was knocked unconscious. (Ezek 1:28, Dan. 10:8, Rev. 1:17).

As great as their power is, it is not without limits.   Only God is omnipotent.   Angels can be bound and trapped by God or other angels.   I know to some people, all these abilities may sound like something that was taken out of a comic book but actually the reverse is true.

The truth is, these abilities were described and recorded in the Bible, thousands of years before anyone ever heard the term, superhero.   When Superman was created in the early forties, many people felt they had stolen the idea from the Bible.   Superman was supposed to be some type of angel because of his tremendous powers. If you read through the Bible, it will amaze you when you read some of the things that angels can do.   God gave the angels all these powers and a free will.

God, the Father, decided He did not want mere robots to worship him, but beings with a will of their own.   He wanted beings who would worship Him from the very depths of their souls.   He wanted beings who would serve Him of their own free will, help Him maintain the order of the universe, and help minister to the creatures less than themselves.   Of course there is a problem when there is a freedom of choice.   You have the freedom to choose evil.

Some of the powers they exhibit in the Bible may only be temporary gifts from God for special purposes. When the Bible speaks about the word *anoint* it also means to temporarily empower.

For instance, Samson did not have his great strength all the time. He only had it when the Spirit of the Lord would come upon him and empower him in certain situations (Judges 13:25, 14:6, 14:19, 15:14). This anointing was not limited to Samson alone. Many others were temporarily anointed by the Lord to do something incredible. So it is possible that this is true to some extent for the angels.

This seems more realistic, because some of their powers are so fantastic it is difficult to imagine them having these powers to use at their discretion, considering they have a free will. But with God's permission, they even have the ability to do such things as alter time itself (Rev. 10:6).

We do not know at what point prior to Creation the angels were created. We only know that they were present and in unity at the start of Creation.

First Day

If you decide to build a house, you must first determine its design and features. After the design has been completed (and you know what it will look like outside and in), then you know what to build. However, before you can build, you must know all the parts that make up the house.

If you do not know all the necessary facts about the building materials (what are they, what goes where, how to assemble them) then the house can never be completed. Just as the most elaborate builder must first start with such basic information as the difference between a nail and a screw, likewise the Trinity first designed and built the smallest particles of nature.

As they prepare to begin creation, it is decided that the atom will be the basic building block of all matter. Yet, what will the matter be made of? All matter is basically electrical in nature. Matter will exist in four states; solid, liquid, gas, and plasma. There will always be such a strong relationship between matter and energy, that matter can be converted back into energy.

God, the Father, prepares to begin His part of creation. Before the Trinity, nothing ever existed. Aside from themselves and the angels they have created, there was nothing in all of existence. Not one grain of sand, not one ray of light, not one atomic particle exist, or one erg of energy is present in all of existence. Now The Godhead prepares to create a universe.

As the Trinity prepares to begin the creation process, all the angels watch with great anticipation. The Father has planned it all out and completed the precise calculations.

For one last time, God, the Father, looks around at the great emptiness of the cosmos. An endless sea of angels watch in hushed anticipation as He, the Lord of Eternity, prepares to begin. How do you create something from nothing? How will He do it? From His own body, He releases the necessary energy to create all that will be.

Like a gigantic living star, He generates the energy from his own body. God, the Father, begins to release the awesome energy for creation. Endless streams of power seem to flow from Him to every corner of the universe. It is energy in its purest form, without heat, without light. Everything will be made up of His energy. He is The Heavenly Father. The fabric of Creation was once part of His body. Since it is an extension of His energy, it will also remain under His absolute control. As easily as a man controls the fingers of his hand, He will have absolute control over every atom, every particle of creation. No wonder He says it is all His.

Psalms 24:1   A Psalm of David. The earth is the LORD'S, and the fullness thereof; the world, and they that dwell therein.

Creation of solid matter requires a tremendous amount of energy. For instance, there is enough energy in one brick, to equal that of an atomic bomb. If you could suddenly release the energy in a brick, it would cause a nuclear explosion equal to an atomic bomb. This is how atomic bombs work. An atomic bomb is a detonation of a mass of uranium^{238} about the size of a brick. The gigantic explosion is caused by the atoms brick-sized piece of uranium being split. Uranium was used because of the huge size of its atoms, making it easier to split. Currently not all the energy is released in an atomic bomb. The uranium's atoms are split in an atomic bomb. Its large uranium atom is split and changed into the smaller atom, plutonium. If you have sufficient power, you can detonate any type of solid matter this way.

If it requires that much power to make a brick, think of what it takes to make a mountain. Think of the amount of energy it requires to make the world. Only God has the power to do this! The amount of energy required for all solid matter is an exact formula. That formula is $E = mc^2$. This means the amount of energy required to make an object, energy measured in ergs equals the objects mass, multiplied by the velocity of light to the second power. ($c = 3 \times 10$ billion centimeters per second.) This will give you the amount of energy measured in ergs that is contained in all solid matter.

Throughout the universe, across unimaginable distances, He places the energy for creation. The energy that will be turned into suns, moons, planets and stars is placed throughout the cosmos. In this energy state everything is useless. It is without form and void. There is no gravity, no particles of any kind. Only the necessary power is released to make the universe.

It is.., THE BEGINNING.

It is now time for the next phase of creation.

Galaxies without end, and the celestial bodies within,
can you imagine how it was to begin
Father, Son and Holy Ghost,
in view of their angelic host,
created stars, sun and all that you see,
in one glorious week of eternity.

It is time for the second One of the Godhead to begin His part in creation. God the Son, begins to use His power to form the energy into the solid particles that will become the atoms. As great as the required amount of energy is to form particles, it requires an equal amount of energy to hold all things together. He begins to form the nuclear particles.

The Father has Jesus to form atoms which resemble miniature planets with moons revolving around them. These atoms form the elements. Everything that is made or will be made whether living or nonliving, water or air, plant or animal, man or metal will be made entirely of the elements. It is the atomic structure of every element that determines all of its characteristics. Because the Son forms every particle, which in turn forms every atom, which forms every element, there is nothing that is made without Him.

John 1:3   All things were made by him; and without him was not any thing made that was made.

Creation is making something out of nothing. Without a binding force atoms will not remain intact. Without something to hold all the atoms together, all of creation would dissolve into nothingness.

Colossians 1:17　And he is before all things, and by him all things consist (held together).

The physical laws that will govern this reality have been discussed and decided upon. Laws that will govern such things as gravity, magnetism, electricity, electromagnetic radiation, and nuclear fusion which allow suns to burn in airless space. The physical properties and characteristics of every atom, element, particle, object and heavenly body are determined by the Trinity.

Christ decides to make the meson. These particles in the nucleus of the atom bind it together with incredible force. Some of them are the electron, positron, photon, proton, neutron, neutrino, and meson. Altogether, there are more than 200 sub-atomic particles. The electrons circle the nucleus of the atoms many thousands of times a second, forming a sphere around it. This is what gives the atoms most of their substance.

The electron circles the nucleus of an atom similar to the way the moon circles the earth. However in the atom the distance is much greater. If the nucleus of an atom were the size of a baseball, the electron would circle 1/4 of a mile away. The distance between the nucleus and the electron is empty space.

There is so much space between the atoms that if the electrons and nuclei in the human body were packed so tight there would be no space between them, the body would shrivel to a dot so small that you would need a magnifying glass to see it. If you took the entire earth and packed all the electrons and nuclei so tight there would be no space between them, the earth would be the size of a basketball.

The outer layer of electrons or shell, in the atom is not bound as tightly as the inner layers. This allows for more chemical reactions. Atoms combine and form molecules.

A molecule is the smallest particle of an element or compound that can exist in the free state and still retain the characteristics of the element or compound. If an electron in the outer layer of a molecule is split through heat or friction, this will cause the electron to split into some of its component parts. It will give off photon particles (light) and energy in the form of heat (infra-red rays). This will be called fire.

Only the outermost layer (shell) of molecules can be destroyed by fire or burning. The inner shells of atoms are bound so tightly that fire can never destroy it. If not, every time something burned, it would be like an atomic bomb exploding. Only the outermost layers are burned, releasing a small amount of the objects potential energy.

God determines the properties and characteristics of every particle, element, and everything in creation. We know this is true not only because He is all-knowing but, if He didn't predetermine what they were going to make, then someone else must have determined it for them. For example, when He said, "Let there be Light," if He did not fully understand what was going to be created, then those words were a magic spell. And what was going to come about was predetermined by a greater and wiser force; who set the laws for that spell. We know that the Bible teaches there is no magic and there are no powers or anything that exist that was not created by Him (Jesus).

"..All things were created by him and for him."
Colossians 1:16

Hebrews 1:1, tells us that God, the Father, had God the Son, to make the worlds. So we can see from these Scriptures and Hebrews 1:2, that God, the Father, was the planner, engineer, architect of creation which was a gift for God the Son, who was the builder of it all.

There are some people who would take issue with the idea that God planned everything to this degree. But nothing could be more ridiculous. Some people would say, "God didn't have to plan anything, He just spoke it and it was done." While we know He did create the heavens with the breath of His mouth (Psalm 33:6), He still has to know precisely what He is doing every time He uses His power. Otherwise He could accidentally destroy everything.

For example, suppose you ask God for power to help you make it through the day. He hears your prayer and decides to answer. But because He does not know precisely the limits of the human body and how much power to give you, He could easily, accidentally fill you with so much power that your body explodes or turns into a star and destroys the world. So we see that God must have infinite wisdom, to control His infinite power. The greater the power, the greater the understanding and control of that power must be, to prevent unwarranted destruction.

The Bible tells us that God created the universe using wisdom or scientific laws, and not just mystical ones.

Proverbs 3:19 The LORD by wisdom hath founded the earth; by understanding hath he established the heavens.

This statement was made at a time when men thought that the world was based on mystical laws. The growth of trees, the rain falling, all seemed to be governed supernaturally. Although God is the ultimate source of all these things, He set up a system which we call nature that governs all these things. We now know that the universe is based not on mystical laws, but scientific ones.

The role of wisdom was so vitally important in the creation of the universe, Solomon personified it in book of Proverbs.

Proverbs 8:22-32 The LORD possessed me in the beginning of his way, before his works of old.
{23} I was set up from everlasting, from the beginning, or ever the earth was.
{24} When there were no depths, I was brought forth; when there were no fountains abounding with water.
{25} Before the mountains were settled, before the hills was I brought forth:
{26} While as yet he had not made the earth, nor the fields, nor the highest part of the dust of the world.
{27} When he prepared the heavens, I was there: when he set a compass upon the face of the depth:
{28} When he established the clouds above: when he strengthened the fountains of the deep:
{29} When he gave to the sea his decree, that the waters should not pass his commandment: when he appointed the foundations of the earth:
{30} Then I was by him, as one brought up with him: and I was daily his delight, rejoicing always before him;
{31} Rejoicing in the habitable part of his earth; and my delights were with the sons of men.
{32} Now therefore hearken unto me, O ye children: for blessed are they that keep my ways.

All is in readiness.   The creation process will as with any activity on a nuclear level, (fission or fusion), create tremendous amounts of heat.   So much heat, that centuries after the earth is created it would still be to hot for anything to live on it.   This will never do for the earth must be created in six days.

Even the dissolving of the universe would release tremendous amounts of energy.   It would be like one gigantic atomic bomb had been detonated.   This is exactly how Apostle Peter described what will happen when God eventually destroys this universe.

II Peter 3:10 But the day of the Lord will come as a thief in the night; in the which the heavens shall pass away with a great noise, and the elements shall melt with fervent heat, the earth also and the works that are therein shall be burned up.

11 Seeing then that all these things shall be dissolved, what manner of persons ought ye to be in all holy conversation and godliness,

Notice how he, by the inspiration of the Holy Spirit, described exactly the effects of the matter of the universe going through a fission (dissolving process).   He described it exactly as he should have.   The dissolving of the universe would cause all of the energy in matter to be released.   The universe would be turned into one gigantic atomic bomb.   The Apostle Peter gave an accurate description of this event. He described a great noise caused by the explosion, the fervent heat that would dissolve all the elements and the destruction of the earth and the entire universe.   This is incredible when you realize this was written 1900 years ago by a simple man who had no concept of nuclear physics.   (Note* by the time Jesus does come back, with the destruction of the ozone layer, toxic waste problems, land, sea, and air pollution it looks like we are going to need a new earth.)

How does the Trinity decide to deal with the problem of the great heat caused by creation?   Although I am certain that they could have used many different means to correct this particular problem (the most of which would be beyond human comprehension) there is one way that would help solve other problems while correcting this one. Having just made all physical and natural laws (or at least something for them to govern) it would be only natural that He would invoke a process that would use them.   God is not anti-natural.   He made the natural world. It is even possible that He was anxious to use some of His newly created laws of physical science to deal with the problem of cooling the earth in one day, which would normally take millions of years.

Ironically according to the Biblical record, God decides to use the same substance that we use to cool our nuclear plants today. It is in great abundance and almost everything contains a significant proportion of it. It is easily managed and very simple to make. It's atomic weight is 18. It is made from two of the simplest elements. Two parts hydrogen and one part oxygen. Its chemical formula is H_2O. Its common name is ... water.

As the Godhead begins, the Word (Jesus) speaks and at His command millions of cubic square miles of oxygen come into existence. Next, He creates even more hydrogen. Hydrogen will also be needed to make the millions of suns He will create. To this day hydrogen is the most abundant element in the universe. As soon as the super-heated hydrogen comes in contact with the oxygen, the resultant effect is, across millions and millions of square miles, water explodes into existence!

It is such an awesome feat that the angels shout for joy at this magnificent sight and they begin to sing. God described this event later to Job in the book of Job, Chapter 38. God has created enough water to cool all the planets that He will later make. He then places it in its predesignated positions to prepare for the earth and the rest of the worlds that Christ will make shortly. The energy for the earth is now placed beneath this great body of water.

Jesus speaks and a ray of power strikes deep within this great ocean of the water. Slowly, beneath this huge dark body of water that is millions of miles long, the earth begins to form. In this state it is pure energy. In this stage there is no cohesiveness because there is no type of attraction, gravimetric or otherwise, within it. It is useless in this present state. It is without form and substance.

Genesis 1:2 And the earth was without form and void; and darkness was upon the face of the deep. And the Spirit of God moved upon the face of the waters.

Next He begins to change the energy into solid matter by somehow turning them into sub-atomic particles. The relationship between matter and energy is $E = mc^2$. They are changed into protons, neutrons, electrons, mesons, neutrinos and others. Just as it takes great heat to weld steel plates together, so does it require an even greater heat and energy to fuse these particles together. As these atoms begin to form, the temperature is above 27,000,000° F and increasing rapidly. These particles unite and begin to form the different elements.

Now this energy has become solid matter. These particles have become atoms which are now the elements. These elements comprise the earth. Because of the heat caused by its initial creation, the earth is so hot that it is liquid and unsuitable for life.

It grows outward because Jesus keeps adding material inside. This way the outer layer is cooled first leaving the inside molten. He begins to form it into a circle. He lays the foundations of the earth. Since there is no heat in space, the Holy Spirit acts immediately. He moves upon the newly created water and circulates it to keep it from freezing in the sub-zero temperatures in space.

The super-heated earth is slowly cooled by the icy cold waters circulated by the Holy Spirit. It is minus two hundred degrees Fahrenheit (-200°F) below zero in space. Therefore, the Holy Spirit has to move these millions of miles of water at thousands of miles per hour to keep it from freezing. So hot was the earth that to this day most of its interior is still molten, thousands of years later.

...And the Spirit of God moved upon the face of the waters.

Genesis 1:2

The Hebrew word *rachaph*, translated *moved* here does not mean to slightly push; but to vibrate, fluctuate or circulate at tremendous speeds. As these waters circulate around the newly formed earth, some of its elements mix with the pure water and becomes seawater. This is why seawater contains every known chemical element. Many of these elements are salts which gives seawater its salty taste. The U.S. extracted one of these salts, bromine from the ocean in World War II to make aviation fuel.

The Holy Spirit is moving like a wind covering this body of water. Since He moved with enough force to move across the entire surface or face of this huge body of water at colossal speeds, the water itself would have an enormous force or current, capable of moving the earth.

Because the earth is still liquid as the water circulates around it, this causes the earth to move also. Gradually this mass of melted earth begins to cool. As it does, some of the water begins to cut deep into it, forming huge impressions. The Holy Spirit hovers over the body of water that covers the earth. The Holy Spirit broods as it controls the circulation of the water that is shaping the earth.

In some places the water cuts a few feet, and some hundreds of feet deep. Some places it piles up earth. This is how hills and valleys and great mountains were created. As the water circulates around the newly formed earth at cyclonic speeds, it causes it to rotate on its axis at its present speed of more than 1,000 miles an hour. This is precisely the right speed. For example, if the earth rotated at 200 miles an hour, all vegetation would burn up during the day and freeze at night.

Much of the water is turned into steam that carries many particles of the newly formed elements high above the earth, forming our atmosphere. Lava (molten earth) is rich in nitrogen. With all the earth being covered with lava that would explain how so much of it got into the atmosphere. The air is 78% nitrogen, 21% oxygen and the remaining percent is made up of small amounts of argon, neon, carbon dioxide and other elements.

Nitrogen is necessary for all plant and animal life. It is part of all protein foods and protoplasm. Have you ever noticed how green everything is after it rains? When it rains the water carries nitrogen back into the soil enriching it so the plants can grow. Every time it rains it is replenishing the soil.

Nitrogen dilutes the oxygen in the atmosphere and hinders combustion. Without it you could not light a match in your house without the whole house bursting into flames, then your whole block would go up in flames! Another reason that we can be grateful that the air is not pure oxygen, is no human can breathe 100% oxygen for more than a few hours and live.

Some of the newly created air mixes with certain particles, condenses and forms the beautiful clouds. Some are white and beautiful, others are dark and imposing. Until the advent of the airplane men believed that the clouds were so high, that once you passed them, you would reach into the heights of heaven. Heaven to them meant space, or dwelling place of God (or gods). From the ground it seems that the clouds are very high, but if you have ever ridden in a jet you will notice that the clouds are actually very close to the earth, almost seeming to hug the ground in proportion to the rest of the atmosphere.

No wonder that when God described this to Job, He said the clouds appeared to him as a garment. And dark clouds as a swaddling band for the newborn earth. God had to tell him this, because there is no way Job or any man in his time could have conceived of this, viewing the clouds from the earth! However, it is easy to see when you are viewing them from 20,000 feet in the air. Before the jet age, no man had ever seen the clouds from this vantage point. As the earth continues to form, it is important to realize that none of this is by chance, but all of it is planned by God.

Even after the earth has cooled sufficiently so that no more water is turned into steam, there still is so much water that the earth is completely submerged. So hot is the newly formed earth, that it must remain underwater for two days before it is cool enough to support any life.

How does the Bible say the earth is suspended? Not by a Titan named Atlas as the Greeks thought. Nor was the sky held up by mountains or invisible pillars as Muhammad wrote in the Koran. These people thought the earth was flat and all the universe was just a small room. The earth was the bottom and the sky was the ceiling. However the Bible said, God sits on the circle of the earth.

Isaiah 40:22   It is he that sitteth upon the circle of the earth, and the inhabitants thereof are as grasshoppers; that stretcheth out the heavens as a curtain, and spreadeth them out as a tent to dwell in:

What does the Bible say holds up the round earth?

Job 26:7 He stretcheth out the north over the empty place, and hangeth the earth upon nothing.

Now the earth has reached its full size. It is a staggering 7,918 miles in diameter. Earth's surface area today is 196,950,000 square miles. It is capable of supporting billions of people, not counting the multiplied billions of other creatures who shall call this planet home. This is especially remarkable when you consider that today 3/4 of its surface is covered with water. If you think this was something, wait to you see what He does next!

Chapter 2

LET THERE BE ...

Prior to this time if we could have been there, we would have seen very little of this because there was no light. The Holy Trinity nor the angels needed light to see. Their powers of perception go far beyond anything we could conceive, but man and most of the life that He would create would depend upon it.

So the Lord Jesus speaks, "Let there be Light" and immediately 93 million miles away from the earth, it happens! It is a phenomenal explosion! God had created a sophisticated mix of hydrogen, oxygen, carbon, nitrogen, and other gases. He starts a nuclear chain reaction at the center of these gases and the sun is created!!! It is a giant nuclear furnace. It is caused by a nuclear reaction creating a fusion process in the midst of some of the remaining hydrogen from when He created the water.

It is a mind-boggling 865,000 miles in diameter. It is so big it weighs 322,000 times more than the earth. It is an unbelievable 1,300,000 times bigger than the earth. The sun gives off heat, light and harmful radiation. Its surface temperature is 12,000 degrees Fahrenheit. In its center it is estimated to be 27,000,000 degrees Fahrenheit. It is estimated that the sun loses 4,000,000 tons of hydrogen a second in the nuclear fusion process. But still at that rate it would take 35 billion years before it consumes its fuel. In contrast if the sun had been made of coal, it would have burned out in a mere 1,500 years.

So powerful is the sun, that one of its flames (some of them reach a distance of almost 80,000 miles) is equivalent to a hundred thousand hydrogen bombs! If not for the newly created atmosphere, the radiation would have made the earth incapable of supporting life. This is why it was necessary to create the earth first. Eight minutes after the sun is created the first rays of light strike the earth. As God watches the light from the first morning strike the earth, He watches the impressions made in the light by objects. These impressions cause shadows. He would later describe this to Job in Job 38:14 The impressions made by light was similar to the impression that a seal makes in clay. The earth is continuously moving as the light strikes it. No wonder God described the effect as, *it is turned as clay to the seal.*

The side of the planet away from the earth is in complete darkness. The rotation of the earth causes each part to have a day and night effect. After the 1st day God looked over all His works and saw that it was good and He was well pleased.

Second Day

On the second day, the earth has cooled sufficiently that God can remove the excess water from the earth. He says let there be a space between the waters. God divides the waters of the earth from the rest of the waters. He calls this space between the waters, Heaven. When the Bible talks about heaven, it is talking about one of the three heavens; the stratosphere, interstellar space and finally the Heaven which is His home.

God separates the earthly waters from the rest of the waters, and He finishes forming the clouds and our atmosphere. Some of the water is placed high above the earth forming an invisible vapor barrier. This has a greenhouse effect that traps heat and makes the entire earth a tropical climate. That is why palm trees and all manner of tropical plants have been found frozen under ice in Polar Regions.

Scientists have studied and written much about the effects of this vapor canopy that once existed above the Earth. Henry Morrison in his book The Genesis Record writes that it would accomplish the following things:

[1] **1. Since water vapor has the ability to transmit incoming solar radiation and to retain and disperse much of the radiation reflected from the earth's service, it would serve as a global greenhouse, main-**

---

[1]Henry Morrison, The Genesis Record (Grand Rapids, Mi: Baker Book House, & El Cajon, Ca: Master Books 1976) p. 60,61

taining an essentially uniformly pleasant warm temperature all over the world.

2. With nearly uniform temperature, great air-mass movements would be inhibited and windstorms would be unknown.

3. With no global air circulation, the hydrologic cycle of the present world could not be implemented and there could be no rain, except directly over the bodies of water from which it might have evaporated.

4. With no global air circulation, and therefore no turbulence or dust particles transported to the upper atmosphere, the water vapor in the canopy would have been stable and not precipitate itself.

5. The planet would have been maintained not only at uniform temperatures but also at comfortable uniform humidities by means of daily local evaporation and condensation (like dew, or ground fog) in each day-night cycle.

6. The combination of warm temperature and adequate moisture everywhere would be conducive later to extensive stands of lush vegetation all over the world, with no barren deserts or ice caps.

7. A vapor canopy would also be highly effective in filtering out ultraviolet radiation, cosmic rays, and other destructive energies from outer space. These are known to be the source of both somatic and genetic mutations, which decrease the viability of the individual and the species, respectively. Thus the canopy would contribute effectively to human and animal health and longevity.

8. Some have objected to the idea of a heavy vapor canopy because of the great increase in atmospheric pressure which it would cause at the earth's surface. Rather than being a problem, however, this effect would contribute still further to health and longevity. Modern bio-medical research is increasingly proving that such "hyperbaric" pressures are very effective in combating disease and in promoting good health generally. There should be no problem in organisms living under high external pressures, provided their internal pressures had time to adjust correspondingly.

9. Later, when needed, these upper waters would provide the reservoir from which God would send the great Flood, to save the godly remnant from the hopelessly corrupt population of that day (the content of water vapor in the present atmosphere, if all precipitated would cover the earth only to a depth of about one inch).

Although the waters above the firmament were condensed and precipitated in the Flood, they will apparently be restored in the millennial earth and in the new earth which God will create. Psalms 148:4,6 speaks of the "waters that be above the heavens" which like the stars will be established "for ever and ever."

Not only does He place water above the troposphere of the earth, but also He positions water in space across millions and millions of miles, preparing it for the ten planets and many moons that He will make in our solar system.

"... And the evening and the morning were the second day."
Genesis 1:8

On the third day God the Son who is the Living Word speaks. He is called that because the heavens are made by the breath of His mouth. The LORD speaks and commands the water to be gathered together in one place. He speaks, "Let the dry land appear." At his command the huge land masses that are submerged underwater began to break apart forming the new continent. It is the Pangea. Europe, North and South America, Africa, Asia, Australia are all connected.

As the new continent breaks and pull further and further apart from the rest of the ground , huge clefts are created that form very great valleys. The water rushes in to fill these new clefts. As these valleys get wider and wider across the earth, some of them form lakes, rivers, seas, and oceans. God left just enough water here from the previous day that by the time all the water fills the newly created ocean bed, the dry land has appeared. He commands much of the moisture to be pulled from this newly surfaced mud so He can create plant life. However before He can do this, He must solve another major problem. The planet is dead and without life. He prepares to create living things. He decides to create living plants.

God prepares to create wonderfully complex organisms. Even the simplest amino acid chains are so complex that they will never occur randomly. A frog will be more complex than a B2 bomber. The complexity of living things is mind-boggling.

Yet, all will be in vain, unless organisms are imbued with a life force. Life is so rare, so unique, that it will never occur spontaneously. It is not heat. It is not electricity. No flame or electrical spark ever has or ever will produce life in dead matter. At this point, nothing is alive in the universe except the Trinity and the holy angels. Without the next step, life would never occur anywhere in the universe.

God the Son, looks at the earth. The Trinity has control over every particle, atom, and molecule in their universe. He gathers different atoms and forms molecule, amino acid chains. He begins to form mitochondria, nucleus, cell walls, and other parts to form complete plant cells. With every cell He forms, He imbues it with the smallest portion of His life force. Otherwise, it would wither away.

"In Him was life and the life was the light of men."
John 1:4

He alters the eternal life force that He places in each organism. Instead of that particular organism living eternally, it passes a portion of its own life force into its prodigy. Instead of a particular organism living forever, in a sense, it can live through its offspring. Only on earth, will He place life. In all the cosmos there will only be found life on earth. Not one meteor, asteroid, comet nor any of the planets in the solar system have life in any form.

Since everything in creation will now be formed out of the existing elements, this aspect of creation does not produce the same amount of heat as it did when He made the earth. All across the planet He began to form the plants; green grass, beautiful sweet smelling flowers, all manner of herbs and green trees. Because of his ability to alter time, He is able to cause trees to become full grown almost instantly. What would normally take centuries to grow, God does it in one second. His knowledge is so complete that He can and does create objects at different stages of their developments.

He has the ability to affect the aging process and to create things with the appearance of age. Genesis 6:3, tells us of the time when He shortened man's life-span time down to 120 years because of his continued sin (He later cut it to 70). Also, when Jesus cursed the fig tree He had to accelerate the aging process in the tree, for it to wither up and die in just a few hours.

So we see that not only can God affect the aging process, but He is able to alter time as well. Any physicist can tell you that time, space, energy and matter are all closely related. His control over all things is so absolute that He is able to control everything, including time. I have personally witnessed this ability.

Time In Time: A Witness Testifies

One fall evening in my home town of Pontiac, Michigan, my mother began to sense that I was in mortal danger. She began to have a tremendous burden for me and started to pray. Because of the tremendous burden she felt for me, she asked God to send a guardian angel to me for my protection. She looked at the clock on the stove and it read 5:00 p.m.

Meanwhile, I was totally unaware of all this and had no idea that I was in terrible danger. I was at football practice. Practice was over and all the other guys had made it to the bus. I was the last one to leave the locker room. I was running, anxious not to miss my bus. As I stepped outside of the building, I saw one of the principals standing there watching the other guys get on the bus. The bus was approximately 40 feet away. Then I saw something coming at me out of the corner of my eye. As I turned my head, there it was, a U.P.S. truck was coming straight at me!

Before I could even complete turning my head, the U.P.S. truck had traveled another 10 feet. Now it was only 4 feet away and didn't seem to be slowing down. I knew the truck was going to hit me in a split second and the only thing I could try to do was leap out of the way as much as possible. I was hoping that when it knocked me down, it would only run over my legs and not my chest or face and kill me. Now it was inches away and I instinctively reached for it with my right hand to push it away.

Before I could move, the angel of the Lord intervened. I never saw him but I know he was there because he used his time altering powers on me. Suddenly, I heard the strangest sound. It was as if someone was playing a tape recorder and suddenly turned it to the slowest speed. All sounds seemed as if they were being made in slow motion. Not only that, but the truck and everything else was in slow motion. I looked around and the whole world seemed to be moving in slow motion. I even saw birds flying at this unbelievable slow rate of speed. My fear left me because everything was moving so slow that it was now child's play for me to avoid that truck. It required almost no effort at all.

It was so easy that I began to laugh. It seemed as if the truck couldn't have caught me in a million years. As I continued to run out of the way, I looked up at the principal. His eyes were bulging with disbelief. To him, I appeared to be moving incredibly fast.

As soon as I stepped clear of the truck I looked back and time had snapped back to normal. The truck went past me and went another 10 feet before it stopped. It had happened so fast that the driver did not have time to brake. I got on the bus and asked the guys, "Did you see that?" They said "See what?" I said never mind.

I looked at my watch because I knew someone had to be praying for me and it was probably my mother. It was about 5:45 p.m. when I got home. I asked my mother what was she doing about 5 O'clock. She told me about her burden and how she interceded for me. Then I told her everything that happened. The next day my mother talked to the principal who had witnessed this. He jokingly told her that she was almost a wealthy woman. My mother laughed and told him that she would rather have her son in one piece. Then he told her "I don't see how in the world he got out of the way of the truck!" He was right. It wasn't because of anything of this world, but an angel of the Lord. For a few seconds I was blessed to be able to view time as He can.

2 Peter 3:8 .. One day is with the Lord is as a thousand years, and a thousand years as one day.

God can do anything. The Bible says that He is able to do exceeding abundantly above all that we can ask or even think (Eph. 3:20). When you take this into consideration you can understand why there are certain things about creation that some scientists mistakenly think took millions of years. Many people think that it took millions of years for the world to be created, because of the great heat of the newly formed earth. However, they did not take into consideration all the water He created to cool the earth, as has been previously explained.

Some of them may be trusting in their equipment. There is no way they can tell the true age of the earth, despite all their equipment, even if it can measure carbon-dating and other things accurately, because of His ability to control all things, including time.

For instance, let us take crude oil that we use to make gasoline. It comes from pre-historic organic fossils. It can be argued that God intended for us to have machines, because He created the physical laws whereby they would operate. Many scientists argue that it took a million years for organic matter to be changed into crude oil. (Scientists working in a laboratory have produced crude oil from a ton of garbage in just one hour). However, let us suppose they are correct; it would normally take millions of years for these changes to occur.

If 6,000 years ago God decided to make crude oil so that we could have it for this industrial age, He would simply cause it to change at whatever accelerated rate He chose. If God wants to cause the earth to age a million or billion years in a few thousand years, He can do it. Jesus caused a fig tree to whither up and die overnight. God has the ability to control all things, including the rate at which everything ages. So, even if the equipment is accurate in measuring the age of materials beyond 5000 years (which it is not), it still can be wrong.

No matter which radiation dating method you use to date objects, you will get different answers, sometimes by as much as a half billion years. The truth is, no scientist can ever prove evolution, because no one was there to observe it happening. Evolution is only a theory, because it can never be proven. The only way they could really know, is to have been there to watch.

"Professing themselves to become wise they became fools."
Romans 1:22

There are some people who would much rather believe in evolution than in God. Why? Because if there is no God, then there is no one to answer to. No God, no Judgement Day. No Judgement Day, no hell. For many proud, arrogant and sinful people, their worst nightmare would be to find out that God is real. That would mean that they would have to change or face eternal damnation.

Now that the Word has finished raising the dry land. All across the world, He has filled it with all manner of beautiful plant life. Now the Trinity prepares to finish the awesome task of completing the solar system, and the rest of the universe as well.

"And the evening and the morning were the third day."

Chapter 3

Mercury, Mars, and the other Stars!

The heavens declare the glory of God; and the firmament showeth his handiwork.
Psalms 19:1

Long before the invention of the telescope the Bible said there were other worlds. There are only six thousand stars that are visible to the human eye from earth. When man could look up in the sky and count these six thousand or so stars, the Bible said the stars were without number. With every new invention to view the heavens come discoveries of countless stars. As beautiful and as vast as the heavens are, God completed them all in just one day.

On the fourth day God, once again, set His sights on the heavens. He finishes His work on the sun. He stabilizes it and establishes its orbit and gravitational field. Next He also the moon to give us light at night. One side of the moon is always facing the sun and its average temperature is 214 degrees Fahrenheit. Now He must complete the solar system and establish the orbits of its members.

Mercury will be the closest planet to the sun and revolves around it every 88 days. Its temperature is between 660°F. He creates the other planets in a similar fashion that He created the earth; from deep within a huge body of water. How much water, was dependant on His designs for that planet.

For instance, when He created the planet which we call Mars, He decided that it would basically be a lifeless, dry and dead planet by our standards. He formed Mars deep within a body of water as he formed the earth. By the time Mars had finished cooling off, there was practically no water on the planet and thin atmosphere that is 95% carbon dioxide. It is red colored with canals that crisscross the planet. Sometimes they go in a straight line for hundreds of miles.

Mars has half the diameter of Earth and one-tenth the mass. That means that a person who weighs 150 pounds on earth, weighs 57 pounds on Mars. Because Mars has one-tenth of earths mass, its gravity is weaker than earths. It cannot sustain much of an atmosphere. On earth, the atmosphere acts as an insulating blanket, keeping the temperature warm. Mars' atmosphere is so thin, much of its heat goes into space. Over the years Mars cooled significantly, and that is why it appears to be a dead, lifeless planet with very little volcanic activity.

Mars has two moons, Phobos and Deimos. The maximum temperature on Mars is 63°F in the summer. Average temperature at the equator is below freezing during the day and -100° F during the night. Mars has the largest known mountain in the solar system. It is called Olympus Mons and is 373 miles wide at the base and 16 miles high. That is three times the height of earth's tallest mountain; Mt. Everest.

Jesus makes each planet. Jupiter is the biggest planet. It is more than 11 times bigger than the earth. It has fourteen moons and a thin ring that goes around the planet. The planet itself is covered with swirling clouds that form different color bands. Also, the planet has a giant red spot. It is 30,000 miles long and 7,000 miles wide. It has constant winds traveling at an average of 800 miles per hour. Its atmosphere is highly poisonous, consisting of frozen ammonia and methane.

Jupiter's density is only one-fourth of earth's. A man weighing 150 pounds on earth would weigh 396 pounds on Jupiter. If Jupiter was as dense as the earth, this man would weigh 1,500 pounds.

Saturn is 750 million miles away from the earth. It is average surface temperature is -250° F below zero. It is the second largest planet at 73,000 miles in diameter. It looks like a giant yellow star with rings around it. The rings are different colors and are 170 miles in diameter. Saturn is made up of such light materials that if it were possible to place it on water, the planet would float.

The winds blow at an amazing 1,100 miles an hour. It has eleven moons, the largest of which is called Titan. It takes 29 and one half years for Saturn to complete one trip around the sun.

He continues to form other planets with different characteristics. By the time Jesus finishes creating the solar system, it contains 10 planets. Their names and order from the sun are Mercury, Venus, Earth, Mars, Eros*, Jupiter, Saturn, Uranus, Neptune, and Pluto.

Since none of these planets will have life on them, as we know it, their creation does require the same amount of time and care, as the earth. We know from the Scriptures that He made the rest of the planets on the fourth day. He didn't necessarily have to complete everything about them, on this particular day. Their creation was complete on this day. However, there may have been changes wrought in their appearance since then. As the earth has changed, so too there may have been in some of these planets. He could have decided to add a few features or more to any planet He desired in the following years, as we continually redecorate our homes.

Next, God decides to create the stars. He has already placed the sun and the moon in the sky for man. Now He decides to place the stars in the heavens. They will represent a change of the seasons, whereby men would one day be able to navigate across the deserts and oceans by them.

Man would one day look up at the stars and imagine that different groups of stars formed different objects, such as the Big Dipper. These groups are called constellations.

Though there are only 6,000 stars that are visible to the naked eye from earth, there are trillions and trillions of stars in the universe. These stars are in groups called galaxies. Our galaxy is called the Milky Way. Our solar system is a little more than halfway to the outer edge from the center of the galaxy. It is 100,000 light years across and has 100 billion stars. There are 100 billion galaxies that are visible from earth.

Even for someone for whom "one day is as a thousand years" this is quite a feat. When you take into consideration the incredible distance between the stars in the known universe and that it was done in less than twenty-four hours, it seems incomprehensible. But there are several possibilities.

1. He only created the six thousand stars that are visible to earth on that day. The rest were created later at His discretion. However, this is unlikely.

2. If, when He was preparing the hydrogen to be made into water, He also created enough Hydrogen and other elements to create the suns. (Hydrogen 92.5% Helium 7% and the remaining 1/2 % is made up of carbon, iron, nitrogen, oxygen, sodium, magnesium and a few others) If they were already prepared, then all He would have had to do was simply ignite them. For Him, it would be as easy as you or I lighting a bonfire. Since God is omnipresent (everywhere) then He is able to bend all laws of time and space; being able to be

at all these suns at once. Thereby igniting all of them at the same time.

Even though a star is much more powerful than the earth, it is much more simple to make. The complexity of living things is incredible. Living things are created not by chance, but by the hand of God. The mathematical odds of evolution occurring over millions of years are impossible. The odds of a frog evolving through evolution over millions of years, are greater than a tornado traveling through a junk yard and assembling a B2 bomber out of the junk. A simple amino acid chain has only five elements but hundreds of combinations. There are some four hundred chain combinations. If you have a two hundred chain combination (which is ridiculously primitive) the odds of that occurring randomly are 10^{375}. That is the number ten with three hundred and seventy-five zeros behind it. Mathematical odds these great, never occur.

When you consider that amino acids are just a basic building block of living organisms, you begin to get the picture of how complex living things are. If you find it difficult to comprehend that God could not possibly have figured all this out in one week, you must remember that God created the universe after an eternity of His existence. If He did need to plan, He had all the time He needed. He would have planned and designed everything within His mind. His calculations would have been perfect and He would not even need a model. He began building when He was ready. This is not unlike what engineers do today. Engineers today design their machines on sophisticated computers before they are ever built. The U.S. just built a new stealth bomber. They knew how to design it and they knew it would fly by their computer programs. They were so confident of their calculations by computers that they spent billions on its development without even testing it to beforehand to make sure it would fly. Fortunately their calculations were correct and the airplane flew. If man can correctly build complicated things using computers, then of course God could do it with His mind. Certainly God is wiser than any man-made super computer.

3. Again, with if the stars were already positioned and prepared, then there would be nothing left to do but ignite them with sufficient temperature. God could have allowed angels to participate. The angels, since their creation, have acted as God's agents. Aside from speaking for Him, they also dispense God's judgement. Disobeying an angel acting under the command of God was as severe as disobey-

ing God, Himself. In the book of Revelation they will pour out judgement affecting the earth, wind, seas and even the sun. Because they are so active, it is possible that the igniting of stars was one of their first jobs. We know that in the Bible, God refers to the angels, several times, as stars. We don't know exactly what is the connection between them. We don't know if this represents their power and/or luminance or something else. However, it is possible, that their power rivals that of a star. (Their power must be somewhere of this magnitude, otherwise how could Satan and the evil angels ever expect to overthrow a God that has power to create the universe, with trillions and trillions of stars.) Heat and light are two of the simplest forms of electromagnetic radiation. So if they could generate anything at all, it would certainly be at least these two forms of radiation. (The record shows they can do much more). If they indeed have the power of a star and are able to generate heat in these quantities, then surely lighting a star would be very easy. It would be as easy for them as you or I, lighting a gas stove with a match. This would not be creation, but rather ignition.

The following is a brief make believe scenario showing how this could have happened.

Betlegeuse

After completing Pluto, the Trinity gathers the angels and together they fly billions of miles out in space.

The Father begins, "Now I have brought you here because I am ready to begin the next phase of my creation: the igniting of all the stars. I have prepared them and placed them throughout the universe. All that remains is for their nuclear fires to be lighted. I will allow each of you to participate in this endeavor. I have brought you here to this spot to show you how."

Their eyes open wide in amazement. Some gasp in utter astonishment. Others are simply too overwhelmed and bewildered to say anything. The angels are deeply grateful and honored to have this opportunity. They are proud, yet feel so unworthy and they have no idea how they can possibly be of service. Their eyes filled with wonder as the Father continues.

The Father says, "We are deep within this sea of hydrogen that I have gathered into this spheroid shape because I am preparing to turn it into a sun. This will be the biggest star in the universe. It will one day be called Betlegeuse. It will be over one million times bigger than the star called Sol, that is the earth's sun. To light a sun is very simple. All we need to do is increase the temperature sufficiently, (27,000,000 degrees°F) and the hydrogen will detonate and form the thermonuclear explosion. When we established the laws for this reality, we designed it so that there are 408,600,000,000,000,000,000 ergs of energy in just one pound of hydrogen. (If you lift your foot 13 million times, you would have used just one erg of energy). If you will focus your eyes on the atoms present here, you will see something strange."

They each begin to strain with their fiery red eyes whose limits we can only begin to guess at. Many of them gasp in awe at what they see. Because of the tremendous air pressure, these atoms of hydrogen are already crashing into each other hundreds of trillions of times a second.

As the temperature rises the molecules move faster and faster, until at 27,000,000°F they move with such force that when they crash into each other, they break apart releasing their energy. (For example, if you were in a crowd of people and I just barely bumped into you, then you would feel no pain and no harm would be done. But if I crashed into you at the speed of 1,000 miles per hour, I would hit you with so much force that our bodies would break apart. Also, we would crash into others destroying them. This is a morbid example of what happens to the hydrogen).

He tells them, "I have given each of you sufficient power to generate this amount of heat. Just simply hold out your hands and do this."

The Father stretches out His hands and they begin to turn red hot as they generate great heat. As it gets brighter and brighter they adjust their eyes to compensate for the tremendous light. They can see the atoms racing madly into each other. Faster and faster the collisions are until finally it happens. The first hydrogen atom splits, beginning the nuclear chain reaction.

Immediately, there is an explosion powerful enough to devastate a world. The star ignites and a huge fireball begins to grow and grow, racing at incredible speed until it forms the biggest sun in the universe. It is a giant red star, more than 400 times bigger than the earth's sun. Its surface temperature is 5,000°F. While no one knows the temperature in the center where the fusion is continuously going on, it has been estimated to be between thirty thousand and one million degrees Fahrenheit.

The power of this explosion is so incredible, that it is difficult to imagine anything surviving. Suddenly rising from the surface of the new star, we see the Trinity and all the angels flying unharmed, rising from the depths of Betlegeuse's nuclear fires. How could they survive?

Perhaps, despite the incalculable forces unleashed here, it was not enough force to move them, let alone harm them. Possibly they turned immaterial and were so insubstantial that the forces of the explosion passed harmlessly through them. Maybe even some remained solid and let the blast hit them full force, but because of their invulnerability were just carried on a nice little harmless ride for several million miles, laughing all the way. Who can say exactly? T'was not meant for mortal men to know such things for certainty.

Now the angels fly off in billions of different directions traveling at hyper-light speeds. Their destinations are the many billions of stars waiting to be ignited. All of the angels are anxious to ignite a star and help finish this awesome task that must be completed in less than one day.

And the evening and the morning were the fourth day.
Genesis 1:19

Chapter 4

Trouble: Thy Name Is Lucifer

After the creation of the heaven and the earth, God brings His angels down to earth to view His wondrous creation. Never before has there been such a sight as this beautiful verdant sphere teeming with life. Many of them glorify God for His wonderful works. The universe is shaping up beautifully. God is preparing to create all the living creatures that will live in the water and the fowls that will fly in the air. There is one angel who is becoming more and more dissatisfied with all that he sees. His name is Lucifer.

Lucifer, who was an anointed cherub (guardian angel), ruled over many trillions of angels. He was beautifully created. Many precious stones covered his body.

Gold, ruby, topaz, diamond, onyx, jasper, emerald, sapphire, and beryl all were part of his covering. Pipes and tabrets (small drums) were also part of his body which allowed him to make the most beautiful music.

He was created without a flaw, but like all the other angels, he was created with a free will. Because of his position, power, and his beauty, he began to get lifted up in pride.

Ezekiel 28:13-17 Thou hast been in Eden the garden of God; every precious stone was thy covering, the sardius, topaz, and the diamond, the beryl, the onyx, and the jasper, the sapphire, the emerald, and the carbuncle, and gold: the workmanship of thy tabrets and of thy pipes was prepared in thee in the day that thou wast created.

{14} Thou art the anointed cherub that covereth; and I have set thee so: thou wast upon the holy mountain

of God; thou hast walked up and down in the midst of the stones of fire.

{15} Thou wast perfect in thy ways from the day that thou wast created, till iniquity was found in thee.

{16} By the multitude of thy merchandise they have filled the midst of thee with violence, and thou hast sinned: therefore I will cast thee as profane out of the mountain of God: and I will destroy thee, O covering cherub, from the midst of the stones of fire.

{17} Thine heart was lifted up because of thy beauty, thou hast corrupted thy wisdom by reason of thy brightness: I will cast thee to the ground, I will lay thee before kings, that they may behold thee.

Lucifer was created perfect, but because of his beauty, power, and position he originated the first sin. Pride. As he allowed himself to be filled with more and more pride, he became filled with contempt for his masters. Like the millions of men and angels who would later follow him into sin, his pride evolved into stubbornness and rebellion against God. This filled Lucifer with contempt.

As Lucifer continued to lift himself up with more and more of this abominable pride, his sins evolved and multiplied. Contempt grew into frustration. Frustration grew into anger. Anger grew into hatred. Once you get into hatred, you are only a hair away from murder. Lucifer was dissatisfied with his current position and he began to crave an even greater one. He no longer wanted to serve God. He decided that he wanted to take over. He would risk all and set himself up as absolute ruler of the universe.

But as vain as he had become, he still knew that he could not possibly overthrow God by himself. Somehow he must obtain help. He must enlist the aide of other angels. Somehow he must win them over to his side.

He decides to talk with his closest cohorts. Some of them are receptive, others are dubious. The Bible says that Lucifer's heart became filled with violence through the multitude of merchandise. (Ezek 28:16) The only thing he had to trade was the positions in his new kingdom.

Some angels already ruled over others. These angels already had kingdoms. Whether or not all these kingdoms were on earth, we do not know. Though the Bible mentions that some of Satan's kingdom being governed by some of his minions, (In Daniel 9 it mentions one spirit who was in charge of Persia and another being who ruled Greece), we do not know exactly how things are divided up between them.

Since not all the angels rebelled against God, we know that they did not all automatically fall in line behind Satan. Some were unwilling, but many of them got greedy for power. It was a very frustrating thing as these angels began to quarrel among themselves for power. Their arguments were so intense that Lucifer had to resort to violence to settle some of these disputes. Actually the bitterness of the disputes filled him with violence.

WHAT IS EVIL

Many people have a misconception of what evil is. Evil is not a mystical force, but it is disobeying God's commandments. Anytime you disobey God's commandments, that is evil. The Bible teaches that Satan was created perfect, without a flaw. There was no evil in him. He chose to do what he did. Since he was the originator of evil, then there was no evil force to overcome him. That means his evil acts were conscious ones, made by choice.

Because of his freedom of choice, he chose to try to further his own ends and in the process committed acts which God had labeled evil. There is no evil force per se. But anyone (man or angel) can become a force for evil. Evil did not have to be created as a force. Evil is not a seducing force, but it is an option.

Whenever you have law, you have the potential for lawbreakers.

God's word and will is His divine law. Any act that is contrary to His law and His divine righteous nature is evil.

James 1:13 Let no man say when he is tempted, I am tempted of God: for God cannot be tempted with evil, neither tempteth he any man.

THE DEVIL MADE ME DO IT

When Adam and Eve ate the forbidden fruit from the tree of knowledge, they committed an evil act. They did not have to eat the fruit to commit evil but of their own free will they chose to disobey God's strict command. They sinned before they ate the fruit.

True they were tempted by Satan's suggestion, but they ate of their own free will and that is why they were punished. When we stand before God on Judgement Day no one will be able to use the excuse "the devil made me do it" because with our will He gave us the power to resist evil.

Animals and other sentient life on this planet only seem to have a few areas of concerns, reproduction and survival of the species. They have no desire to challenge man for intellectual superiority. They do not try to build airplanes or learn to write. Generation after generation they remain the same with no intellectual improvement, unlike man. They do seem to have a certain innate knowledge that we do not possess.

Once, when I was a little boy, my father told me that if our dog ever got bitten by a snake to turn him lose and he would go into the woods, and find a certain plant that would cure him of the snake bite. I asked him, "How does the dog know that?" He said he just knows. Another example is the salmon. When it is time for them to reproduce, they have an irresistible urge that drives them to swim upstream. They must return to the very same spot where they were born to mate. They either succeed or die trying. How can a salmon know how to find the stream where it was born, to spawn?

When Adam and Eve ate of the forbidden fruit, they and their descendants were forever altered. Prior to that time, their level of awareness seemed to be only slightly above the animals, (They didn't know they were naked. This implies that among other things, their awareness was limited). Perhaps the fruit changed the area of our brains where we would just have instinct like the animals, into our great capacity for reason. It gave us the gift (or curse) of knowledge of good and evil. Man's desire for knowledge of good things is strong and so is the desire for evil. It has been said that man is the only predator species which preys on itself.

Babel

God saw at the tower of Babel that this technological age was coming (Gen 11:6). He said if man continued unchecked, the day would come when man could do whatever that he could imagine, ahead of God's cosmic timetable.

When you look at what man has done with CD's, microwave ovens, vcr's, and especially in the field of genetics, space exploration, etc. you can see that we are quickly approaching that point (When you consider these and other advances that we have made in science, just imagine where we would be in another 100 to 1000 years, if, we have that much time left).

So God confused them and instantly caused them to speak in different languages to separate them and send them to the different parts of the earth. In the process this hindered them intellectually. Imagine if we had come into the atomic age a few centuries ago while we were still in our totally barbaric state what could have happened. We certainly would have destroyed ourselves. So God allowed us to have the industrial revolution at this time.

WHY?

The Bible tells that Jesus was the Lamb slain before the foundation of the world. This means the fall of Lucifer and man, which led to Jesus dying on the cross, was all planned by God before the world was ever formed. This may seem cruel to some people, but Romans 8:28 says, "And we know that all things work together for good to them that love God, to them who are the called according to his purpose."

If you can accept the fact that God is all-knowing, loving, and good, then you must concede that for God to allow all these things to happen, it must be for a greater good. Not just for mankind, but for all creation, and ages to come. Six thousand years of suffering the effects of evil is not too much when you consider that from the lessons that we will eventually learn, will ensure peace and righteousness for billions of years to come.

Christ's suffering demonstrated the blessedness of obedience, humility, and suffering for righteousness sake.

Though he were a Son, yet learned he obedience by the things which he suffered;
Hebrews 5:8

Therefore (because He stooped so low), God has highly exalted Him and has freely bestowed on Him the name that is above every name, That in (at) the name of Jesus every knee should (must) bow, in heaven and on earth and under the earth, And every tongue (frankly and openly) confess and acknowledge that Jesus Christ is Lord, to the glory of God the Father.
Philippians 2:9-11
Amplified Bible

At the risk of oversimplifying it; An inherent evil of a free will is the ability to chose evil. God allowed all these things to happen (including millions of souls being lost forever) and all this evil to come upon the world. Perhaps so that in the future times when people will still have a free will, they will remember the lessons from this time and forever chose good over evil. Sometimes the lessons that are learned "the hard way" are the easiest ones to remember.

We know that one third of the angels rebelled against God. It is obvious that with these many defections of intelligent beings, they must have thought that they would succeed.

As Lucifer prepares his rebellion, he realizes that he must have something, an ace in the hole to use against God. The power of the Father had never been tested. No one had ever seen Him angry, let alone tested his strength in a fight. Lucifer also realizes there is no way after taking over, that the Father would sit idly by and do nothing. So he looks for some means by which he hopes to destroy the Godhead.

He was a murderer from the beginning and abode not in the truth, because there is no truth in him. When he speaketh a lie, he speaketh of his own; for he is a liar and the father of it.

---Jesus concerning Satan
St. John 8:44

Who, or what did Lucifer murder? Was it one or many? Was it some of the angels? (The Bible never mentions the death of any angel). Was it some other form of life?

FACTS ABOUT THE WAR

The Bible does not tell us very much about what actually happened during the angelic war, but it does tell us a few things. From what it does tell us, if we examine the facts carefully, we can figure out many things and get a clearer picture.

Lucifer was reduced to Satan

Lucifer and some of the angels' physical, supernatural bodies were forever changed. Perhaps they were destroyed by a tremendous force. Their power to affect the physical world became limited. Their ability to affect things spiritually, including men's spirits, remained strong. For some reason this group of angels was not allowed to affect physical things significantly.

The only time the Bible records that they can affect things physically, is when there are many of them involved. For some reason, this group which includes Lucifer, was no longer entrusted with the ability to affect things in the material world.

There are some evil angels who have been imprisoned every since the war. Some of them are never released, and others are. Those that will be released, can and will affect the physical world upon their escape. This will have disastrous affects for those remaining upon the earth.

So we see there are four different groups of fallen angels.

1. Lucifer and the group that are free to roam the earth as devils or demon spirits.
2. Some that are never let out of hell.
3. Some that are let out when the angel sounds the fifth trumpet (Revelations Chapter 9).
4. The 200,000,000 angels that are let out when the angel sounds the sixth trumpet (Revelations Chapter 9). Since these angels were handled differently, perhaps they attacked differently; meaning there was more than one plan of attack. If Lucifer had

a brilliant plan, this would explain why so many of God's angels (1/3), were willing to take part.

PROOF?

A war between such powerful creatures that took place in heaven and in earth, could have left some traces. (Unless they were covered up). Do we see any results of great devastation in heaven or in earth? Yes.

1. In space we see the asteroid belt between Mars and Jupiter. It has thousands of different asteroids. They are different sizes, ranging from the smallest which is ten miles in diameter to the largest which is almost 500 miles in diameter. Many scientists feel these asteroids are the remains of a planet or planets that exploded for some unknown reason long ago.

2. You also have the rings of Saturn and the recently dis-covered rings of Jupiter, Uranus, and Neptune. Scientists believe that perhaps some or all of these rings were formed by the destruction of moons or other heavenly bodies above the planet's surface. When this cataclysm occurred, the debris was scattered in layers around the planet and formed rings.

When did the war take place?

We know that this took place sometime after the first day. Job 38, tells us that all the angels were in harmony on that day. Since Lucifer had already become Satan by the time he enticed Adam and Eve just a few days later, we know it must have happened by this time.

A popular theory is that there is a time gap between Genesis 1:1 and verse 2. This is called the age-gap theory. Proponents of this theory believe during Gen.1:1-2 the prehistoric age occurred and Satan's rebellion happened during this time. This theory was invented to accommodate the evolutionists theories of the prehistoric age. The Biblical argument of those who believe in the age-gap theory centers around the statement the earth was without form and void. They ask, why would God create the earth without form and void. They believe the earth was without form and void because it was destroyed in the war with Satan. After the earth's destruction they believe it was recreated into its present form. But this theory does not take into consideration the creation process.

You cannot build a house until you first obtain the parts. When these parts are delivered, they do not look like a house. Anyone who has ever visited a new construction site knows it looks a scattered mess or without form and void. In much the same way, God created the sub-atomic particles first that made up the elements, which in turn formed the earth. Besides, even if the earth was so devastated by the war that it was reduced to a gaseous state like Saturn (or the sun), it would still have a form. If the earth was destroyed to the point that it was without form and void, it would have been at a state less than a gas. If the earth was destroyed to the point that it was less than a gas, no relic of the prehistoric age would have survived.

When you consider all these facts, it becomes much easier to envision what may have happened. In the next two chapters we will describe what **may** have happened.

I have taken the position that the war occurred on the sixth day, just before God created his last creature, man. A schemer such as Lucifer would have waited until the best possible moment, which I will explain in the next chapter, would be the sixth day. The following story is a theoretical account based upon the facts we have just discussed (as well as a few others), and what light the Scriptures shed upon this subject. As to whether how much is fiction or how much is fact, what mortal man can say?

Chapter 5

War In Heaven
(As It Might Have Happened)

Isaiah 14:12-17 How art thou fallen from heaven, O Lucifer, son of the morning! how art thou cut down to the ground, which didst weaken the nations!

{13} For thou hast said in thine heart, I will ascend into heaven, I will exalt my throne above the stars of God: I will sit also upon the mount of the congregation, in the sides of the north:

{14} I will ascend above the heights of the clouds; I will be like the most High.

{15} Yet thou shalt be brought down to hell, to the sides of the pit.

{16} They that see thee shall narrowly look upon thee, and consider thee, saying, Is this the man that made the earth to tremble, that did shake kingdoms;

{17} That made the world as a wilderness, and destroyed the cities thereof; that opened not the house of his prisoners?

He enters the solar system flying under his own power, travelling at hyper-light speeds. He can hardly contain himself, as he streaks toward earth. He is overjoyed at the success of his secret mission. He was heading straight toward earth, but he feels like celebrating. He sees the burning star and decides to make a slight detour of several million miles. He heads straight for the giant nuclear furnace, that will one day be called the sun, and flies toward it. As the temperature rises thousands of degrees, he merely smiles for he seems impervious to the heat. Faster than a streaking meteor, he plunges into the depths of earth's star. The million plus degrees temperatures, the nuclear explosions, and nuclear radiation only seem to invigorate the anointed cherub, (guardian angel).

Here, he reasons it will be safe to let out his scream of unbridled joy, for surely it would be drowned out by the din of the nuclear explosions. He does not wish to draw undue attention to himself yet. Soon he will command all the attention he needs, but not yet. He shouts his song of triumph, and sounds the pipes and tabrets that are part of his body. He sounds as only he can, for he is Lucifer, and soon he will make the universe tremble.

Lucifer flies from the depths of the sun and continues his journey to earth. He has changed so much in the time since the creation. He is ready to take the biggest gamble of all. He has schemed, lied and fought to forge this rebellion. He has had to become very violent to maintain control of the angels that have joined with him. He has made many promises. He feels only the strong and crafty will survive. He is ready to do anything to achieve his goals. He has reasoned the only way to defeat the Almighty is to become something totally different from Him, evil. The fate of the universe hangs in the balance. He streaks to earth to make the final preparations for his war with God.

As daylight begins on the earth for the sixth day, there is a great deal of discussion going on in Lucifer's palace. He is meeting with all his generals to prepare for their attack on the forces of the Almighty. His generals' names are Mammon, Beelzebub, Abaddon, who now calls himself the Destroyer, the four angelic kings; Baal, Vinshi, Jorgamunde, and Endoc.

Mammon begins, "It is rumored that on this 6th day the Trinity will complete creation."

Beelzebub says, "Yes, that's right. Not only that but today I'm told, they will make a creature that will dominate all others on this planet."

Endoc asks, "What is this creature supposed to look like?"

Beelzebub says, "No one knows. All we know is that he is supposed to be something special. He will be wiser than any of the creatures so far and is supposed to have a very special place in God's plan for the universe."

Jorgamunde asks, "What do you mean?"

Beelzebub says, "We don't know exactly. We do know that God is supposed to love this creature more than any of these others so far."

"Will these creatures be as powerful as us?" someone asks.

"I'm not sure," Beelzebub tells him.

"Explain yourself!" Lucifer demands.

"Well we've heard that eventually it will be allowed to eat the tree of knowledge and the tree of life," Mammon tells him.

Lucifer says, "If this is so then one day they have the potential to become nearly as powerful as we."

Abaddon asks, "What is to be our relationship with these creatures."

Mammon says, "In some way we are supposed to minister to them."

"Minister? You mean as in serve?" they ask.

"Yes, I suppose," Mammon says.

Lucifer says defiantly, "I refuse to serve any creature less than myself."

Baal says, "Perhaps we can turn this new creature on our side and against the Trinity. After all, we have almost a third of the angels on our side."

Lucifer shouts "NO! We can't take that chance. Soon the Father will take action against us. Suppose He creates new creatures to shift the balance of power totally against us. We must act now!"

Vinshi says, "I agree. We must act before He completes His plans for the universe.

About that time, one of Lucifer's minions enter the room abruptly saying, "Master! The Father has just put His new creation all across the globe. As Lucifer and his men rush outside to view God's newest creation, even they are surprised at the shape and size of these creatures.

Even though God had already created some of the different types of animals, none are as large and as powerful as these. They are huge lizard-like creatures. Some of them are eighty feet tall. God had just created the dinosaurs!

Because Lucifer has no idea as to the form or the name of man, he confuses the dinosaurs for man. Since he knows that God's special creature is supposed to have dominion over all other creatures he assumes because of the dinosaur's size they must be the ones. For with their great size they could easily dominate all the other animals on this planet.

"Listen we must slay these creatures before it is too late," Lucifer tells them.

"Slay them?" Mammon asks in startled disbelief.

"Yes. Quickly, while they are still mortal and before they can be used against us! Look at their size! If they were to made immortal, they might even be more powerful than us! We must kill them."

"But how?" some of them ask.

"Watch," Lucifer tells them. Nearby is a giant tyrannosaur. It stands a full fifty feet tall. Lucifer flies toward it, de-materializes, and slips inside it. The tyrannosaur reels back and roars. It then charges a nearby brontosaurus and begins to fight it and kill it. The tyrannosaur begins to eat the other dinosaur. As it rips the living meat from the dying creature, it almost seems to smile through its blood-soaked teeth. Slowly it breaks into a devilish grin. It has tasted meat and now it will desire meat for the rest of its brief life.

Lucifer then rises from the tyrannosaur. He solidifies, and forms razor sharp claws on his hand, harder than the purest diamond. The tyrannosaur is covered with scales that a sword or today's bullets would not pierce. Angrily Satan rakes his hand across the dinosaur's neck, slashing through the scales like they were blades of grass, slitting the creatures throat. The poor creature falls back screaming and twitching as its blood spews out.

"You see!" says Beelzebub. "Lucifer has shown us the way. We can easily manipulate them into killing themselves. Not only can we slit their throats, but we can rip out their hearts or drive them into tar pits where they will be trapped and drown. But Lucifer was right, we must move quickly before these creatures can be used against us."

As Lucifer watches the helpless creature's death throes, the other angels anxiously fly to him. Beelzebub says, "Master you were right. If you wish, Mammon and myself will take your forces and oversee the destruction of these creatures."

Lucifer turns to them and shouts, "NO!" They stop and stare at him in stunned silence. They are confused.

"You will not touch them," he commands. They pause in obedience to him. They wonder if Satan will give them an explanation, yet they dare not ask for one.

Satan, now satisfied with their unflinching obedience, begins to explain. He says, "When I possessed this creature's body I analyzed its mind. I realize now that its brain was too primitive for it to be God's special creation. Even though it is of tremendous size, it simply cannot be the one. We have no need to fear them and no time to waste."

"Well, what is it then?" asks Endoc.

Lucifer thinks for a second. "I do not know exactly," Lucifer answers him. He says, "I think that it believed itself to be some sort of creature called a dragon." Lucifer looks at the creature as if he admired it.

In total surprise they ask, "A dragon?"

He seems lost in thought, admiring the creature's power and ferociousness. He responds, "Yes. That is what it said when I read its mind while inside."

Lucifer realizes that time is elapsing. He says to his followers, "Listen! One thing is certain. I do know that we can waste no more time. We must move now if we hope to achieve success."

Endoc questions, "But Lucifer, the Father is said to be all-knowing. How can we hope to succeed if He is indeed omniscient?"

"If He was omniscient, wouldn't He have stopped this rebellion before it got started?" he asked them angrily.

"That's right." Vinshi agrees, the thought having never occurred to him.

Lucifer knows he has them now. He smiles within himself and says, "I tell you, don't believe those rumors and exaggerated stories about His power. I don't. Listen, we can defeat Him. The Trinity has expended great energy in creating the universe and is noticeably drained. Now they are nearly finished and have said tomorrow will be the Sabbath when they must refresh themselves. We must attack now while they are weak. We may never have a greater chance."

Lucifer continues to deceive them. Many lies and blasphemous things he speaks. Some are too foul to be mentioned. Nothing is beneath him in his quest for universal domination. He continues, "We must free ourselves from God's tyranny. We are free to do as we choose. We are not His slaves, but masters of our own destiny. He cares nothing for us. To Him we are playthings which He will one day tire of and destroy. He has told me this Himself."

Satan adds with great sincerity, "He does not love us. I do not trust Him. Don't believe His lies about Him being a good and benevolent God. I don't! Nor do I believe He is eternal. He may have somehow evolved from the universe itself. How do we know what He says is truth? We only have His word for it. Don't be like those other gullible fools that believe everything He says. He may just be a type of angel like us. Once we have defeated Him, we will make Him tell us all the truth.

Lucifer, the deceiver, knows that he has the angels completely in his power. His words and arguments thoroughly convinces them. Lucifer proclaims, "After we have forced Him to share with us His great knowledge, then the universe will be ours for the taking. All we need is a plan; and I have a great plan.

Listen. Abaddon, you take your forces and fly across the other end of the universe and attack Heaven from the rear. By that time we will be finished here and we will attack Heaven from the front. Baal, Vinshi, Endoc and Jorgamunde, I want you to gather your forces of 200,000,000 and divide them between the four of you. Then tell them to use their size-changing abilities to shrink as small as they possibly can."

"For what purpose my lord?" Vinshi asks.

Lucifer explains, "I want them to hide inside your bodies. Then, I want you to go to Heaven and warn the Godhead of our attack."

They cannot believe their ears. "What?" they ask.

"Yes. Yes," he rolls his head back and laughs sinisterly. Then, beginning to clench his fist he instructs them, "By then He will be aware of it anyway. Perhaps you can gain their trust. When we attack, you release the angels inside you. I also want you to take two thousand of my most powerful angels with you. You must be especially convincing. You and the two thousand must deceive the Trinity into thinking that you have turned against me and have come to warn them. You have the most dangerous task because you will be severely outnumbered. When we attack, you attack the Son. Destroy him if you can. But at least occupy Him that I may assault the Father. Even though we are outnumbered we shall yet win this day."

"But Lucifer, none of us has the power to overcome the Trinity. We know that your power is great indeed, but please, don't be angry." Vinshi carefully asks, "Are you sure you have the power?"

Lucifer looks at him with a gaze that seems it could obliterate a world and retorts, "Do you remember the stones of fire near the mountain of God. The stones that temporally increase the powers of any angel many times that walks upon them. So that we can do special jobs for the father which would ordinarily be beyond our abilities."

"Yes. Of course, we remember." One of them says.

Lucifer, full of pride and arrogance brags, "Well, I have stolen most of them. While you are fulfilling each of your appointed tasks I will fashion these fiery-red stones to my body, increasing my strength even more. Since I am, by far, the strongest of all the angels I am sure that this will give me all the power I need, and coupled with our three pronged attack, we will prevail against the forces of God this day.

I am called the son of the morning while you are called stars, because as the morning light is greater than the stars at night, by the same proportion is my power greater than yours. I am the most beautiful and the most powerful as well. It is my destiny to rule the cosmos. They were fools to create me with this much power and I will not be denied any longer.

Finally, I will ascend above the clouds. I will exalt my throne above the stars of God. I will have a name above every name, above everyone in the universe. I will go to heaven to the holy mountain where God rules the universe from His throne. Then, I will destroy the Father. Once He is gone, the others will join us. And if they do not, they will die as well. Either way, the universe will be mine."

The fallen angels begin to cheer and laugh as they fly off, convinced that they are going to certain victory; unaware that all of their doings has been observed by the Trinity.

Looking at the mangled bodies of the two dinosaurs, God decides that even though He still has plans for them, Lucifer and his angels are too powerful and too dangerous to leave in their present state. He begins to prepare for what He must do.

As Abaddon and his forces approach Heaven from the far side of the universe at hyper-light speeds, they are met by one solitary angel. It is Gabriel, the archangel. He has a black disk shaped, metal type object on his left arm that Abaddon mistakes for a shield.

"Look, it is Gabriel," one of Abaddon's men cry out.

Abaddon shouts to Gabriel, "Gabriel, we know that you are mighty indeed, but I'm not sure that you can defeat me, let alone my 100 million friends. You'll need more than a shield to defeat us.

Gabriel smiles and says, "Perhaps it is not a shield. Maybe it is a bottomless pit."

"I've no time to joke with you Gabriel," Abaddon says.

"Neither have I with you, evil one," Gabriel answers back.

"Well then, mighty Gabriel," Abaddon says with a smirk on his face. "Then surely you have to come to join us," Abaddon mockingly laughs with his men.

"You know me better than that!" Gabriel answers angrily at the mere suggestion that he would ever turn evil. He proclaims, "The Father has sent me to stop you!"

Abaddon not concerned at all about Gabriel's words says, "Well, living all those ages must have finally made the Father mad..."

"Mind your tongue!" Gabriel angrily interrupts.

Now Abaddon is angry and he shouts, "And you must be touched by the madness as well if you hope to stop us with one shield or are you expecting some more help. Are there more angels approaching?"

"I am alone," Gabriel calmly replies. Give up this madness and surrender yourself and perhaps the Father will forgive you."

Abaddon and his soldiers begin to laugh mockingly. Then He becomes indignant and spews, "We spit on Him and His forgiveness! You surrender to us archangel!"

"Never!" he shouts.

One of Abaddon's men cry out "Enough of this. Let's tear him apart," and lurches forward.

Abaddon holds up his arm signalling him to wait. He smiles wryly and says, "You see, I can't hold them back much longer. These are my final words."

There is something about the sound of Abaddon's voice that lets you know the extent of his cruelty. He makes you feel like he enjoys the sound of breaking bones and ripping flesh. Abaddon, the Destroyer, leans forward and says, "If you turn and flee perhaps you can find a real weapon and maybe you'll last three seconds before we destroy you."

"I have all I need," Gabriel rebuts confidently.

Angered by Gabriel's seeming over-confidence Abaddon yells, "You pompous arrogant fool! You will be the first to die! Destroy him!" With that cry, 100 million screaming angels fly at the seemingly helpless and outnumbered Gabriel.

Gabriel, whose voice is already like a multitude of voices, begins to raise his voice to an unbelievable degree. He shouts and boldly speaks with great authority proclaiming, "It is not I that shall be destroyed but it is you, O Destroyer and all those with you! Hear ye the word of the LORD. Because you act like demons, demons you shall become!"

Gabriel raises the round metal object and presses the blinking red light. Then amazingly from the disk comes a blinding red light. As it strikes the evil angels, they scream in agony. The ray of power stops them dead in their tracks.

They scream and cry "NO!" as the ray twist them and horribly deforms their bodies. In vain they strain against the ray's effects, as it causes all of them to shrink and change against their will.

Smaller and smaller they dwindle until they are only about a foot long. They've become locust-like creatures. They have the legs of a horse, the tail of a scorpion, the face of a lion with long hair like a woman, and insect like wings.

Before they can move, Gabriel presses the black button on the disk and this time a solid black beam erupts from it. Only when it strikes the demons, do we understand its function. It immediately begins to pull the demons by the thousands into the disk. In vain do they scream and struggle against its irresistible pull. Wave after wave of them are sucked into the bottomless pit's irresistible maw. Finally, the last of demons are sucked in.

Gabriel switches the beam off and turns and flies toward the earth as the Father had previously directed him. As he approaches the ground, he is flying straight down, head first pointing the pit towards the ground in front of him.

He slams into the ground burrowing into it. Down and down he goes, forcing the disk mile after mile beneath the surface. He descends until he is at the right depth. He then presses the green light and the disk expands to its rightful size of 15 feet across. Next he turns the key and the disk begins to vibrate. Then the bottom of disk shoots downward like it has been shot out of a cannon.

It is expanding downward at a rate of several hundred miles per second. It bores through the rock and mire. Through lava, down and down it goes, slicing through everything in its path. It slices through the hardest rock like it is not even there.

Finally it reaches its full size. It is a cylindrical tube 15 feet wide and 7,800 miles long, going almost the length of the entire earth. He then turns the key in a complete circle and removes it from the lock. Now the pit is fully activated.

Immediately, the other end of the pit is activated and it pulls the demons toward it. Because of its gravity-like effect, it feels as if they are falling downward. Before they can reach bottom however, it shuts off and the other end begins to pull them in the opposite direction towards it. We don't know how long it takes them to fall from end to end, for the normal rules of time and space do not apply within the pit. As they approach the other end, gravity again switches 180 degrees.

They are never able to touch the bottom because it keeps changing direction on them. It is a true bottomless pit where they will remain for thousands of years. These are the demons that are let out when the 5th trumpet sounds, (Revelations chapter 9). The Father will send an angel to release them to punish rebellious men near the end of time. When the demons attack men, their sting will put men in agony. They will be in such pain that they will wish for death, but the sting will render them temporarily incapable of dying.

As Gabriel turns and leaves, he can hear their screams for they are forever falling. When he rises to the surface, he pivots and stretches back his hand over the pit and closes the ground to hide it from mortal eyes. He then streaks back to heaven as fast as he can anxious to see what has taken place during his absence. He has a feeling of great urgency, as if he is desperately needed.

Assault On Heaven

When Baal, Vinshi, Jorgamunde, Endoc, and two thousand of Lucifer's strongest warriors left the earth, they flew to their forces of 200,000,000 angels who where hiding on the planet Eros. Eros is the planet that lies between Mars and Jupiter. Their forces are hiding there, and trying not to arouse too much suspicion by being on the same planet as Lucifer and his angels. They have been anxiously awaiting a word concerning the upcoming battle. They wait in tense anticipation as the Four Angelic Kings descend to the planet's surface. Some of them have been testing their powers while they were waiting to hear from their masters.

Quickly, they inform them of Lucifer's brilliant plan. The 200,000,000 demons are to shrink down to their smallest possible size and enter the four kings' bodies. With 50,000,000 angels inside them, the four kings are to go to heaven and warn the Father of Lucifer's impending attack. When the attack begins they are to release the angels inside them and try to kill the Son.

With 2,000 angels already with them, they will never suspect they have brought another 200,000,000. The angels think it is a wonderful plan and it is assured to be a great success. They reduce themselves and enter the four kings' bodies. Then the four kings fly off with Lucifer's finest 2,000 warriors. As they leave Eros far behind, no one bothers to look back. If they had, they would have noticed that strangely, the whole planet was being moved out of its regular orbit. Now it was in direct line between Earth and Heaven.

As the four kings and the two thousand approach Heaven's outskirts, they see the celestial sea. As they pass over it, they see the mountain of God. They land at the base of it and climb the steps to the holy mountain. None are allowed to fly up the steps. They must all climb them in reverence to God. Even though they no longer reverence Him, they must pretend to do so if they wish to succeed. The mountain is immense, higher than any other in the universe. There are 144,000 steps leading up to the top of the holy mountain.

As they approach the final steps, they come to the gate of God's courtyard which is atop the mountain. They are met by the cherub (guardian angel) of the gate. The angel greets them and asks what brings them there. Endoc tells him "We have urgent business with the Father. We bring Him news of Lucifer's rebellion. We know his plans. He plans to invade Heaven today. We have come to warn Him."

The angel allows them to enter. He says, "You four follow me. The others will be escorted by the four seraphims."

They look up the final steps, and waiting at the top are these frightening looking creatures. These are the angels that Prophet Ezekiel described in Ezek 1:5-14 They are the seraphims.

Their feet are hoofed, similar to a cows feet, but they are sparkling and are the color of brass. Their legs are straight. As they look up, they realize that these seraphims are huge and powerful looking. Their power is so great that it radiates through their amber colored skin.

It looks like there are bright torches moving underneath their skin, with lightning coming out of the flames running all up and down their bodies. They have two sets of wings, four wings altogether. Each set is joined together. Two wings cover their faces and two large wings cover their bodies. Under their large wings they have a set of hands. The seraphims open up their huge wings and reveal their bodies.

On the four sides of their heads they each have a different face. One is the face of a lion, another is the face of an ox, the other has the face of an eagle, and the last is the face of a man. Their whole body is full of eyes.

In their hands they have a crystal staff. The seraphims tell the two thousand to follow them in formation. The four-winged seraphims lead the formation to the throne of God. As the seraphims move they never turn, but energy comes out of the bottom of their feet, lifts them up and propels them forward. When the two thousand march, each seraphim is on the four corners of the formation. They are on the left bank of the crystal river, while the four kings are on the right bank.

In the center of the courtyard is God's throne. Flowing from His throne is the river of crystal. The Father is sitting on His throne with the rainbow about His body. Standing on His right is the Son. On the left is the Holy Spirit, who appears as a tornado of fire. Standing on each side of the throne of God are two more of the seraphims. These are six-winged seraphims and they are larger than the others.

Endoc says, "Father, we have come to tell you about Lucifer."

The Son says, "Yes, we have already dispatched Michael and the other angels to meet him."

The angels smile thinking everything is going according to plan.

Then Jesus says, "We also know you and the 200,000,000 have been sent in a foolish attempt to kill me." Suddenly the smile leaves their faces. But before they can act, Jesus moves.

Immediately, Jesus throws a red cube from His hand that expands and traps the four kings before they can release the fifty million demons they each contain. Then, He turns to His left and fires a beam of light that energizes the crystal staff, held by the closest seraphim. The seraphim, whose strength is great enough to lift whole worlds, struggles to hold the crystal staff, as the power of God shakes the staff like a thing alive.

Suddenly, the power explodes from the staff, flowing to the other staffs held by the other seraphims, trapping the evil angels in an energy fence. The evil angels are temporarily stunned and before they can think to fly over the fence, the seraphims stamp the crystal staffs on the ground. When the staffs strike the ground, there is a loud clap of thunder.

Immediately the energy that looks like fire and lightning, runs from each staff across the floor. The flow from each staff expands until it finally meets in the middle of Lucifer's finest angels. The two thousand are completely stuck to the floor and cannot move.

The evil angels are very angry and some of them say, "This won't stop us. You cannot hold us for long."

The Father says, "I can, and will imprison you for all eternity.

"No you won't. Lucifer will be here any moment. He will free us and then we will kill you all."

"You won't be here when he arrives. I will send you to earth, where you will burn for all eternity."

"Nothing can burn angels. No flame nor nuclear fire can begin to harm us," they insist.

"You are all so foolish," the Father says at their incredulous stupidity. "I have powers and abilities which no angel or any creature could ever dream of. Behold!"

Then the Father reaches out with His left hand and tears a hole in space. Through the portal they can see the earth. The Father fires two beams from His eyes through the portal that strike deep beneath the earth. He energizes the lava beneath the surface and begins to form the kingdom of Hell. The lava is now energized so it will burn, but not consume any angel or spirit that enters it.

As the evil angels watch, a great sense of dread begins to overcome them. In vain they struggle against the power that binds them fast, but to no avail. In horror they watch this inescapable prison being formed right before their eyes. They see cells being formed with chains.

Then suddenly, the chains leap through the portal and begin to clamp on the angel's wrist and ankles. Next the chains yank them through the portal, down to hell. Row after row is pulled through the space-warp. As some go in screaming, others begin to beg for mercy. Unfortunately for them, it is too late.

After the last one goes in, they can see them lying in the supernaturally charged lava, screaming to the top of their voices, straining against their unbreakable chains. They would not accept God's love so now they must accept His judgement.

God, the Father, speaks and says, "The wicked shall be turned into hell and all the nations that forget God."
Psalms 9:17

Then the Son stretches His hand toward the cube which has the four kings trapped. It flies towards His hand. Then He almost casually flings it away and it flies across the universe until it gets to earth. There it crashes into the Euphrates River and sinks to the bottom. It sinks below the ground where it will remain until the end-time. Then all these angels will be released when God's angel blows the sixth trumpet.

When the 200,000,000 angels are released, they will incite the army of the kings of the east to go on a murderous rampage. They will transform themselves into horse-like creatures with tails like snakes that will bite men. Instead of horses' heads, they will have a lion-shaped head from which they will breathe out fire and sulfur. This army of demons will inspire the 200,000,000 Oriental Army to kill 1/3 of earth's remaining rebellious population.

Chapter 6

IT'S SHOWTIME

As Lucifer and his forces approach the outer edge of Heaven, they are met by Michael the archangel. With him are more than two hundred trillion angels that are placed in his command. Lucifer's body has grown many times its normal size to compensate for the awesome energy it now contains.

As the confrontation prepares to begin, it seems as if time itself stands still, and all the stars appear to dim, as the forces of evil try to conquer the universe. There is an eerie silence that sweeps over the cosmos, as the forces of death prepare to battle the forces of life.

Is it imagination, or does eternity seem as if it is about to weep, as all the angels prepare to go to war? If the universe had eyes to cry, it would weep galaxies of oceans, as its heart breaks. For Lucifer, the Deceiver, has manipulated a third of the holy angels to become a force for evil, and to dare rebel against God. Save for the sound of the cosmic winds, nothing can be heard for a billion parsecs.

As the opposing forces face off, their fiery, red eyes are blazing like flaming meteors. The holy angels are hurt and enraged by the treachery of Lucifer. They are prepared to defend the Giver of Life at all cost. They are determined not to let the evil angels proceed no further.

Finally, Michael speaks in a voice that sounds like thunder. He orders him, "Turn back Lucifer! Heaven is no place for you and your traitorous minions. The Father has blessed us, and given us all gifts and powers beyond mortal keen. We can plunge into the depths of the hottest star and outrace the fleetest comet. We can do all these things and a thousand more and this is how you repay His kindness?!" the outraged Michael says in disbelief.

Lucifer says nothing, unaffected by Michael's words. Michael says, "And you, Lucifer whom is blessed to be the mightiest of all of us, how can you prepare to commit such heinous and barbarous acts?"

Lucifer, who is unmoved by Michael's words replies, "To do evil, one must become evil. My actions are my own. If in serving my own ends, you and the Father call us evil, then let it be known forevermore, evil shall we be.

You are right, I am the strongest; mightier than the Father, Himself," Lucifer proudly exclaims.

Defiantly Lucifer blurts, "I will go to God's holy mountain, attack the Father, and defeat Him. Then, when He begs for mercy, I will make Him tell me all His secrets. Then the universe will be mine. If you join us now, I will give you a great position in my new kingdom. If you do not, then I will kill you myself, by disrupting the energy matrices that hold you together, and you shall go down into oblivion."

With tears in his eyes and defiant rage in his heart, because of the undying love for the Father, Michael emotionally proclaims, "I would sooner taste death's bitter cup myself than to betray my Lord and Master."

As a cry of "So say we all" rang forth from the rest of the holy angels, it seems as if the Father and the Son's hearts would burst with pride at their unswerving loyalty.

You see, Lucifer saw something in God, but because of his blind arrogance, he mistook it for weakness. Gabriel, Michael, and the remaining angels saw it too. But they recognized it for what it truly was...LOVE! He loves all His creation. But for the good of all, sometimes love must be tough.

Lucifer says, "My destiny is at hand. It was meant for me to rule this universe."

"Your power has corrupted your reason, foolish one. This day will see the end of Lucifer," says Michael.

Lucifer shouts in anger, "Enough talk! If you will not aide us, then you shall die. Attack!"

As the two forces collide, they strike each other with such force, the resultant shockwave reverberates throughout a dozen star systems. It is a ferocious battle. No quarter asked, none given. Lucifer's forces are badly outnumbered. But no number of angels seem to be able to contain the evil cherub. With one blow, he fells dozens of angels. He seems tireless. But he knows that the other evil angels cannot continue at this pace. He begins to wonder when will his other forces arrive.

Michael shouts to Lucifer, "Lucifer you have sealed your doom. Your other agents, Abaddon and the four Kings have all been neutralized." They charge toward each other, and begin to fight in hand to hand combat.

As they begin to grapple Lucifer smiles, "I told you, I would kill you. Prepare to die."

Michael, straining with all his might says, "Do your worst. My only regret is that I don't have a thousand lives to give for my Lord." As valiantly as Michael fights, he knows it is not enough. Once, he might have stood a chance. But not now, with Lucifer's formidable strength being multiplied by the *stones of God.*

Finally, Michael goes down and Lucifer transforms his hand into a celestial axe. He raises his hand to cleave Michael in two and disrupt the energy matrices which hold his body and spirit together, thereby, sentencing him to oblivion. He laughs and prepares to deliver the final blow.

From a million miles away, Gabriel, who is just now returning from earth, having completed his mission, sees Michael's imminent demise. He strains with all his might, flying as fast as he can, to save his fallen friend. He strains and pulls every bit of his reserve energy, as he desperately flies to save Michael. The very atoms about him seem to burn, as he streaks toward Lucifer.

He flies with his fist outstretched, crossing a million miles in the space of a heartbeat. With the force of a supernova he crashes into the dark angel. Lucifer plummets into the ground creating a huge smoking crater at the base of the God's Holy Mountain. All the combatants cease their struggling to see the fate of the dark angel. For a moment it seems as if the battle is over.

Then suddenly, Lucifer rises from the smoking pit completely unharmed. Gabriel has saved Michael but at what cost? Lucifer is within sight of God's throne. Gabriel, Michael, and the others prepare to renew their assault against him. As they hurtle towards him, Gabriel and the others realize that something is wrong. For even with the stones, no angel should be this strong. They immediately surround him to try to prevent Lucifer from advancing any further.

Enter: The Dragon

With Lucifer's final goal in sight, it is time for him to use his final secret plan. Unknown to all, Lucifer had secretly stolen the energy from a dozen stars, reducing them to black holes. He has stored that energy within the stones of fire.

There is enough energy in one pound of hydrogen to power six million homes for one year. Our sun is an average star that burns four million tons of hydrogen per second. That is enough energy to power twelve quadrillion homes (12,000,000, 000,000,000) for a whole year. Imagine all this energy burning at this rate for thousands of years. Lucifer stole all this energy from a dozen stars. He now has hundreds of thousands of years worth of energy from a dozen stars stored in these fire-stones. Can anything stand against him?

He fully activates the fire stones and his body begins to grow and change. Bursting with power he changes his form into a form similar to the tyrannosaur he had possessed earlier. It is a great, giant, red dragon!

And there was war in heaven: Michael and his angels fought against the dragon; and the dragon fought and his angels.
Revelation 12:7

Immediately the angels engulf him, fighting furiously. Never before, nor ever again, will there be such a battle. But despite all the thousands that have swarmed over his body like a swarm of angry bees, it feels to him like the sting of a gnat. He shrugs them off, and with his final goal in sight streaks toward the Father. This giant, burning, red dragon is roaring and flapping his wings ascending the Holy Mountain with an ease that defies description. He flies so quickly that seraphims, who are near God's throne have no time to intercept him before he reaches the Almighty. Lucifer can feel the universe within his grasp. He roars, with his wings flapping and his jaws slavering, this great, red dragon opens wide his mouth, as if he means to devour the Almighty. As the angels watch in transfixed horror, it seems as if evil has won this day.

As he leaps, the Father draws back His right hand and it glows with unimaginable power. Suddenly there is an incredible blast. The blast was so immensely powerful that all of reality shook at the force of the blow. The light was so blinding that even the angels, who can look into an exploding star without blinking, have to shield their eyes. After a few moments their eyes adjust and realize what happened. The Father smote Lucifer and he was blown away.

It happened so fast that no one saw just what, and how the Father struck the evil one. No words, no division of time, whether thousands or billionths of seconds could do justice to the speed at which the Father struck Lucifer. The Father smote him so quickly that no one knows whether it was a right cross, left hook or if He just blasted him with some beam of unimaginable force. Even to the Son, all he saw was Lucifer cast out of Heaven like lightning. (Luke 10:18)

Immediately the Holy Spirit transforms into a cloud of plasma-fire and gathers around Lucifer's angels. It then picks them up and hurls them in the same direction, and with the same force that the Father cast out Lucifer.

As the holy angels watch the evil angels being cast out, they realize there is no force or power that can stand against the Father. All at once, they fall down and worship Him.

Then the Son proclaims for all to hear, "Let it be known from henceforth and forevermore, that the Father has prevailed and all of Lucifer's plans have come to nought, for there is no wisdom or understanding, or counsel against the LORD. He is the Master of the Universe and none may say Him nay."

Lucifer and the fallen angels have been cast down. As they hurtle across the universe, they appear to be blazing comets. The Father has caused their own energies to begin to burn from beneath their skin. Like a cancer, it eats their physical supernatural bodies. They are on a collision course straight for our solar system.

A Hard Fall

As they enter the solar system, they streak past Pluto, Neptune, Uranus, Saturn, and Jupiter. There are trillions of fallen angels whose speed and trajectory will take them almost to the heart of the solar system. They are on a collision course straight for Earth, but Eros lies in the way; having just recently been moved into position by the Father.

With the force of a million thunderbolts, they crash into the doomed planet. Because of its decaying state, their bodies become broken and mangled from the murderous impact. As they continue boring through the planet, they are in excruciating pain. They have been cast from Heaven with such force that they bore completely through the planet, causing it to explode into millions of pieces.

The shattered planet is scattered across millions of miles in all directions. Some pieces become huge asteroids many miles long. The largest that remains is 480 miles long. To this day more than 1500 asteroids have been charted with the smallest being 10 miles long. One of them is the closest heavenly body to the earth besides the moon. It is a mere 33 million miles away from Earth. It was discovered in 1898. Its name is Eros.

Some of the planet is reduced to dust. The earth gains hundreds of thousands of tons of meteorite dust a year from Eros. Eros will not be recreated. It will remain in its destroyed state to remind all the angels of the time when Lucifer dared to rebel against God and the terrible price of his folly.

The angels hit Eros with such force that most of their bodies were destroyed. Where Lucifer hit, his body energized the rock and as it was hurled towards the sun in an elliptical orbit these meteors became flaming comets.

As Lucifer and the angels crash to earth bringing some asteroids and much cosmic dust with them, they land with thundering impact. Through re-entry of the atmosphere and the crash, their supernatural bodies have been destroyed. Though they have power on the spiritual plane, their power is very limited on the physical plane. Because they are immortal their spirits do not die, even though their bodies have been destroyed. They are angels no longer. Their main power is only deception and manipulation. Lucifer, the son of the morning, is gone. He is only a shadow of his former self. He is no longer an archangel. He and the other fallen angels have been forever changed into something horrible. Their outward form now matches the evil in their souls. They have become devils and demons.

The Father tells the holy angels to rise. He blesses them and praises them for fighting the good fight. He was aware of all Lucifer's doings from the beginning and could have stopped him at any time. Yet, all this was necessary for them to prove their faith and loyalty to the Trinity.

He wished to show that no scheme or all the greatest plans contrived by the wisest of minds, could prevail against Him. He allowed Lucifer to gain all the extra power and confront Him directly to prove a point. Rebellion is futile, for in all the universe there is no power to equal His. Despite His disappointment in Lucifer, the holy angels have made Him very happy, for they have justified His faith in them, and have proven themselves worthy to be His holy angels.

Lucifer was cast out of heaven with such force that even after traveling countless miles, he crashes to earth with the speed and force of a thunderbolt. In his bid for universal domination, he has failed, and his hopes have ended in ashes. His cohorts have either been reduced to disembodied spirits or imprisoned. As Gabriel, Michael, and the rest of the holy angels view Lucifer and his minions, they are awestruck at the changes that God has wrought upon the rebellious angels. They are unconscious and perhaps would remain so for ages, but the Father wakes them, and prepares to pronounce His final judgement upon them.

As Gabriel, Michael, and the other holy angels look upon Lucifer, they can hardly believe their eyes; his actual form has changed and he is a mere shadow of his former glory. As he grovels before them, he is fearful for his life. The Father makes them aware of the punishment of the other fallen angels. They are allowed to see those in the bottomless pit and those chained in hell. In transfixed horror, they view the doomed angels who are in agony. Their screams are horrible.

The Father speaks, "Because you dared to rebel against me, this too shall be your fate. This is my law and my eternal decree: Let it be known that you, and any who shall come after you throughout time; those who sin against me, shall spend an eternity in hell; where there is weeping and gnashing of teeth. This is the final fate of all those that dare oppose me."

They immediately beg for mercy. "Mercy! Please Father have mercy! We will do anything, but please spare us! Forgive us. Give us another chance."

They begin to blame one another. Finally someone says, "It was Lucifer. He tricked us all. He lied to us and deceived us into following him."

"Yes, it was all his fault. He started it all," they begin to cry out.

"If you wish Master, we will punish him for you," another one pleads.

"Yes. Let's do it! Then perhaps the Father will forgive us." some of them advise.

"No!" the Father interrupts; angry at their continued treachery. He says, "There is no forgiveness for fallen angels. You have seen too much and experienced too much for your sins to be forgivable.

To whom much is given, much is required. Only if you had been mortal could there be a possibility for forgiveness; and only then with an acceptable blood sacrifice to offer in atonement; for the wages of sin is death. But, because you left your first estate and followed Satan, there is no forgiveness.

Since all of you were foolish enough to follow him in his quest to become God, it is My command that he shall have dominion over you and all that sin. You chose him as your God and now keep him as such.

You were all gifted to be holy angels. You witnessed creation. You were there when I caused the waters to burst forth into existence. You saw Me in all My glory and witnessed the birth of the universe. Yet, viewing all My mighty and wondrous acts, and experiencing all My goodness, did not stop you from rebelling against Me.

You were created perfect, but you listened to the lies of Lucifer, and allowed him to steal your faith in Me. Then you let your hearts be filled with the pride of life, and dared to rebel against your God.

So you see, experiencing My goodness and witnessing My miracles did not ensure your faithfulness to Me. If witnessing My power and experiencing my blessings does not guarantee faithfulness in you, then certainly it won't in creatures less than you. You angels rebelled against Me because you have no faith in Me.

I AM GOD!!

I demand faith. I decree, the just shall live by faith. He that has no faith is not worthy of Me. Without faith it is impossible to please Me.

Lucifer! You sought to rise above the clouds, above the stars and rule the kingdom of heaven. But instead, you shall descend into the lowest part of the earth. I give you a kingdom. It is not the kingdom of heaven, but the kingdom of hell."

Suddenly the ground begins to rumble beneath them. It begins to crack and split. As it opens beneath them, the angels fall into the ground screaming. Down and down they go. Just about the time it seems they would fall forever, they crash into the ground. Some of them have fallen on top of each other. They have fallen straight into hell.

As they struggle to rise, they realize they are not burning. They are in hell all right. It appears to them as a very old, damp filthy castle. They are in a great room. A shaft of brilliant white light is coming through the hole in the roof which they have fallen through. The deepest part of hell called Tartarus, is below them. In that level are imprisoned the other fallen angels. Satan and the rest of his followers are not imprisoned in hell. While the stars are denied them, they are free to roam the earth. As they lift their eyes to behold their new surroundings, once again their attention is diverted to the blinding light. They are startled as God's voice seems to come from the light. He finishes telling them the details of their awful judgement.

"You thought the proud would prevail, but it is the meek that shall inherit the earth. You sought to rule even the righteous, but you shall only rule the wicked. Who you set in authority under you, I give you to choose. It is in your power; I care not.

I shall not destroy you now, for it pleases Me to allow you to continue for a season; lest they say I immediately destroyed you out of fear. You are no threat to Me. You never were. I gave you the greatest of wisdom. I gave you greater intelligence than any mortal mind can contain or imagine. Yet, your wisdom was corrupted by your pride. I resist the proud, but give more grace to the humble.

These followed you because of your wisdom. But in the end I shall show all of creation that your wisdom is nothing compared to Mine. As you have used these for your own ends, I shall use you as the greatest of fools. Your name is changed to Satan, which means adversary.

The fear of the Lord is the beginning of wisdom. Wisdom fled from you the moment you lost your fear of me. But I... shall teach you fear. I will allow you to continue for a season as immortals go, but each day you shall live in fear; knowing that each day may be your last; for your time is but a season.

When that day finally comes and all of creation views your final fate, they shall not remember your beauty or wisdom; but you shall be remembered as the greatest fool of all time."

As the Father leaves them, the ground closes up and the light from the surface shrinks with it. As it finally disappears with the closing of the ground, a terrible sense of dread comes over Satan, and his devils, and demons. For even though they have some time left, they know in their heart of hearts, they are doomed.

Conference

Now the Holy Trinity have a conference. God, the Father, says, "All that We have foreseen has come to pass; Lucifer's rebellion, the defection of 1/3 of our angels to Lucifer and their dismal defeat. However, his defeat was only physically. My Son, only You can defeat him totally. All that he sought to attain through rebellion, You can achieve through submission. All that he sought through lies, You will gain through truth. All that he sought to gain with selfishness, You will gain through love for those who are undeserving of Our love. Lucifer was an archangel, yet he yielded to sin. You will remain faithful. You will be tempted and tried. You will commit the most selfless act and save a world. Evil will strive against good until the time of evil is no more. When men have finally learned that only the meek shall inherit the earth, then Satan's defeat will be complete."

Time Capsules

It may seem strange to some that the entire rebellion from start to finish was over in just a few days. But, you must keep in mind the speed at which the angels and spirits can communicate and act. If one day is *as a thousand years*, then one hour is as 41.6 years. If you find it difficult to believe that the angels can communicate at these great speeds, just consider Judgement Day.

The Bible has a lot to say about Judgement Day. Jesus said that men would have to give an account of every idle word. The dead are all raised, no matter when or how they died. Hitler, Kennedy, Capone, Roosevelt, Napoleon, and Abraham Lincoln will all be there. All these, and billions more, will be raised from the dead, to be judged. This will be an amazing event for sure, but have you ever considered how long this could take?

If this happened at normal human speed, then it would take a lifetime for one person to be judged. But on Judgement Day, everyone who has ever lived will be judged. There are three billion people alive in the world today. Some estimate the total number of people who have ever lived, is forty billion people.

Since we must *give account*, this means that the judging is done at a speed at which we understand every issue that is raised concerning our words and deeds. If this is done at normal human speed, then the Judgement Day would actually be billions of years long. That would make it longer than the Millennial Reign of Jesus Christ, and longer than any of man's ages. This would be a Judgement Age and not a day.

This would certainly be unbearable for everyone involved. (I am sure some would say, "I know I'm going to hell anyway so let's just get it over with)." If the preceding age of peace is only a thousand years then certainly God would not want to drag this out for billions of years (Despite the fact that after the judgement, begins the eternity of peace). It is not called a Judgement Age, but Judgement Day.

Therefore, we must conclude that the judging is done at tremendous speeds, communicating to our spirits, going over each lifetime in just a few seconds. When you consider how different time is for those in the supernatural realm, and the fact that 40 billion people's lives can be judged in one day; then it is easy to understand how the rebellion, from beginning to end, was able to be completed in just a few days.

Chapter 7

To Finish The Work

Now, the Son prepares to complete creation. The earth had been formed from beneath a huge, swirling body of water. As the icy cold waters circulated around the molten earth, making it solid, some particles broke lose and made the waters very murky. Eventually much of this material would settle to the bottom, however, God does something to expedite the matter. He takes sufficient amount of the elements out of the ocean and forms the fish and all the birds. All the birds and fish were formed on the previous day. The Bible tells us that the birds and fish were formed out of the sea. So we can conclude that they were formed out of the elements in the seawater.

Many writers incorrectly thought that these two forms of life were created out of nothing. The sea is not made of nothing. Not only is the sea made up of hydrogen and oxygen, but the oceans are made up of every chemical element. During World War II, America got bromine from the ocean to make airplane fuel and magnesium from the ocean to make incendiary bombs. There is more gold in seawater than there is in some gold mines in California. Until recent centuries, this was not understood. The writers who claimed the birds and fish were created out of nothing, did not consider the fact that seawater consists of every element.

Another reason we know they were not formed out of totally nothing is because this would require a fusion process of atoms; releasing the heat of a hydrogen bomb. Each one of these birds and fish being created would have generated that kind of heat, causing world-wide destruction. So from this, we know they were formed out of elements in the water.

He forms all types of fish, dolphins, whales, piranha, sharks, salmon, bass and hundreds of others. He forms all types of birds. From the great eagle to the small hummingbird. Some fly thousands of miles a year. One type of geese flies from the North Pole to the

South Pole every year. He completes their creation on the fifth day. Now He prepares to create the animal life.

From the dust of the earth, He begins to form different animals and insects. Everything is made up of the different elements. So He begins to take the different elements out of the ground to form the different creatures. The Bible places them in three categories, creeping things, cattle, and beasts of the field.

Lions, tigers, bears, elephants, cows, sheep, and many others He creates, including dinosaurs, with different shapes and abilities. He creates them with different characteristics. Many people assume, because they are not mentioned by the name dinosaur, that they were not created during the age of man. But, the Bible never mentions hundreds of animals and fish by name. Rather they are categorized by their relationship to man. Creeping things included all insects and smaller animals and small reptiles. Cattle probably included all domesticated animals. Beasts of the field include; larger animals such as lions, bears, dragons, and other large wild animals.

There is a large type of lizard living in the East Indies today, called the dragon of Komodo. It can grow to ten feet long and weigh 150 pounds. It has a long tail and is covered with small dull-colored scales. When it opens its wide, red mouth it shows rows of teeth that are curved like the edge of saw. The dragon comes out only in the day when the sun is high. With its strong claws it digs caves, which it hides in at night. It has a keen sense of smell and sight and it hunts other animals.

Though it is so powerful that it can tear off the hind quarters of a wild boar and swallow it, bones and all, this is probably not the dragon the Bible refers to. The same Hebrew word 'tannin' that is translated as "great whales" or "great sea monsters" is most frequently translated as dragons. Since the same word was used, then they were probably of similar size. They were most likely dinosaurs.

Every ancient nation has stories about dragons (whose descriptions sound amazingly like dinosaurs). Dinosaurs bones have been found on every continent. When you consider that dinosaurs were actually dragons, you can understand why more and more human footprints are being discovered alongside dinosaur bones. Human footprints have been found with dinosaur bones in Kentucky, Texas, and many other places across the earth, much to evolutionists dismay.

Many people who believe in dinosaurs will argue that dragons never existed. Tell me what is the difference? None. They are both very large and extremely powerful, lizard-like creatures. If the dragon of Komodo at two feet tall is extremely powerful, imagine how powerful one would be if it were 40 feet tall, like the tyrannosaur.

If all the Scriptures in the Bible that mention the word dragon were printed here, it would fill up five pages. That is quite a bit for something that supposedly never existed. The mightiest type of creature that ever existed was a dragon that lived in the sea, called the Leviathan. He was the most ferocious of all the species on earth, and totally without fear. The same God that made the electric eel give electrical charges, the firefly to give off light, and the little skunk an odor that can travel for miles, gave this dragon the ability to breathe out fire. Read here how the Leviathan is described in Job chapter 41, of the New King James Version of the Bible.

> **Job 41:1-33** Can you draw out Leviathan with a hook, or snare his tongue with a line which you lower? Can you put a reed through his nose, or pierce his jaw with a hook?
>
> Will he make many supplications to you? Will he speak softly to you?
>
> Will he make a covenant with you? Will you take him as a servant forever?
>
> Will you play with him as with a bird, or will you leash him for your maidens?
>
> Will your companions make a banquet of him? Will they apportion him among the merchants?
>
> Can you fill his skin with harpoons, or his head with fishing spears?
>
> Lay your hand on him; remember the battle; never do it again! Indeed, any hope of overcoming him is vain; shall one not be overwhelmed at the sight of him?
>
> No one is so fierce that he would dare stir him up. Who then is able to stand against Me?
>
> Who has preceded Me, that I should pay him? Everything under heaven is Mine.
>
> I will not conceal his limbs, his mighty power, or his graceful proportions.
>
> Who can remove his outer coat? Who can approach him with a double bridle?
>
> Who can open the doors of his face, with his terrible teeth all around?
>
> His rows of scales are his pride, shut up tightly as with a seal; One is so near another that no air can come between them;
>
> They are joined one to another, they stick together and cannot be parted.
>
> His sneezings flash forth light, and his eyes are like the eyelids of the morning.

Out of his mouth go burning lights; sparks of fire shoot out. Smoke goes out of his nostrils, as from a boiling pot and burning rushes.
His breath kindles coals, and a flame goes out of his mouth.
Strength dwells in his neck, and sorrow dances before him.
The folds of his flesh are joined together; they are firm on him and cannot be moved.
His heart is as hard as stone, even as hard as the lower millstone.
When he raises himself up, the mighty are afraid; because of his crashings they are beside themselves.
Though the sword reaches him, it cannot avail; nor does spear, dart, or javelin.
He regards iron as straw, and bronze as rotten wood.
The arrow cannot make him flee; slingstones become like stubble to him.
Darts are regarded as straw; he laughs at the threat of javelins. His undersides are like sharp potsherds; he spreads pointed marks in the mire.
He makes the deep boil like a pot; he makes the sea like a pot of ointment.
He leaves a shining wake behind him; one would think the deep had white hair.
On earth there is nothing like him, which is made without fear. He beholds every high thing; he is king over all the children of pride."
Job 41:1-33
New King James Version of the Bible

Some scientist believe that the leviathan may have actually been a Kronosaurus or something like it. A Kronosaurus was a large crocodile-like creature more than 60 feet long. We know more about the surface of the moon than we know about the bottom of the ocean. The last official sighting of a creature like this was in 1915. It was reported during World War I by a crewman on a German submarine. Captain George von Forstner described what happened:

[2]"On July 30, 1915, our U28 torpedoed the British steamer *Iberian* carrying a rich cargo in the North Atlantic. The steamer sand quickly, the bow sticking almost vertically into the air. When it had gone for about twenty-five seconds there was a violent explosion. A little later pieces of wreckage, and among

---

[2]Paul Taylor, **The Great Dinosaur Mystery and the Bible** (El Cajon, Ca: Master Books, 1979), p.46

them a gigantic sea animal (writhing and struggling wildly), was shot out of the water to a height of 60 to 100 feet. At that moment I had with me in the conning tower my officers of the watch, the chief engineer, the navigator, and the helmsman. Simultaneously we all drew one another's attention to this wonder of the seas...we were unable to identify it. We did not have the time to take a photograph, for the animal sank out of sight after ten or fifteen seconds. It was about 60 feet long, was like a crocodile in shape and had four limbs with powerful webbed feet and a long tail tapering to a point."

In the early days of China, people of royalty rode in wagons driven by medium sized dragons on special occasions. Ancient people from all over the world, with no contact with each other, had stories about dragons. The Chinese, Greeks, British, Germans, and Vikings all have stories about great dragons. Since every ancient race and nation of antiquity had stories about dragons, can these be shrugged off as mere fairy tales? It is highly probable that these were stories about dinosaurs handed down by people who remembered them before they became extinct.

There are many ancient legends of young men like Hercules, Siegfried, Beowulf and others who fought and killed dragons. These were probably exaggerated stories about young men who hunted smaller dinosaurs and killed them. This coupled with environmental changes that occurred would explain their eventual extinction.

Today, if a young man wants to gain fame and fortune for his courage and physical strength, all he has to do is play football or some other sport. In ancient times one gained fame and fortune on the battlefields. Poor Goliath! He was born three thousand years too soon.

If he had been living today, instead of David's time, he never would have had to face that dangerous shepherd boy. Since his height was at least nine and a half or maybe twelve feet tall, all he would have had to do is learn to drop the ball in the hoop. He could block the tallest players shots. Can you imagine how much money they would pay him? I'm sure it would be enough to make Michael Jordan envious.

Ancient literature is full of men who fought dragons to gain fame and glory. The Bible mentions a famous hunter. His name was Nimrod. We don't know what type of creatures he hunted, however if they were dragons, they were only medium sized ones. The larger dragons such as behemoth and leviathan mentioned in Job 40 and 41 could not be killed with a sword. At this point, however, Jesus had created all the different types of dinosaurs, and they were alive and well in the earth.

Jesus finishes creating the animal kingdom. He is having a wonderful time forming all these beautiful, wonderful creatures. Like a decorator, who truly enjoys his work, and a veterinarian with a consuming love for all animals the Word continues to form the different species of animals. Elephants have long noses. Giraffes have long necks. Some have hoofs, some have paws. He decides to give the apes arms, legs, hands, and feet.

A full grown chimpanzee will be five feet tall and have seven times the strength of a normal man. A gorilla, which grows to a height of six feet, and a weight of three hundred pounds, has fourteen times the strength of a normal man. The apes love to hang out in trees. Some, like the hippopotamus and the water buffalo, love water. Some creatures like the sand. The pig loves mud. Some are gentle, like the deer and some are ferocious, like the lion.

Because of his great strength and regal manner, the lion is called the king of beasts. When it stands on its hind legs, the lion is seven feet tall and weighs 300 pounds. One strike of its paw can break a zebra's neck. The lion is strong, powerful, and was given a ferocious roar.

Few are privileged to hear their roar. If you go to a zoo what many people think is a roar, is actually, for a lion, more like a grunt! Not all the ferocious animals are as large as the lion. Some are small. The wolverine, which lives in and around Michigan and Wisconsin, is said to be pound for pound the deadliest fighter on earth.

Jesus has made the horse strong and fast. It will become man's principal means of transportation for thousands of years. He has given horses a docile nature, making them among the most loyal of animals. When tamed, they will literally run themselves to death for their masters. Here is God's description of the horse when He was talking to Job in Job chapter 39.

Have you given the horse strength? Have you clothed his neck with thunder?

Can you frighten him like a locust? His majesty snorting strikes terror.
He paws in the valley, and rejoices in his strength; he gallops into the clash of arms.
He mocks at fear, and is not frightened; nor does he turn back from the sword.
The quiver rattles against him, the glittering spear and javelin.
He devours the distance with fierceness and rage; nor does he stand firm, because the trumpet has sounded.
At the blast of the trumpet he says, 'Aha!' He smells the battle from afar, the thunder of captains and shouting.

Job 39:19-25
New King James Version of the Bible

Another loyal animal is the dog. Although, in ancient times they were despised and treated badly by people, dogs will eventually come to be known as man's best friend.

With great love and affection, Jesus has created all these animals. He even has created all types of creeping things. He creates the reptiles, lizards, dragons, turtles, snakes, alligators, and also the insects.

Some insects fly, some crawl. They are formed with many different shapes and sizes. The fly has a compound eye which allows it to see in many different directions at once. There are millions of different kinds of insects. Each one with different shapes, sizes, characteristics, and functions.

The bee's job, who can see ultraviolet light which man can't, is to pollinate flowers. Some, like ants and spiders, are arthropods; meaning their skeleton is on the outside of their bodies. This gives them such great strength that they can lift forty-seven times their own weight. Some, like the bees and ants, have social structures. Black ants and red ants have wars with each other. Now that the animal and insect world have been created, He prepares to create the final creature; man.

A Man Called Adam

Man will be the Trinity's special creation. He will play a very special role in God's plan for the universe. Because of man's special place, they decide:

"..."Let us make man in our own image, after our likeness: and let them have dominion over the fish of the sea, and over the fowl of the air, and over the cattle, and over all the earth, and over every creeping thing that creepeth over the earth."

Genesis 1:26

Many people believe that when He spoke of man being formed in "our image", it only meant man's spirit, and not necessarily his body. But the writer makes a special notation here by writing *in our own image, after our likeness*. The writer wanted to make it perfectly clear. Man was created after God's image physically and not just spiritually.

From the dust of the earth, He pulls the necessary elements. Oxygen, iron, calcium, hydrogen, magnesium, sodium, nitrogen and many others are needed to form man's body. He draws the necessary elements from the ground to form complex molecular combinations. It is an amazing sight as these different molecules begin to form all the body's components.

Genes, proteins, amino acids, blood, hemoglobin, antibodies, skeleton, muscles, tendons, ligament, lungs, heart, nerve fibers, eyes, and all the other organs, body parts and bodily fluids. He forms the feet, legs, torso, arms, hands, neck, and finally the head. He is perfect. Yet, he lacks the final and most important ingredient, Life.

To give him life, God does something which He has not done before. He breathes into man's nostrils the 'breath of life,' and man becomes a living soul. The same word that is translated from the Hebrew that means *spirit*, is also used for breath. So man is in some way, a living extension of God's Spirit.

This sort of explains why some of the prophets were able to do miraculous things in accordance with His will. From having fellowship with God, they got so close to Him that their bodies and spirits were charged with His power. This may seem strange, but remember

Jesus reminded the Pharisees in St. John 10:34, about the scripture in Psalms 82:6,7

"6) I have said, Ye are gods; and all of you are children of the most High
7) But ye shall die like men.."

The scripture says, "ye are gods." Man is not meant to be separated from God. But he is meant to have fellowship with him.

God names the man whom He had formed, 'Adam'. He then takes him, places him in the garden of Eden, and commands him to dress and keep the garden. As God watches Adam, He realizes that it is not good for man to dwell alone.

So God brought all the animals that He had created to Adam, to see what Adam would call them. Whatever name Adam called the animal was its name. But still, there was a longing in Adam's soul that could not be satisfied. None of these animals could be a suitable help meet for Adam. So God decided to make him a mate.

As He prepares to operate, He applies the anesthesia and causes a deep sleep to fall on Adam. He takes one of his ribs and makes him a mate. This process was similar to cloning. When Adam awoke, God presented the woman to him. He called her woman, because she was formed from man.

Genesis 1:27 So God created man in his own image, in the image of God created he them.

28) And God blessed them, and God said unto them, Be fruitful, and multiply, and replenish (fill to capacity) the earth, and subdue it...

God gives every creature that He has made the ability to reproduce after its 'kind'. This will allow for some variations in genetic duplication. It allows species to adapt according to environmental changes if necessary and breeding but it is always after its 'kind'. It cannot evolve into other types of animals. It can only reproduce according to what is programmed in the genes.

For example, you can breed certain dogs to form new breeds (pit bull is one example of a new breed), but you can never mate dogs with sheep to form a new species that will reproduce itself. However, dogs will never mutate into cats, people, or any other type of creature. They will always be dogs.

The garden was one of the most beautiful places on earth. In the garden was all types of plants, flowers, every herb, and tree that was good for food. In the middle of the garden He placed the two trees with supernatural fruit: The tree of knowledge of good and evil and the tree of life.

God instructed Adam and Eve that they and the animals could eat all types of herbs, plants and fruit for food. They could eat everything in the garden except the tree of knowledge of good of evil. God commanded that they were not ever supposed to touch them.

Everything was going according to plan. The war was over and Lucifer had become Satan. He had failed in his plans for universal conquest and his armies were defeated. Although they (Satan and his angels) were unaware of God's divine plan, they were fulfilling his eternal purpose nonetheless.

God's plan (which is for the overall benefit of His entire creation) was proceeding according to schedule. Much pain and suffering will eventually come. To be truthful, the hurts, sorrow, death, and destruction that will come is incalculable in human terms. No one will be exempt. Even The Trinity will experience anguish, grief, and suffering. One of Them will taste death. But They in their omnipotent wisdom, know that there is no better way. For the peace, safety, and survival of billions of creatures who will live in eternity; the Eternal Plan must be carried out.

God looks over all His works and He is well pleased. The universe is perfect. The earth is a paradise. Because of the water vapor canopy causing a green-house effect, the earth's entire climate is tropical. Because there are uniform temperatures throughout the planet, there is almost no wind, if any.

In its original state, earth has no deserts, and no storms of any kind. There are no hurricanes, snowstorms or even thunderstorms. Even the North and South poles have tropical temperatures with fruit trees in great abundance. It does not rain. The land is watered by a mist that comes up from the ground daily from rivers, streams, and by the many underground waterways. These underground waterways or "great fountains of the deep" would later be broken up in the Flood. The earth is not only pleasant, but incredibly healthy.

There is no disease, sickness, or death. If things remained the same, Adam and Eve would live forever.

31 And God saw every thing that he had made, and, behold, it was very good. And the evening and the morning were the sixth day.

Now it was the seventh day and He was finished creating the universe and He rested from all His works.

Chapter 8

Paradise Lost

From deep in hell Satan watches Adam and Eve. Adam has dominion over all the earth, and Satan hates him for it. To think that this man; such a fragile creature should experience an eternity of bliss, is unthinkable. How he would love to rend the flesh from Adam's bones and feast on his living heart; but that is beyond his power now. Still there must be a way. Somehow he will make Adam, God, and the world pay for his present predicament. He hates all that lives. And he feeds on his hate. He begins to ponder a way to make everyone suffer.

He remembers God's decree; that he would only have dominion over all those that sin.

He realizes, "If I could trick Adam into sinning, I would gain dominion over him and all his seed."

Adam was given only one commandment: Don't eat of the two trees in the midst of the garden. If he could deceive Adam into eating the tree of knowledge, he would not only be disobeying God, but he would be forever altered.

They both are naturally curious. However, the woman seems more so. The way to Adam's heart is through his wife. Since Adam and the woman were friends with all the animals, he decides to approach the woman using an animal form. But which one? It must be one that would arouse the least suspicion. They must not know that it was Satan who would possess this creature and was speaking through it. He decides to use the craftiest, most subtle beast of the field, the serpent.

Satan leaves hell and spies a suitable serpent in the garden. He enters it and tries to possess it. He can never control any creature totally against his will. Yet, if the creature surrenders his will to Satan, he will control it.

The woman is strolling about in the garden and she hears a voice calling out to her.

"Woman," the voice calls to her in soft seductive and almost hypnotic tones. Intrigued by the voice she turns to see who is speaking to her. It is the serpent. He speaks to her and says,

"Isn't it true that God said you cannot eat of every tree in the garden?"

"Yes. God said we must not eat of the two trees in the midst of the garden. We shall not eat of it them lest we die," Eve answers.

"But do you know why He told you this?" the serpent asks her. "You shall not die. God knows the day you partake of this fruit your eyes would be opened and you would be like gods, knowing both good and evil," the serpent answers.

The woman looks at the fruit. It certainly looks delicious. She reaches out ever so gently. She wonders to herself, "Perhaps if I just barely touch it, nothing will happen?" She lightly touches it and nothing happens. She does not die. Was God's command and warning untrue? If this was not true, perhaps she could eat of the fruit and still live. Why did God say in the day she would touch the fruit she would die? What the woman was about to learn and what ten billion of her children yet unborn would learn, was if you touch the *forbidden fruit*, it is not long before you eat it. In the centuries to come, her children would face their own versions of *forbidden fruit*. It's name would change to cocaine, alcohol, drugs, adultery, murder, rape, and greed to name a few. As complex as the circumstances become, it always begins with touching the *forbidden fruit*.

The woman looks around to make sure no one sees her. Surely there could be no harm in tasting something that looks so delicious. She plucks the fruit and slowly puts it to her mouth, after all, one little bite can't possibly hurt. She eats it and nothing happens. She goes and finds Adam and tells him everything. She persuades him to eat the forbidden fruit. When he does, their eyes are opened. Their understanding and knowledge increase many times.

They stagger and drop the fruit as their new sense of awareness overcomes them. They look at each other and realize, for the first time, that they are naked. New emotions overcome them; shame, guilt, and fear. Not only that, but death sets in. Although it would take some time for their lives to fully end, their days are numbered.

Before, they would have lived forever. Now Adam will be dead in 930 years. Suddenly, they realize they have made a terrible mistake. While hiding in the bushes, watching everything, the serpent smiles with glee.

The serpent is glad.

God returns to the garden and calls out to Adam.

Aware of their nakedness for the first time, they gather fig leaves and sew them together to make aprons.

God continues to call out to Adam, "Adam. Adam where are you?"

Adam and the woman try to hide among the trees of the garden. God keeps calling to him. Finally, he answers.

"I heard you calling, but I was afraid to answer because I was naked, and I hid myself" he answers.

God asks him, "Who told you that you were naked? Have you eaten of the tree that I commanded you not to eat?"

Adam knows he is in trouble now. He says, "The woman that You gave me, she gave me the fruit and I did eat.

"Do you know what you have done?" God asks.

The woman says, "The serpent beguiled me and I did eat."

God begins to pronounce His terrible punishments.

Because you have done this, cursed shall you be of all cattle and every beast of the field. God removes the legs from the serpent and says, "Upon your belly you shall go, and dust shall you eat all the days of thy life. And I will put enmity between thy seed and the seed of the woman; it shall bruise thy head and thou shalt bruise His heel.

This was the first prophecy of Christ. Many have wondered about this passage because a woman has no seed. This was the first prophecy of the virgin birth of Christ. Christ, who will be virgin born, will be the seed of the woman who will bruise the head of the serpent.

Unto the woman He said, "I will greatly multiply thy sorrow and thy conception; in sorrow thou shalt bring forth children; and thy desire shall be to thy husband, and he shall rule over thee.

And unto Adam He said, "Because thou hast hearkened unto the voice of thy wife, and hast eaten of the tree, of which I commanded thee, saying Thou shalt not eat of it: cursed is the ground for thy sake; in sorrow shalt thou eat of it all the days of thy life;

18 Thorns also and thistles shall it bring forth to thee; and thou shalt eat the herb of the field;

19 In the sweat of thy face shalt thou eat bread, till thou return unto the ground; for out of it wast thou taken: for dust thou art, and unto dust shalt thou return.

20 And Adam called his wife's name Eve; because she was the mother of all living.

Genesis 3:18-20

Adam and his wife had sinned. God killed an animal and gave Adam and Eve the animal skin to wear for clothes. Not only did this cover their nakedness, but it covered their sin as well. God instituted a law that without the shedding of blood, there should be no remission of sin. The consequences of sin are so devastating, bringing death and destruction, that God instituted a law. In order for sin to be covered, innocent blood must be shed. This can only be done by an acceptable blood sacrifice. God explains this to Adam, who will later pass this knowledge on to his future children.

Now, the Holy Trinity have a conference.

And the LORD God said, "Behold, the man is become as one of us, to know good and evil: and now, lest he put forth his hand, and take also of the tree of life, and eat, and live for ever."

Therefore, the LORD God sent him forth from the garden of Eden, to till the ground from whence he was taken.

So He drove out the man; and He placed at the east of the garden of Eden Cherubims, and a flaming sword which turned every way, to keep the way of the tree of life.

Adam was driven out of the garden and the presence of the Lord. Never again would he have fellowship with God as before. Never again will he feel as near to God. He has lost the beauty of the fellowship in the spirit with the Father. As much as he, tries it will never be the same. The grass will never seem as green, the flowers will never be as beautiful, nor will a rose smell as sweet. Adam has become a sinner, and he is separated from God.

God cannot have fellowship with sinful men. Man can never understand how horrible sin is to God. To God, the Father, sin is like a horrible stench in His nostrils. It is so foul to His righteous eyes that He cannot bear to look directly upon the face of iniquity.

Habakkuk 1:13 Thou art of purer eyes than to behold evil, and canst not look on iniquity...

From time to time, God tries to reach men. He tries to get men to leave their sin, and turn to Him. The Holy Spirit always tries to reach men through their spirits. However, they will not have the fellowship that was first available to man in the garden.

For a while, Man was able to look at the entrance of the garden of Eden and view the cherubims who guarded it. This would remind man and his future generations of his fall from grace. The garden may have endured for centuries.

Satan has gained dominion over man and now the earth. He has extreme intelligence. No human being, whether scientist or doctor, will ever be the equal of his intellect. He witnessed the creation. Because of this, he understands much of it. His understanding of chemicals, hormones, genes, DNA, germs, and microbes is greater than any mortal genetic scientist can imagine. Although he can create nothing, he can make some changes in things that already exist. Many of life's biological processes he completely understands, and what he does not understand, he is determined to learn. His power in the physical realm is quite limited, yet he will make the world tremble underneath his foot.

The Order Of Things

Now man has been cursed to work by the sweat of his brow. He will succeed, if he works. In the centuries to come, those who apply themselves, will prevail. No matter what the area, success will not necessarily come to the good or the bad, but those who diligently strive to succeed in their endeavors.

Proverbs 13:4   The soul of the sluggard desireth, and hath nothing: but the soul of the diligent shall be made fat.

God will generally cause His rain to fall on the just as well as the unjust. Although there will be times when God will super-naturally intervene in the affairs of men, man will generally be left on his own to determine his fate. If a man seeks after God, the Lord will bless the work of his hands. He will be blessed in what he sets his hands to do. What he does not set his hands to, he will not be blessed in. In centuries to come, many will mistake the success of diligent men for favor with God or false gods. Some will blame God for their lack of success, when many times, it is a question of their own diligence, or wisdom.

Men will suffer the consequences of their actions. Sometimes they will be rewarded in this life, sometimes not until in the hereafter. It is man's responsibility to subdue the earth. He can succeed if he tries, but he must be diligent. In his trying, there is no substitute for wisdom, however.

Proverbs 8:11 For wisdom is better than rubies; and all the things that may be desired are not to be compared to it.

All the trying in the world will not make up for lack of wisdom. God is the source of all wisdom. Some will only seek after knowledge of war, science, and other things, while not seeking after the source of all wisdom who is God. Without seeking after Him, their knowledge will always be incomplete.

They are like a mouse who has wisdom to know he is hungry. The mouse has enough wisdom to know he must do something about it. The mouse seeks after food and has wisdom to recognize it when he finds it. He has wisdom to go after it and tries to gather it. However, he does not have wisdom to recognize that he is on a mousetrap. He is snared by the trap because he did not have wisdom to see the big picture. So is everyone who does not have wisdom to seek after the Lord. Ultimately, he will be snared in a trap, because he did not seek the greatest wisdom, knowledge of God.

Proverbs 9:10   The fear of the LORD is the beginning of wisdom: and the knowledge of the holy is understanding.

As time passed, Adam knew his wife and she bare a son. His name was Cain. Later as time passed and she bore another son named Abel. There came a time after they were both grown that they gave their offerings unto the Lord. Abel was a keeper of sheep and Cain was a farmer. Abel gave the acceptable blood sacrifice and God was well pleased. Cain, however, gave a grain offering and this was not acceptable unto God. Cain was very angry because his offering was not accepted. The Lord spoke to him and said,

"Cain why are you angry? Why are you pouting with a long face? If you do well, shall you not be rewarded?" And if you do evil, sin lies at the door."

In other words, Cain's rejection was his own fault. He had no right to be angry at anyone, but himself, because he knew what he was doing was wrong.

Later as Cain talks with his brother Abel, they begin to argue. They are in the field alone. Cain tells Abel all about his ordeal. He is still angry. Abel says to Cain, "What right do you have to be angry. God's words to you was as plain as day. You know that God told our father that only a blood sacrifice was acceptable. Yet, you had to do it your way."

Cain becomes so angry that he picks up an large stone.

"Shut up!" says Cain.

Cain picks up a large stone and holds it high above his head. He says, "I told you, I do not want to hear it."

Cain hurls the stone at his brother with all his might. It strikes Abel on the top of the head. For a split second, Abel feels the pain of the blow on his head. Intense pain continues to radiate through his head as Cain continues to mercilessly strike his brother, again and again. Abel drops to the ground. He remembers the feel of his warm blood as it flows down the side of his face. A strange drowsiness overcomes him. It feels like a deep sleep, is coming over him. This deep sleep brings with it a strange peace. He surrenders his will to the weakness that overcomes him.

Abel awakes to find himself standing upright in a strange mist. He looks around for something that he may recognize. He is in a strange place. He recognizes nothing. He cannot see the sun. Everything seems real, yet unreal. Initially, Abel assumes he is having a strange dream. He suddenly feels that is not the answer. He begins to walk, to see if he can find a way out of this strange place. He walks faster and faster. There seems to be no escape out of this strange place.

Meanwhile, the Lord calls out to Cain. And the Lord said unto Cain, "Where is Abel, your brother?"

Cain wishes to hide his evil deed from God. He is still angry and unrepentant. He does not know that God is testing him. Cain answers disrespectfully to God, "Am I my brothers keeper?"

At that moment, Abel realizes that this is no dream. He cannot escape. He travels and finds no one. Not one creature is visible. He does not know where he is. He is all alone. He is getting scared. The thought dawns on him that he is no longer alive. He cries out to God, "Lord where am I?" His panic mounts and he screams, "GOD HELP ME!"

The cry of his spirit travels upwards. It continues to rise until it hits a roof of some sort. Above this roof is a huge layer of stone. The cry of Abel is not muffled by the objects it must pass through. It goes through rock and earth for mile after mile. As we follow the path of his righteous cry, we realize where Abel was calling from; From deep within the bowels of the earth. He is in Sheol, the land of the dead, and Abel is the first to arrive. It is not mere sound, but something far more potent. It can travel across the universe to the ears of God in less than a heartbeat. It is the *cry of the righteous*, and it has reached the ears of God.

God says, "What have you done? The voice of your brothers blood cries unto me from the ground. And Now art thou cursed from the earth, which hath opened her mouth to receive thy brother's blood from your hand. When thou tillest the ground, it shall not henceforth yield unto thee her strength; a fugitive and a vagabond shalt thou be in the earth."

And Cain said unto the Lord, "My punishment is more than I can bear. Behold, thou hast driven me out this day from the face of the earth, and from thy face shall I be hidden; and I shall be a fugitive and a vagabond in the earth; and it shall come to pass, that every one that finds me shall slay me."

And the LORD said unto him, "Therefore whosoever slays Cain, vengeance shall be taken on him sevenfold."

And the LORD set a mark upon Cain, lest any finding him should kill him.

And Cain went out from the presence of the LORD, and dwelt in the land of Nod, on the east of Eden.

According to tradition, Adam had 33 sons and 23 daughters. The Bible only mentions three of Adams sons by name. It does mention that Adam had many sons and daughters. Cain was well aware of God's command for them to be fruitful and fill the earth. Perhaps this is why God did not slay him. He was driven by God from the area in which he and his family had always lived in. To him, this land was the only world he had known.

To him going to a far distant place to him, seemed like he was being driven off the face of the earth. He took his wife with him, who was one of his sisters. He dwelt in the land of Nod which was east of Eden. He and his wife had children. The first child's name was Enoch. Cain began to build a city and named it after his firstborn son, Enoch.

Adam lived a hundred and thirty years and he had another son, whose name was Seth. Seth looked just like Adam. Eve said, "God has appointed me another seed instead of Abel whom Cain slew."

Adam lived after he had Seth another eight hundred years and then he died and all the days of Adam were 930 years. Here are the generations from Adam unto Noah and how long they lived.

Adam (930 years)
Seth (912)
Enos (905)
Cainan (910)
Mahalaleel (895)
Jared (962)
Enoch (365 years*)
Methuselah (969)
Lamech (777)
Noah (950)

*Enoch did not die of natural causes nor was he killed. Enoch was so perfect before God that one day God took him to heaven without dying.

The Bible tells us that each of these men (except Noah) had other sons and daughters besides those mentioned here. However, their names were lost through time.

Satan has called a conference in Hell. All his demons are there. He begins to instruct them on their various positions. He divides up the jobs of the various devils. He divides the earth into various sections. Each section is assigned to his generals. Weaker spirits will have the task of tempting men to commit violence and other acts of sin.

As time passes, men begin to multiply across the face of the earth. Many ignore the teachings of Adam and forsake God. Man is blessed with a long life-span. The average man lives over 900 years. Perhaps a 400 year old man only looked like today's 31 year old. Yet, few men use their time to draw closer to God. However, there were a few. Enoch walked and talked with God continually for most of his life. His desire was to be closer to his God. In 365 of his years he had pleased God, as no other man had before him. Finally, one day God translated him. He was taken straight to heaven without dying.

The Bible says a curious thing began to happen. The sons of God began to look upon the daughters of men and began to mate with them. From this strange union, giants were born in those days. These giants were mighty men. While it is not understood exactly how this came about, there are a few possibilities.

First of all, we know that these sons of God were not His holy angels but fallen ones. If we take this verse literally, it does raise many questions. The Bible does not specify if the women realized there was anything different about their appearance. It just mentions the demons' influence. It is possible that these fallen angels possessed certain men. They were selected by their genetic potential for great size and violence. They may have even manipulated the genes to increase the size and strength. It is possible. through demonic influence, that only the sperm with the potential for these evil giants were allowed to fertilize the egg. This experience served the demons' own ends, and they took pleasure in doing it.

From their efforts these giants were born. With their help, mankind fills the earth with violence. Man's only thought, his every imagination becomes evil continually. He has become so wicked, God can no longer stomach His creation. God is forced to withdraw from His creation.

And the serpent is glad.

And the LORD said, "My spirit shall not always strive with man, for that he also is flesh."

The situation only gets worse. Men have multiplied across the face of the earth. Imagine if you could live for 900 years and at 500 you were still in the prime of life. Think of all the wonderful things you could accomplish and all the wonderful things that you could learn. No wonder the Bible tells us that men were already making music and working with metals, and apparently they were skilled in shipbuilding. Imagine if the great minds of this world Einstein, Newton, and others lived 900 years, instead of 70. Yet, instead of using this wonderful gift of time for constructive humanitarian purposes, they used it to kill, maim, and murder. They strive to invent new ways to destroy their fellow man. They use their years to perfect their evil ways. They have become hopelessly corrupt.

And the serpent is glad.

And GOD saw that the wickedness of man was great in the earth, and that every imagination of the thoughts of his heart was only evil continually.

And it repented the LORD that He had made man on the earth, and it grieved Him at his heart.

And the LORD said, "I will destroy man whom I have created, from the face of the earth; both man, and beast, and the creeping thing, and the fowls of the air; for it repenteth Me that I have made them."

There is nothing left for God to do, but start over. He has given them a free will and they have exercised their will to destroy. Man has grown increasingly violent. They will not listen to the voice of reason. They are without a conscience. They are not interested in God. Even though every one on earth is a descendant of Adam and he has been dead for less than one of their lifetimes, they ignore his teachings. For example, Noah's father, Lamech talked with Adam for 56 years before Adam died. The story of Creation and the fall of man is known to the entire human race. Finally, God comes to a fateful decision.

The end of all flesh is before me.

Chapter 9

Noah and the Ark

God decides to destroy the entire world. He has decided to send a great Flood to destroy the planet and end all life. Yet, there is one man worth saving before the flood. His name is Noah and he found grace in the eyes of the Lord. Noah had three sons, Shem, Ham, and Japheth. Noah had walked perfectly before God all his life. That is why he found grace in the sight of the Lord. God speaks to him and tells Noah His plans.

Genesis 6:13   And God said unto Noah, The end of all flesh is come before me; for the earth is filled with violence through them; and, behold, I will destroy them with the earth.

"Make yourself an ark of gopherwood; make rooms in the ark, and cover it inside and outside with pitch. And this is how you shall make it: The length of the ark shall be three hundred cubits, its width fifty cubits, and its height thirty cubits.

"You shall make a window for the ark, and you shall finish it to a cubit from above; and set the door of the ark in its side. You shall make it with lower, second, and third decks.

"And behold, I, Myself, am bringing floodwaters on the earth, to destroy from under heaven all flesh in which is the breath of life; everything that is on the earth shall die.

"But I will establish My covenant with you; and you shall go into the ark; you, your sons, your wife, and your sons' wives with you. And of every living thing of all flesh you shall bring two of every sort into the ark to keep them alive with you; they shall be male and female. Of the birds after their kind, of animals after their kind, and of every creeping thing of the earth after its kind, two of every kind will come to you to keep them alive. And you shall take for yourself of all food that is eaten, and you shall gather it to yourself; and it shall be food for you and for them."

Genesis 6:22　　Thus did Noah; according to all that God commanded him, so did he.

Noah gets his sons and tells them what God told him. Together they begin to build the ark. After many years, the day finally came when they completed the ark. Building the ark had been a monumental task. Even with the help of his three sons, it had taken over a hundred years for them to finish the ark.

He had constructed the ark as God commanded him. He built the ark out of gopher wood. This wood was found near the banks of the Tigris River. It is nearly water tight, and it is excellent wood for making boats. The ark was huge. A cubit was between 18 and 21 inches long, depending on which version of the cubit you used. That would mean the ark was at least 450 feet long, 75 feet wide and 45 feet high. It would have been large enough to hold over 30,000 living creatures. It is estimated that Noah only needed to bring less than 2,000 creatures on the ark.

Then the LORD said to Noah, "Come into the ark, you and all your household, because I have seen that you are righteous before Me in this generation. You shall take with you seven each of every clean animal, a male and his female; two each of animals that are unclean, a male and his female; also seven each of birds of the air, male and female, to keep the species alive on the face of all the earth. For after seven days, I will cause it to rain on the earth forty days and forty nights, and I will destroy from the face of the earth all living things that I have made."

And Noah did according to all that the LORD commanded him.

Now begins the most famous procession in history, as all the species of earth's creatures begin to enter the ark. From all over the globe, they have come. They have been drawn here by an irresistible urge at the command of God. Two of each kind, a male and his female, to preserve their species. Of cattle and sheep and other domestic animals, there were seven of each kind.

Even though God had told Noah it would be like this, he can hardly believe his eyes. Every land creature has come. There are the great dragons; tyrannosaur, brontosaur, and other types. The ark is big enough to accommodate the largest of the dinosaurs and all of earth's species of land animals. Noah and his family march this wonderful procession of animals to their cages inside the ark. Every type of animal, bird, and creeping thing enters the ark. Even insects such as ants, beetles, bees, butterflies, and others enter two by two. All these creatures move in this procession as if guided by some unseen hand, and indeed they are. Meanwhile, more than 12 million miles away something strange is happening in the asteroid belt.

God, the Father, looks at the world He is about to destroy. There is no turning back. Resolutely, He reaches with His mighty power and grabs hold of a huge asteroid, more than a hundred miles across, and hurls it at the earth. It is but the first of many. Simultaneously, He gathers comets and asteroids, and sends them on a collision course straight for earth. These asteroids and comets are all that remains of Eros. The remains of this dead planet have become instruments of His divine judgement. These are but a few hundred of the tens of thousands of asteroids from the Asteroid Belt. He will not need all of them now. Some, He will save for thousands of years in the future, to use during the Great Tribulation. Even then, He will only need a few of the asteroids.

He blows with the breath of His mouth, and thousands of meteors and asteroids are sent on their way to doom the earth. Their average distance is 12,000,000 miles away from the earth. Their average speed is 70,000 miles per hour. In seven days, three hours, and 6 minutes they will strike the earth. As they speed toward the earth with the force of a thousand hydrogen bombs, the angels watch in awe and perhaps fear, at the judgement of God. This barrage of space debris speeds past the planet Mars, on its way to end all life on earth. As they speed toward the earth, Noah continues to load the ark. He has seven days left.

If ever Noah doubted the coming of the Flood, his doubts are put to rest as God gathers these creatures into the ark. Amazingly the lion lays next to the lamb. Nor does the wolf attack the sheep. He has soothed all the savage beasts. You can almost feel God among the animals. They seem to understand exactly what is going on and resolutely march to their cages. Noah looks at the animals and can't help but wonder, "How much do they know?" They are supposed to be the savage beast. Yet, it is because of the sins of man that God is preparing to destroy the world. As Noah thinks about the irony of the situation, he is almost embarrassed to belong to the species of man.

Now Noah and his family are preparing to enter the ark for the final time before the flood. They look around for one last view of the world about them. Little do they realize, the world will never be the same. Land, rivers, continents and seas will not be the same as before. The Land of Eden will never be recognizable again. Some of the rivers that mark its boundaries will not exist. Nothing on the planet will be the same. Was there a place, a continent called Atlantis? a whole continent that was destroyed when it sank beneath the ocean according to legend? Who can say?

The last of the animals have entered the ark. Two of each kind, except for the "clean" beasts. There are seven of each clean animal. The animals were selected by God. He probably gathered those that were the healthiest and most genetically fit. The rivers begin to overflow near the ark, and Noah knows it is near the time. He gathers everyone and they enter the ark. They go inside and wait for the Great Flood. After they enter, God shuts the door of the ark and seals in Noah and everyone.

Seven days have passed from when the first animals entered the ark. None except those on the ark believed the warnings of Noah. They have no idea of the doom that is to befall the whole planet. An unimaginable distance away, God, the Father, looks down upon the world He is about to destroy. Man has become hopelessly corrupt. He has filled the whole earth with violence. His only thought has become evil continually.

God has been trying to reach them by His Spirit but they have ignored His gentle pleading. Man is too confident, too stubborn, too proud, and too arrogant. The average life-span of a man is over 900 years. He is rarely sick. The earth is so stable with no violent storms or earthquakes, that most men feel no need for God. He has no fear for his own mortality. Even now, man has totally ignored Him. On the day of their destruction, they are still marrying and making plans as if they had the rest of their lives. God is so angry He is about to destroy the whole world. Yet, mankind has grown so insensitive to Him, that they have no idea the extent of his displeasure.

Mankind has taken for granted that they still have centuries left, instead of hours. None, save Noah, even listen to Him. Man has become such a disappointment, that God is sorry He ever made man. Of all the creatures in creation, none have failed Him more. There is nothing left to do, but start all over. He is so grieved by man's wickedness that He has repented that He ever made man.

The Great Flood

With Noah and His family safely in the ark, it is time for the end. The first of the deadly meteors are entering earth's orbit. They speed past the moon, 285,000,000 miles above the earth. In just four hours, they will strike the earth. They continue to hurtle to the earth and begin to pick up speed, being caught in Earth's gravity.

They engage the invisible water vapor barrier 450 miles above the earth's surface. As they encounter the Earth's atmosphere, the friction begins to make the meteors burn. These burning mountains of death begin to disrupt the water vapor barrier. The dust and meteors condense the water vapor barrier and the rain begins to fall. This huge supply of water is so vast that it will take forty days and forty nights before the barrier finally empties itself. On the ark, Noah sees the great downpour. Noah knows this is it. The day he has preached about for over a hundred years has finally come. The water vapor barrier has finally condensed into this great deluge from heaven. With the water vapor barrier pierced, the heat that was trapped begins to escape.

Violent winds begin to sweep across the planet as the temperature drops. The temperature change is worst near the poles. The greenhouse effect from the water vapor canopy was the only reason the poles were ever warm. Now that it is destroyed, the previously trapped heat escapes into space and the shrill of howling winds is heard across the land.

Near the North Pole the temperatures drops so fast, that some mastodons are frozen solid with leaves still in their mouths. The freezing rain, the extreme cold, and the wind chill factor all combine into such a force, that nothing has a chance to escape. The temperature drops 150 degrees before they realize what is happening. Some are frozen kneeling, some are standing, as they are frozen almost instantly.

Some of the inhabitants of the earth see the burning asteroids, just seconds before they hit from all sides. They appear as huge falling stars, or great burning mountains crashing to earth. It is the last thing they will ever see.

All over the planet, this deadly barrage of space missiles strike the earth. One asteroid strikes the bottom of the ocean, off the coast of Nova Scotia, creating a huge crater 28 miles across. Gigantic tidal waves sweep across the continents, destroying everything in its paths.

This barrage from space is so powerful, that the earth's crust is broken from its onslaught. Massive volcanic eruptions begin across the planet. Near Siberia, a herd of mastodon are feeding. Before they can react, they are caught in the midst of a volcanic eruption. In a moment of time, these mighty creatures are blown apart by the violent explosion of gases released by the volcanic upheaval. The gases erupt from the ground with such force, that the herd is literally blown to pieces and then buried before any decomposition can set in. They will remain buried for thousands of years, until 20th century scientists discover their remains.

Another huge asteroid that is many miles across, crashes near Eastern Europe. It is one of the largest asteroids to ever strike the earth. It strikes with such force that the entire planet shudders under the impact. The earth teeters like a drunken man from the blow of this burning mountain of death. It creates a crater so huge, that from the ground it would never be noticed. Only from space, looking at satellite pictures of the area, can this crater be seen. It was not until 1989, that this huge 200 mile crater was recognized by scientists studying satellite pictures of Europe.

The impact of these heavenly bodies striking the earth is so great, that the air flattens everything for miles around. Even trees are laid flat by the impact. They spew tons of earth into the air, and millions of creatures are buried alive. Some are buried for many centuries, to become fossils, to remind man of the day the earth died. Miles of forests are buried under tons of earth. The great pressure applied to them, changes them over the centuries.

In time these will become great coal deposits in the earth. Some of the buried animals and other organic matter goes through a similar, though different change. Water and hydrocarbon natural solubilizers (soap), break the organic matter down. The great pressure from tons of earth and rock buried over them changes them into crude oil.

Even though more than a thousand times a thousand of earth's creatures are killed by the meteors, this is but a portion of the planet's population. The meteors strike with such force, that the earth's crust, which is more than 80 miles thick, cracks like an eggshell, and the great fountains of the deep are broken up. Now the great underground reservoirs of water are released, and gigantic tidal waves sweep over the earth, and every living thing knows fear.

Deep in the belly of the ark, Noah and his family cower as they hear the screams of a dying world. With the window and door of the ark shut tight, they never see the streaking meteors and comets passing overhead. Those in the ark never see the asteroids or comets striking the earth. God does not allow any to strike near the ark, lest it too be destroyed. Noah feels the earthquakes caused by the crashing of the huge meteors. When he hears the crash from their impact and the rumble of earth, Noah never realizes what God is using to cause it. Nor does he care. It is their survival that concerns him most.

Now it has begun to rain on the ark. It is raining unbelievably hard. This rain does not fall a distance of five miles, as our rain today. It is the water vapor barrier falling from space. It falls a distance of 450 miles to the earth. It actually hurts when it strikes the people outside the ark. Those in the ark hear the violent winds and this torrent of rain as it beats unrelentingly upon the ark. It is the worst rainstorm the world will ever see, and only those on the ark have a chance of surviving.

For a hundred years, he has preached about this terrible day. He tried to warn them, but none would listen. They cared nothing about God, and less for His commandments. His relatives and friends all thought him mad. Only his three sons and their wives would listen to him. Now all his relatives outside the ark are dying and he is helpless to save them. He is glad his father Lamech, had died five years earlier and had not lived to see the death of so many of his children. Noah's grandfather Methuselah, had died only that year. He too, was spared the agony of this terrible day.

If only his remaining relatives had listened to him. Tears begin to well up in his eyes. For a moment he questions himself and wonders if he could have done more to save them. Yet, he knows in his heart he did his very best, and wipes a tear from his eyes. He gathers his composure, and reminds himself he cannot afford to show his emotions. He must be strong for his wife, sons, and their wives.

There is no time for further reflection, for all the animals are stirring. From the great dragons to the weakest chicken, they are all afraid. They know something is about to happen. Suddenly, Noah hears it too. A huge wave is approaching. He shouts, "Hold on!" as finally the ark begins to move.

The howling winds and the rushing waves sweep up the ark and carry it on its journey. The waters begin to rise above the tallest hills. Higher and higher still, the water rises. God remembers those on the ark and protects them from the devastation of the planet.

Thirty, forty, sixty feet and more, the waters continue to rise. The terror that sweeps across the planet is nigh tangible, as billions of living creatures breathe their last breath. Fish in the sea, birds in the air, man, creeping things, and all who have the breath of life die, as the waters continue to rise. Most of the fish survive, but some are picked up and slammed into rocks by the gigantic tidal waves.

It is an awful sight as a living planet enters its death throes. There is no joy from the angels, as they watch this grievous sight from space. No angel would ever question God's resolve or hatred of sin again. Watching the souls of billions of living creatures perish, the angels and demons alike, give pause at the terrible judgement of God.

This is His universe.

HE..IS...GOD!

If mankind will not fulfill God's divine purpose, then man will cease to exist. He does not need earth. For countless ages, the Trinity had existed alone. Everything was created for His purpose and pleasure. All souls are His: The souls of the fathers and the souls of the sons. He did what was necessary. Yet, watching the flame of life being snuffed out of all these creatures troubles Him.

He sees what no mortal eyes can see, and what He sees troubles Him. He sees the souls of all living creatures cry out as they are forced from their dead bodies. As the last of the earth's creatures gasp their last breath, and the screams of the dying fade, the God of Eternity is deeply sadden by what He was forced to do.

The earth is a mess. The tallest mountains are buried beneath miles of water. Plant life, animal, and some marine life have all been destroyed by an angry God. Man's wickedness has brought total devastation to the planet. The earth is broken and ruined. Everything is either buried in a watery grave or underneath layers of earth. As the Lord of Eternity looks upon the judgement of the earth, He makes a promise. He bows His head in quiet resolution and decides this will never happen again. He swears that He will never again destroy all life on earth by water.

Noah keeps track of the days as they pass. It rains for days and days, and there seems to be no end it. The sound of pouring rain can be heard continuously, day and night for weeks. There is no let up. Finally the forty days are up and it stops raining. To Noah's surprise, the water levels continue to rise. Even though the rain has stopped, the great fountains of the deep continue to empty themselves. These huge underground waterways that cover the earth, are emptying themselves. From the window of the ark, Noah can see huge water-spouts shooting hundreds of feet in the air.

Five months have passed since the flood began. Noah and his family have fared well inside the ark. They have taken good care of the animals in the ark. With the rolling action of the sea and the sound of continual rain, the animals sleep most of the time. Since they are not awake most of the time, they do not eat much. This makes Noah's job much easier. All this time the water continues to rise.

For a hundred and fifty days, the flood waters have continued to rise. Now God remembers Noah, and every living thing upon the ark. From the heights of heaven He sees the ark floating like a great barge on the waters. God causes a wind to pass over the earth. Finally, the great fountains of the deep stop flowing. There is no more rain falling from heaven. Now God prepares the waters to recede from off the earth.

During the Flood, the earth had been unstable. Now the ground has settled. Finally the water stops flowing from the great fountains of the deep. It is time for God to end the flood. At his command the mountains begin to move. At His rebuke they flee. He begins to lay the foundations of the earth again. The earth must be stabilized. At His behest, new mountain ranges are created. He speaks and the ground near what will be the western shores of North America, is thrown 90 degrees. This is the beginning of the Rocky Mountain Chain.

As this chain rises, the water drains into the descending ocean beds by means of newly formed rivers. Water flowing eastward from the Rocky Mountains help to form the Missouri, Arkansas, North and South Plate rivers. To the southeast, the Rio Grande River is formed. To the southwest, the Colorado River is formed. So much water flows down the Colorado River that it slices into the ground, forming the Grand Canyon, eventually flows into the Gulf of California, and then the Pacific Ocean. Thousands of square miles of earth begin to descend. The waters of the flood must go someplace. These will become the new ocean beds. This process was described in Psalms 104.

Psalms 104:5 Who laid the foundations of the earth, that it should not be removed for ever.
6 Thou coveredst it with the deep as with a garment: the waters stood above the mountains.

7 At thy rebuke they fled; at the voice of thy thunder they hasted away.
8 They go up by the mountains; they go down by the valleys unto the place which thou hast founded for them.
9 Thou hast set a bound that they may not pass over; that they turn not again to cover the earth.

It will take sometime for the waters to drain. Some drains underground. As this water drains underground, it will separate those creatures who perished in the flood by size and weight. The draining water helps to separate the remains of the creatures which are becoming fossilized. The larger creatures, such as the dinosaurs, will tend to remain near the surface. The smaller creatures drain to lower levels. The draining water shapes the landscape. In some places it creates underground caves, such as Mammoth Cave in Kentucky. Most of the water goes into the rapidly descending ocean beds.

It is the seventh month, the seventeenth day of the month, since the flood began. Noah and his family have wondered many times, "When will the Flood be over?"

Suddenly, there is a sound of the creaking wood and everything is thrown slightly forward as the ark comes to a stop. They have hit something. The ark has landed. It has completed its six hundred mile journey from the banks of the Tigris River. It has landed on the top of Mount Aarat. Noah knows that it is only a matter of time now for their ordeal to be over. He looks out his window and can see only water. Yet, the water continues to recede from the earth.

On the first day of the tenth month, Noah looks out and he sees the tops of the mountains. He must wait a little longer. Forty days pass, and Noah decides to try something; he gets a raven and sends him from the ark. The raven flies out of sight, past the nearby mountain tops. He flies far, looking for someplace to land. The raven never returns. The next time Noah gets a dove. He sends the dove from the ark. The dove flies for some time. Yet, it could find no place to land, for the waters still covered the whole earth. The dove gives up and returns to the ark. Noah reaches out with his arm and the dove hops on his hand. Noah pulls him in and closes the window.

Seven days pass and Noah decides to try again. He takes the dove and releases it once more. Late that evening, the dove returns to the ark. It has an olive leaf in its mouth. Now Noah knows that the earth was beginning to dry. Noah waits another seven days, and sends forth the dove from the ark. This time, the dove never returns.

It is now the six hundredth and first year, the first month and the first day of Noah's life. He decides to take the covering off the ark. Noah looked and behold the ground was dry! One month and twenty-seven days pass and the Lord speaks to Noah, "Go forth of the ark, thou, and thy wife, and thy sons, and thy sons' wives with thee. Bring forth with thee every living thing that is with thee, of all flesh, both of fowl, and of cattle, and of every creeping thing that creepeth upon the earth; that they may breed abundantly in the earth, and be fruitful, and multiply upon the earth."

Now Noah, his sons, and their wives leave the ark. They gather every creature that was in the ark and bring them out. It has been estimated that, including the dinosaurs, there was only about 10,000 different species of creatures alive at this time. The ark had room for over 30,000. Does this mean that they came from evolution? NO. When God made all creatures, He decreed that they would reproduce after their own *kind*. This is not necessarily exact duplication, but allows for genetic variation. For instance, the bear's genes that came out of the ark has the ability to produce offspring that will eventually become all different types of bears.

Noah and his family were people of color. They were not a specific race of people, but all of earth's races of people were within them. The Bible never mentions the word race, that is man's term. God never makes a distinction on the basis of color. God loves all His creation equally.

So Noah went out, and his sons, his wife, and his sons' wives with him. Every animal, every creeping thing, every bird, and whatever creeps on the earth, according to their families, went out of the ark.

Then Noah built an altar to the LORD, and took of every clean animal and of every clean bird, and offered burnt offerings on the altar. And the LORD smelled a soothing aroma. Then the LORD said in His heart, "I will never again curse the ground for man's sake, although the imagination of man's heart is evil from his youth; nor will I again destroy every living thing as I have done. While the earth remains, seedtime and harvest, and cold and heat, and winter and summer, and day and night shall not cease."

So God blessed Noah and his sons, and said to them: "Be fruitful and multiply, and fill the earth. And the fear of you and the dread of you shall be on every beast of the earth, on every bird of the air, on all that moves on the earth, and on all the fish of the sea. They are given into your hand.

Every moving thing that lives shall be food for you. I have given you all things, even as the green herbs. But you shall not eat flesh with its life, that is, its blood. Surely for your lifeblood I will demand a reckoning; from the hand of every beast I will require it, and from the hand of man. From the hand of every man's brother I will require the life of man.

Whoever sheds man's blood, by man his blood shall be shed; for in the image of God, He made man. And as for you, be fruitful and multiply; bring forth abundantly in the earth and multiply in it."

Then God spoke to Noah and to his sons with him, saying: "And as for Me, behold, I establish My covenant with you and with your descendants after you, and with every living creature that is with you: the birds, the cattle, and every beast of the earth with you, of all that go out of the ark, every beast of the earth. Thus I establish My covenant with you: Never again shall all flesh be cut off by the waters of the flood; never again shall there be a flood to destroy the earth." And God said: "This is the sign of the covenant which I make between Me and you, and every living creature that is with you, for perpetual generations: I set My rainbow in the cloud, and it shall be for the sign of the covenant between Me and the earth. It shall be, when I bring a cloud over the earth, that the rainbow shall be seen in the cloud; "and I will remember My covenant which is between Me and you and every living creature of all flesh; the waters shall never again become a flood to destroy all flesh. The rainbow shall be in the cloud, and I will look on it to remember the everlasting covenant between God and every living creature of all flesh that is on the earth." And God said to Noah, "This is the sign of the covenant which I have established between Me and all flesh that is on the earth."

At last, the Flood is over and the world has been remade. The waters from the water vapor barrier will remain on the earth. This has raised the sea level. The Pangea is broken up and has formed the new continents. God will send the animals to different continents walking on the land bridges that connect them. Eventually the land bridges will separate and fall into the sea as the continents drift further apart.

The New Earth and Carbon-14

The composition of earth's atmosphere is changed by the flood. The air pressure is different. It is reduced to 14.7 lbs. per square inch. This will allow more harmful organisms to grow, meaning there will be more diseases than ever before. Men and animals will not live as long or be as healthy. The change in atmosphere will be so pronounced that it will make it difficult for men to measure the age of objects before the Flood. Carbon 14 dating will be effective in dating objects that existed after the Flood. However, when they try to measure objects that existed before the Flood or the fossils that died during the Flood, the readings are deceptive and give false readings of extreme age.

Instead of one continent, there are many. They are now called North and South America, Africa, Europe, Asia, Antarctica, and Australia. These new continents only take up 29.1% of the earth's surface area. Water now covers 70.8% of the earth or 139,400,000 square miles. While most of the world until the modern era, believed the bottom of the ocean was bowl shaped, the Bible said otherwise.

The Bible describes channels in the sea or undersea canyons. There are many of them. One of them in the western North Atlantic, near Greenland, travels for 2,500 kilometers.

The Bible also said there were mountains in the sea in Jonah 2:3,6. Some of them are 10,000 feet tall.

There are now *paths in the seas* as the Bible calls them in Psalms 8:8, or ocean currents. Sometimes these currents lie on top of one another, traveling in different directions. The Florida Current, for example which travels northward of the coast of Florida, is the size of 10,000 Mississippi Rivers. It is along these currents where the fish live. In the middle of the ocean called the Sargasso Sea, there are no fish at all. It is a dead zone in the middle of the ocean.

It will be a few years before the earth's orbit stabilizes. Although God has the ability to immediately stabilize earth's weather, He chooses to let these things occur over a period of time. Like a spinning top, the earth's tilt on its axis will eventually correct itself. However, the immediate effect will be to cause droughts in some areas, and ice ages in others.

Years pass and men begin to multiply across the earth. Within a few centuries, the earth's weather patterns have stabilized and is similar to what it is today. Now the planet's poles are covered with ice, hurricanes now occur near the Caribbean. Tornados, freezing winters, droughts, lightning, rain, hail, and snow storms, are all common place.

Most of earth's creatures adapt to the changes in the environment except one, the great dragons (or dinosaurs). As cold-blooded creatures, they cannot endure the cold weather that now covers much of the earth. The cold weather begins to eliminate many of the tropical jungles that most of the dinosaurs need to survive. Many of their favorite plants are now extinct. Where tropical jungles were abundant, they are now scarce. These gigantic creatures need a tremendous amount of food and water to survive. Without it, they begin to die out. After the flood, the large dragons never gain the foothold they once had before the flood. Though the giant dragons once covered the earth in great numbers, they will be scarce from now on, until they finally become extinct.

Why were they created in the first place? Who can say? Perhaps they were necessary for the pre-flood food chain. Before the flood, most of the world was covered with tropical forest. These gigantic creatures, with their huge appetites, were needed to keep the tropical forest in check. They would have cleared paths through the thick forest for men and smaller creatures to pass through. The dinosaurs with long necks could have eaten the foliage at the tops of tall trees. In a thick forest, this would let light come down to the ground so smaller plants would have a chance to grow. Whatever the case, these creatures began to die out.

Chapter 10

SATAN'S PLANS FOR MAN

And it came to pass that men once again began to multiply across the face of the earth. As they begin to multiply, Satan once again begins to make his plans for humankind. He sits on his throne in hell. He has pondered long and hard. Now he is ready. He jumps off his throne and signals for the great horn, called the horn of Lucifer.

It once was part of the pipes from Lucifer's body. It is all that remains of his former glory. He looks at it and his thoughts drift back to how it was broken off his body, in his fight with the Father. He remembers his pain and his crushing defeat at the hands of the Almighty; another reason for his undying hate for the Godhead. His thoughts return to the business at hand, and he puts the horn of Lucifer to his lips and blows. Its sound is unlike any in the universe. It is not meant for mortal ears, only for the ears of devils.

The horn signals the gathering of demons. From all over the earth, every manner of devil and foul spirit comes. They are anxious to hear the plans of Satan, the Prince of Darkness. The foul stench of this gathering of evil is more putrid than the stench of a thousand maggots, in the midst of a room full of rotted flesh.

This congregation of evil in one place is more foul than the mind can conceive. If a human was so cursed to behold the face of such a gathering of evil, it would surely make him mad. None but they, could behold such an awful sight as this gathering of demons. They are so foul that they not only tolerate it, they revel in it. At the center of it all is Satan. He once was Lucifer, the greatest of archangels. Now he is only the lord of devils, ruler of hell, and he means to make the universe tremble. The demons gather around him and listen with great anticipation as the prince of darkness begins his evil plans.

"Men are not unlike the animals. They will follow leaders. We must seek out those who have leadership qualities; those who are intelligent, strong, and wise. We must try to influence them. If we can influence the leaders of men down the path of darkness, then mankind will follow. When they are successful, we must fill them with pride. They must believe it is solely because of their abilities that they succeed. This will drive them away from God, and unknowingly, turn them towards us.

God hates pride, He cannot tolerate it in men. He will not have fellowship with the proud; this leaves the door open for us. We will do all that is within our power to make evil men succeed. We must make them thirst for power and wealth. They must be willing to trample underfoot the weak and innocent to reach their goals.

As they succeed, we must cause others to worship them because of their success. In this way we can make evil men prosper. As men worship their evil leaders, this will alienate them further from God. If we can make the world a hard place, then men will not obey the laws of God. They will become selfish and hard. They will only look out for themselves. Of course, this will cause the righteous to resist them. We will cause the leaders to turn on the righteous; to kill if possible, but certainly persecute them. If we make those who love God outcasts, we will negate their influence and certainly turn men against God."

Cyphonnus, one of Satan's chief demons, seems confused. To work in conjunction with men is appalling to him and other demons. He asks him, "Satan, are these men that we use to be our friends?"

Satan responds, "You know better than that! We have, nor desire, any friends among the human filth!"

"What are we to do?" Cyphonnus asks. "You know how we hate the very nature of humans. He has two natures; the evil one we can tolerate, but it is his good nature that we abhor. How can we keep from turning on them?"

Satan clenches his teeth, shakes his fist and says, "You must control your hate! You must control your desire to destroy. Humans to us are merely fools and tools. When a human whom we have exalted has fulfilled his purpose, we will turn on him as well. Save your hate! We will torment him and laugh at his destruction. After all, they are only mortal. We can only use one man for so long. We must raise up another in his place. We will either raise up his friend who admires him, and will be just like him, or his enemy who hates him. When his enemy hates him, he opens the door to us and we will use that human fool as well. Either way, our purposes are served.

I hate all human scum, but those that serve God, we hate the most. In the heart of every man is the deadly poison of goodness.

He can be evil all his life, yet if we leave him alone, God may get to him and change him for the good. Then he will try to undo all the evil he has done. That is why every man born of woman is dangerous to us, for the desire for goodness that lurks within his souls.

Even if a man does willingly serve us all his life, he may yet have a child that will try to undo all his father's evil works. I hate all of them. I wish they would all die. We must continually tempt them to satisfy the lust of their flesh so they do not notice the hunger in their souls. Remember all men are dangerous to our cause, even those who become stupid enough to become our willing servants; and there are none more dangerous than the righteous.

"We must isolate and persecute the righteous. We must tempt them and try to turn them. If they fall, we must expose them to destroy their ministry. We must work on their followers, or children if they have any. The children of the righteous must not follow in their parents footsteps. If nothing else, we must discourage the righteous. Nothing is as dangerous to our cause on earth, as a hard-working, zealous, righteous man.

"When we cannot get to them, we must use the next best thing; the innocent. I love the screams, the torture, the cries of anguish of the innocent. It is like music to my ears. Nothing fills me with such joy as the cry of an innocent victim crying out for help, when there is none. I rejoice when they strain to scream to the top of their voice for help, and no one saves them. The unbelief in their eyes when something so painful and horrible is happening to them they can't believe it, makes us feel good. Don't you just love it when they are in so much pain their nerve endings light up and they overload their pitiful little brains and go into shock?" Satan asks his fellow demons. They all laugh and chuckle at the thought of torturing people to these cruel extreme.

"Yes, we love to torture the innocent," Satan continues. "I love it when they have that pitiful look in their eyes like, 'How could this be happening to me?'" He burst into a maniacal laugh and all the other demons laugh with him. They continue for several minutes. Satan suddenly stops and asks them a question.

"Listen," he says. "What is more innocent than a child? The younger, the better. In their innocence they are close to God. We must cause them to be molested, tortured and murdered. If we can pervert these innocent children, we can insure that they will be instruments of our wills for all their lives. Molested children will grow up to be adults who molest children." Satan's evil glee continues to mount as the demons listen with great fascination and delight at his fiendish plans.

Satan continues, "Suppose we whisper to some of the human fools to have success 'you must sacrifice your children?' We will tell them that the forces of nature will be against them unless they give the supreme sacrifice; an innocent child.'" He bursts into laughter and dances and all of the demons laugh and dance with him at the prospect of man's destruction.

"Wait!" one of the demons interrupts. "What will we do when man becomes intelligent enough to understand the workings of nature and he will no longer kill his children to sacrifice them to false god's. How will we get them to kill their children then?

Satan responds, "Don't worry about it. We'll think of something. We will give them another reason. Even if they don't realize they are doing it for us. Whenever men are proud and arrogant, we can sift them as wheat.

Now we must organize. There are trillions of us. I will assign you different jobs, according to your power levels. The weaker spirits will influence men with their power. You cannot control them, but you can tempt them. You will become specialized and operate only in certain areas. Some of you will become demons of hate. You will teach men to hate all men who are different than themselves. Use everything and anything you can. Spirits of hate can work hand in hand with those that will become demons of jealousy and envy.

We will tempt men to violate all the laws of God. We will pervert his natural desires, and fill him with all the lusts of the flesh. We will pervert their reproductive drives. We will make them lust after children and even their own sex, turning them into homosexuals."

"Can we do that?" one of them asks.

"If they are STUPID enough to listen to our lies long enough, WE CAN MAKE THEM BELIEVE ANYTHING!" Satan tells them. "We have a city in the plains called Sodom where we are already achieving this. I have a big plans for the cities of Sodom and Gomorrah. Right now, we only have a handful, but with our manipulation, we will cause their numbers to grow.

Though you cannot control, you can tempt and influence. When these foolish creatures yield to your temptations, they surrender their will and unknowingly open the door of their souls to you. As this door opens, you can call other spirits and gradually we can possess individuals.

We must do our best to make their existence on earth miserable. In our reduced state, our power over physical things is quite limited. We can only move things of small size. One would think that this would hinder us, but it shall not. I have figured a way around this. What is more important to the future of man than his own genes? We were present at Creation. No mortal mind can, or ever will, be as wise as us; and I am wiser than all. With my understanding of human physiology, we shall alter genes of men and microbes to create deadly diseases.

We already effectively alter him chemically. Everything in the human body is controlled through chemical reactions. We cannot fill his heart with lust, except we release those chemicals. His depression, hunger, pain, joy, and everything he feels, all require chemical reactions. We will practice and experiment and continually invent new diseases. Because all the earth is under the curse of Adam's sin, we have the ability to pervert life on this planet. Some of you will be dedicated to causing deformities in man and nature. When people see needless suffering, this will cause them to question God. That is why we will work to form harmful mutations, that will cause deformities and diseases. Many of you will be devoted to this cause. Some diseases will only be strong enough to merely make men suffer.

Because the soul of man will always cry out for God, we must give him alternatives. Some of you will become religious spirits. You will inspire men to create alternate religions. Anything to keep him away from God. Worship of the dead, worship of nature, stars and idols, are all to be included in the destruction of men's souls. We will use our power to impersonate the dead when possible. We do not care if man does not believe in us, as long as he does not believe in God either.

When this fails, we will fill him with pride and make him worship himself. We shall use our invisibility and intangibility to our advantage. What proud and arrogant man will believe he is being manipulated by something he can't see, something he can't feel? In his blind arrogance we will lead him like sheep to the slaughter. We shall drive him down the path of unrighteousness until his death. Then because of God's law, he will be cast to the other side of Geena, where the flames of hell will consume him for all eternity.

For some mad reason, God loves every human soul. It is the evil of man, He abhors. Every soul we cause to be lost into eternal damnation bothers Him. I don't know about you, but I love to bother Him."

Through clenched teeth Satan says, "I love to hurt Him."

Many of the demons smile and nod their heads in agreement.

"I will do anything to hurt him," He says.

Satan continues, "Because of his stupid law, I only have dominion over the wicked, including mortal souls. Those who die in their sins are doomed to hell. Well, I shall not be satisfied with a few souls. I wish to fill hell to capacity with the souls of the doomed and the damned."

A cry of "Yes" fills the hall as some of the demons can no longer contain their joy at the brilliant plan of Satan. Some of them begin to dance, with evil delight at the thought of the havoc they can wreak on the world. After a few moments, after they have calmed down, they pause to hear the rest of Satan's evil plans.

Caught up in the ecstacy of the moment, Satan lifts his head, clenches his fist and says, "We will be true to our malefic destiny and make this world as a wilderness."

The demons shout, "Yes!"

Satan smiles and says, "Perhaps God does not understand man as well as we do. I do not believe He understands the evil within the heart of man. His heart is desperately wicked and extremely deceitful. Because of the evil within their hearts, most men find righteousness boring, and evil exciting.

Most of the time when a man is tempted, he will yield to the temptation. God cannot change this without changing the hearts of men. Therefore, we must always be on the look out for the plans of the Trinity. They will try to stop our plans. They will try to redeem men at every turn, but we must stop Them. Although we do not understand God's plans completely, we do know something. We know that man is essential to God's ultimate plans for the universe. If we destroy man, we destroy His plans. If we destroy His plans, then shall not his destruction follow?" With great conviction Satan says, "Our only hope is for the destruction of mankind."

With great contempt Satan says, "God has a vision of the world. His vision is a united humanity, living in harmony full of brotherly love. Satan continues saying as if the thought of this fills him with disgust, "God's vision for earth is a paradise. It is one of kindness, peace and compassion.

Satan joyfully raises his arms and shouts, "I have another vision for the fate of this planet. My vision is one of DESTRUCTION!" Satan's ecstacy continues to build saying, "I see a divided mankind with hatred for all that is different. I see a mankind that despises those who talk different, who look different, different nations, different colors. I see a mankind with a legacy of war. I see the world as an unforgiving and cruel place. If we make the lives of men hard, we can make them doubt the very existence of God. My vision is a world full of iniquity and violence, one that hates God and His commandments." Satan stops for a moment and snarls defiantly, "We shall see whose vision of earth comes to pass."

The demons jump up and roar in triumph at the conclusion of Satan's speech. These vile devils are so excited, they begin a celebration that will last for three days. Satan the prince of darkness stands in the midst of them, hands on his side, laughing maniacally. He laughs, gloating at all the sick things, he and his followers shall do to the world. The demons rejoice at the magnitude of suffering and terror they shall heap upon mankind. These evil monsters laugh and dance at the thought of the destruction, they shall heap upon mankind.

Meanwhile, at the surface, for reasons unknown to them, all across the planet, men stop and pause for a fleeting moment.

It seems that a cold chill passes through men everywhere. They all shiver for a moment, as if they had just heard, the voice of doom!

Chapter 11

The Tower of Babel

As time passes, the sons of Noah begin to have children. As these children grow and multiply, they have children and the evil rises in mankind again. Cush, a grandson of Noah, has a son whose name is Nimrod. Nimrod's name means "let us rebel." Nimrod becomes a mighty hunter of men and animals, and eventually becomes king and builds the city of Babylon. His wife's name is Semiramis.

The people settle in the plain of Shinar, the Mesopotamium plain around the Euphrates and Tigris rivers. The whole earth is one people and one language. Nimrod and his leaders see that the people have a desire to scatter and explore the earth. Nimrod and his leaders do not wish to see this happen. They wish to keep their kingdom intact. Therefore, they invent a project; one that will keep the people occupied, and give them a reason to stay. They say, "Let us build a great zigguart (or tower). Let us build a tower that will reach into heaven."

The people like the idea, and they begin to build the great tower, which will one day be called the tower of Babel. It works beautifully. It is an enormous project. They continue to build until the tower is more than 770 feet tall and 1/4 mile wide at the base. They build a wall around the city of Babylon.

While this is going on, Nimrod, the servant of the devil and his leaders, are in open defiance of God's commands to Noah. They have no desire to serve the Lord, nor do they wish the people to serve him. They are inspired by Satan to give the people an alternative. They invent a new religion, idolatry. They deny God as the creator and teach the universe evolved without benefit of a creator. Because of his numerous conquests and legendary battle prowess, Nimrod becomes worshipped as a god. His wife Semiramis is worshipped, and called the queen of heaven. They set up a priestly system whereby men come to confess their sins to the priests. Sex is used in the religious rites to entice men and women to participate. The priest gain wealth from the tribute from the temples. For centuries they wield great power, and Babylon remains a theocratic state even up to crowning of Nebuchadnezzar.

With their fascination with heights, they look up at the heavens and study the stars. They imagine certain groups of stars form figures. These 12 figures later become know as Virgo, Sagittarius, Leo, Ares, Cancer, Taurus, Scorpio, Pisces, Aquarius, Capricorn, Libra, Gemini, the signs of the zodiac.

Eventually, Nimrod dies a violent death, presumably by wild animals. To preserve their false religion, Semiramis teaches that Nimrod becomes a child-god, while she is the mother-goddess. Their wickedness increases until it comes like up stench into God's nostrils. The cry of wickedness is so great, God decides to investigate. The Trinity decide to personally go down and inspect. To gauge the impact of Babel upon the men living there, God decides to take on near human proportions to better evaluate the problems. Unknown to all the citizens of Babel, The Trinity descends to the tower.

It seems that most of the people have forgotten all the lessons of the Flood. They observe the religious practices that has been set up; the paganism, astrology and child sacrifice that the Babylonian priests have established. They are in defiance of God's command's to spread out and replenish the earth. On top of all this, while they have become totally depraved, socially and spiritually, they have advanced technologically. This imbalance gives them a potential for incredible destruction.

At this pace, they will unlock most of the secrets of the world within a matter of centuries. A united mankind with the minds of the entire human race working together will soon find out the scientific laws whereby God established the universe. In this atmosphere of scientific advancement, they will soon be able to do whatever they can imagine. If this scientific advancement continues, it will totally disrupt God's cosmic timetable. Their spiritual depravity, coupled with their scientific advancements, threaten man's survival. There is only one thing left to do. Man must be separated, somehow and fulfill the command of God to replenish (fill to capacity) the earth.

The FATHER waves His hand and the miraculous happens. There is confusion at Babel. Suddenly, workmen in the tower are unable to understand one another. Priests cannot understand priests. There are arguments and fights. The work on the tower is suspended because no one can communicate. He confused their languages. It is as if everyone is speaking gibberish. Fortunately, when people go home they find that their families can communicate with them. It is an intolerable situation. Eventually many of the families pack up their belongings and leave Babel. They do not know what drives them or where they are going. They only know they must leave. They gather what they can and scatter across the earth.

This has happened so suddenly, that many of them are ill-prepared for the journey. As they would stop to rest or settle in new places they would have to make whatever tools they needed out of stone. This would give their villages a very primitive look. Later, when they discovered where the ore was in the ground, they would make their tools out of metal.

For those who stay in Babel, they now call their land Sumer. These ancient Babylonians now call themselves Sumerians. Nimrod's became worshipped as Merod-ach or Marduk. Nimrod was also worshipped as Tammuz. It is from Babel that Satan spreads his poisonous gospel around the world. It is Babylon the great, the mother of harlots, the mother of idolatry. Unfortunately, the former Babylonians carry their false religions with them around the world. These are some of the names that Nimrod either as king of gods, or infant god, and Semiramis as a celestial madonna, become known in different nations.

[3]From Babylon, the worship of mother and child spread to the ends of the earth.

Nation	Nimrod	Semiramis
Babylonian	Kronus or Saturn	Rhea
	Marduk	Ishtar
Egypt	Osiris	Isis
India	Iswara	Isi
Asia	Deoius	Cybel
Pagan Rome	Jupiter-puer	Fortuna
China	infant son	Shing Moo
Greece	Plutus	Ceres or Irene

---

[3]Alexander Hislop, **The Two Babylons** (Neptune, New Jersey: Loizeau Brothers, 1959),p.20

As the former Babylonians took their knowledge of idolatry with them, Nimrod takes on many names. In some lands, Nimrod becomes known as Baal. Some believe that Nimrod the hunter is unquestionably Orion, the great Titan whose constellation is in the sky. Ishtar's worshippers addressed her as "The Virgin," "The Holy Virgin," "The Virgin Mother."

Semiramis also becomes the inspiration behind Aphrodite and Venus. For a time, every Babylonian woman had to be a prostitute at least once. Before their marriage a woman had to go to the temple of Venus and wait for the first stranger to come by. The stranger would offer her a piece of silver and ask for her in the name of the goddess. The woman could not refuse.

Nimrod and Semiramis become the inspiration for many idols. Over the centuries the number of idols continues to multiply. By the 9th century B.C. the number of gods worshipped in Babylon was 65,000.

The Sons of Noah

SHEM'S SONS	The principal nations which sprang from them were:	They settled in:
Elam,	Persians,	Assyria,
Asshur,	Assyrians,	Syria,
Arphaxad,	Chaldeans-Hebrews-	Persia,
Lud,	Lidyans,	Northern Arabia
Aram,	Armenians,	Mesopotamia.
	Syrians.	

HAM'S SONS:		
Cush,	Ethiopians,	The continent of
Mizraim,	Egyptians,	Africa and Arabia
Phut,	Libyans,	
Canaan.	Canaanites.	Asia Minor, Asia

*note It is believed that two of Canaan's sons, Heth and Sin, are the ancestors of the Oriental peoples. Heth (Hittites = Khittae = Cathay) and Sin (Sinites = Sinim = China) While some of Heth's and Sin's descendants went south into the land of Canaan, others migrated eastward. The Bible says the families of Canaan were spread abroad. Since the Bible only made this distinction for Canaan, they probably spread out more than any other family. Isaiah 49:12 mentions a people in the Far East named "Sinim." Chinese people have always been known by the prefix "Sino-". The name "Sin" is frequently encountered in Chinese names in the form "Siang" or its equivalent. The descendants of Canaan also formed the Mongoloid peoples (and therefore the American Indians).

JAPHETH'S SONS:		
Gomer,	Russians, Germans, Britons.	Asia Minor,
Magog,	Scythians,	Armenia,
Madai,	Medes,	Caucasus, Persia
Javan,	Ionians and Athen-	Europe,
Tubal,	ians,	
Meshech,	Iberians,	
Tiras.	Muscovites,	
	Thracians.	

Some of the Persians migrated into India and became the progenitors of the Indian peoples.

Originally, the children of the sons of Noah were all one people. They were not a particular race, but had all the races of the world within them. After Babel, the families separated. As with all families, each family had different facial and genetic characteristics.

Eventually through breeding, different characteristics became looked out.   Families grew and eventually became the different nations.   Some people had erroneously thought Noah's three sons were white, brown, and black. Actually each of Noah's sons had dark descendants.   To insure the continued spread of man, the curse of Babel continues.   Mankind is given a compunction to continuously change his language. Evolutionist are at a complete loss to explain the miracle of the different human languages.

The Table of Nations described in Genesis chapter 10 is a confirmed historical fact. Genealogist have confirmed its accuracy. It gives the true roots of over 70 different ancient nations.

The Story of Job

There was a man in the land of Uz whose name was Job. Job was a perfect man in the eyes of God. He feared God and hated evil. He prayed and worshipped God continually. Because he was so faithful, God blessed him and multiplied the work of his hands. God multiplied him so, that he was the richest man in the East.

Job had seven thousand sheep, three thousand camels, and five hundred yoke of oxen, five hundred donkeys, and many, many household servants.

Job was a man of great wisdom and influence, a great benefactor to the poor and unfortunate. When he visited the city, people rose to meet him. When Job came near, princes and the nobleman held their peace. He was held in great esteem. When he spoke man kept silent and listened intently to his advice. Job's word was always the final word.

Job helped the poor and the fatherless. Many came to Job who were destitute and he helped them. He helped the fatherless and made many widows sing for joy. He was eyes to the blind and feet to the lame. He would break the jaws of the wicked and take the spoils out of their teeth.

Job's righteousness was as evident as a man's clothes. His judgement was as a robe and diadem. Job was a great light to all that saw him, and Satan hated him for it.

There came a time when the sons of God came to present themselves before Him. Every angel from across the universe was there. Unto this gathering of angels, Satan requested an audience with the Almighty. He has come alone. None of the angels trust Satan, so he is escorted with angels on each side of him. All of heaven knows that the purpose of Satan's visit is not to bring good to anyone.

The Father asks Satan, "Where have you come from and what have you been doing?"

Satan says, "From walking back and forth, all over the earth."

God asks Satan, "Have you seen my servant Job? There is none like him in the earth. He is a perfect and upright man. He is one who fears God and shuns all evil."

Satan says, "Does he serve You for nought? Haven't You made a hedge about him, and his house and all that he has on every side?

Haven't You blessed the work of his hands and his substance increases in the land?

"But if You stretch Your hand toward him now, and touch all that he has, Job will curse You to your face!"

God's love for Job is so great that He cannot allow this slanderous accusation to go unanswered. Satan has accused Job in the presence of all of heaven. Satan would like nothing better than for Job to fall. It would seem that God is on the spot because He has already proclaimed that Job is the best on the earth. If Job should fail, then it would be a reproach on all men, because Job is the best. Nothing would disturb Satan more than for Job to pass every test. For Job to pass this test, it would be a great victory for men. The story of Job would be told for generations and it would embarrass the fallen angels, for this man to have more faith than they did.

God does not have the heart to strike Job, so He temporarily gives Satan the power to afflict him. God says, "Go! All that he has is in your power, only touch not his life."

With a smile of malevolent glee upon his face, the prince of darkness turns and leaves, anxious to afflict Job.

Shortly after this, there was a day when the children of Job were eating and drinking in their oldest brothers house.

Suddenly, a messenger comes running to Job.

He says, "The oxen were plowing and the donkeys were feeding beside them. The Sabeans came, stole the animals and slew all the servants, I am the only one who escaped to tell you."

While this servant was still speaking, another servant arrived. He said, "The fire of God fell from heaven and burned up all the sheep and the other servants. It totally consumed them and I am the only one that escaped alive to tell you."

While he was still speaking, another servant came, and said, "The Chaldeans came in three groups and attacked us. They killed the servants and stole all the camels. I am the only one who escaped alive to tell you what has happened."

Another of the servant came running to Job. He was frantic. He said, "All your children were feasting in the house of your oldest son. Suddenly, a great wind came. It struck the house on its four corners. The house fell, and all of your children and their servants were killed. I am the only one who escaped alive."

Job is in shock. He gets up and tears his clothes. He goes and shaves his head. Then, he falls on the ground and worships God. He says, "Naked I came out of my mother's womb, and naked shall I return. I came in the world with nothing, and I will leave with nothing. The Lord gave and the Lord has taken away, but blessed be the name of the Lord."

In all this, Job did not sin, nor did he charge God foolishly.

When it came time for the sons of God to present themselves before the Lord, Satan came also.

The Lord asks Satan, "Where have you been Satan?"

He answers God, "From traveling all over the earth."

The Lord answers him, "Have you considered my servant Job, how there is none like him in all the earth. He is a perfect and upright man, one who fears God and hates evil. He still holds his integrity, although you moved Me against him to destroy him without a cause."

Satan knew that this was coming. He cannot stand it. Job has resisted all Satan's pressure to turn against God. He hates losing, neither can he accept the fact that Job can continue to resist his pressure. He say, "Skin for skin. A man will give everything he has to save his life. If You smite him now and touch his bone and his flesh, he will curse You to Your face."

Satan has never believed that God could see into the future. He does not believe that God is omniscient or that God knows more than he does. He has challenged God's wisdom in front of all of heaven and he has slandered Job, the most faithful man on earth.

God says to the accuser of the brethren, "Satan. Behold all that he has in your hands, but save his life."

Satan immediately left the presence of God and afflicted Job. He caused boils to come upon Job that covered his entire body. Job is in great pain from the boils. He takes the sharp edge of a broken piece of pottery and scrapes his boils.

His wife, who is very bitter about what has happened speaks to Job. She tells him, "Do you still retain your integrity? Curse God and die. He has let all these things happen to us. At least curse Him, before you die."

Job looked up at his wife and said, "You speak as one of the foolish women. What? Shall we receive good at the hand of the Lord only. Sometimes evil must come our way."

In all this Job sinned not with his tongue. Even though Job gets depressed and sometimes wishes that he were dead, Satan never gets him to curse God. Job's condition remains the same and news of his misfortune travels. Days, weeks and months pass. Job's prestige is gone. There are some who are glad at his misfortune. Other's are grieved.

Three of Job's closest friends, Eliphaz, Bildad, and Zophar, hear of his misfortune and come to visit him. Job's friends talk to him. They tell Job to confess his sins. They are convinced that he has secretly sinned. Despite Job's insistence that he is innocent, they do not believe him. They are sure that Job has done something to warrant this judgement. They talk at length about the goodness of God.

Job is so depressed that he does not listen to their advice. At one time he had the respect of everyone. He was admired and feared. Now, the sons of men who were so low down that Job would not have let them keep his dogs mock him. Despite his friends' encouragement, he is frustrated. He wonders "Is it worth it?" He comes to the worthless conclusion that the righteous have no more advantage than the wicked.

God appears to Job in a whirlwind. He says, "Who is this that darkens counsel by words without knowledge?" He says to Job, "Job, pick up yourself and answer Me like a man. if you are able. Where were you when I laid the foundations of the earth. Where were you when I created the waters and they burst forth like they had been issued out of the womb, when the Sons of God shouted for joy?" God asks Job many more questions and tells him the glory of His creation. The Lord then says to Job, "Shall he who would find fault with the Almighty contend with Him? He who disputes with God let him answer it."

Job replies unto the Lord, "Behold, I am of small account and vile. What shall I answer You? I lay my hand upon my mouth. I have spoken once, but I will not answer. No twice, but I will proceed no further."

The Lord speaks to Job out of the whirlwind, "Gird up your loins and answer Me like a man. Will you disannul my judgement? Will you condemn Me, that you may be righteous? Do you have an arm like God? Does your voice thunder like His? Since you question My judgement, will you deck yourself with majesty and excellency?"

God asks Job many more questions. He goes on to describe more of His wondrous creations, including the behemoth which is a tyrannosaur and the leviathan, which is a fire breathing sea monster. After God finishes with His speech, Job is humbled.

Job answered God and said, "I know that You can do everything, and no thought can be hidden from You. I have darkened counsel by uttering words without wisdom, therefore, I have uttered that which I understood not. Things which were too wonderful for me to understand.

Lord I have heard of Thee with my ears, but now I see you with my eyes. I know how wrong I was, and I abhor myself, and I repent in dust and ashes."

The Lord tells Job's three friends, Eliphaz, Bildad, and Zophar that they had not spoken right concerning Job. The Lord told them they needed to make a sacrifice of seven lambs and seven bullocks and then come and present themselves to Job.

They do as the Lord commands and Job prays for them. God turns Job's captivity captive. The Lord gave Job twice as much as he had before.

Then all of Job's brothers and his sister came to him. All of his former acquaintances came and ate bread with him in his house. They mourned with him and comforted him over all the evil that the Lord had allowed to come upon him. They each gave him some money and everyone of them gave him an earring of gold.

So, the Lord blessed Job more in the end than he was in the beginning. He has fourteen thousand sheep, six thousand camels, a thousand yoke of oxen, and a thousand donkeys. He had seven more sons and three daughters. In all the land were found no daughters as fair as the daughters of Job. After this, Job lived an hundred and forty years and saw his sons, and sons' sons, even four generations. So Job died being old and full of days.

These are the generations on Noah unto Abram.

Noah (960 years)
Shem (600 years)
Arphaxad (438 years)
Salah (433 years)
Eber (464 years)
Peleg* (239 years)
Reu (239 years)
Serug (230 years)
Nahor (148 years)
Terah (205 years)

*It was during the days of Peleg that the dispersion at Babel occurred.

Terah had three sons, Abram, Nahor and Haran. Haran had a son named Lot. Terah took his son, Abram and his wife Sarai, Lot the son of Haran, left Ur of the Chaldees and went to the land of Canaan. They went to Haran, and dwelt there. Terah stayed in Haran until he died at the age of 205.

The Calling of Abram

After Terah died the LORD spoke unto Abram, "Get up and take your wife and leave your father's house, leave your relatives and go into a land that I will show you. And I will make of you a great nation, and I will make your name great. You shall be a blessing. I will bless them that bless you and curse them that curse you. Through you shall all the nations of the earth be blessed."

So Abram departed, as the Lord commanded him. At this time Abram was 75 years old. He took his wife, and his nephew Lot, all their possessions, and servants. Abram traveled to the land of Canaan. The Canaanites were there.

The LORD appeared unto Abram and said, "Unto your seed will I give this land."

One night God began to speak to Abram in the desert. He said, "Look at the sand, and count the grains of sand."

Abram said, "Lord, I cannot count the sand."

The Lord said, "Look up and count the stars in heaven."

Abram began to count the stars but he lost count. He gave up and said, "Lord, I can't count the stars.

The Lord said unto Abram, "If a man can count the grains of the sand, or the stars in heaven, then he will be able to count your descendants.

After Abram had lived in Canaan for ten years, Sarai came to Abram and said, "The LORD has restrained me from bearing. Please go into my maid, that I may obtain children by her. Abram listened to his wife and took her handmaid, Hagar, to wife. Hagar conceived and began to despise Sarai. The tension between them increased, until Sarai went to Abram. She said, "My wrong be upon you. I gave my maid unto your bosom, and when she saw that she had conceived, I was despised in her eyes. The LORD judge between me and you."

Abram said, "Behold, your maid is in your hands. Do as you please with her."

Sarai took Hagar and dealt severely with her. She humbled her and began to beat her, and Hagar ran away into the wilderness.

The angel of the LORD appeared unto Hagar in the desert near a fountain. The angel said unto her, "Hagar. Where do you come from and where are you going?"

She answered, "I have run away from my mistress, Sarai."

The angel of the LORD answered her, "Return to thy mistress, and submit yourself into her hands. I will multiply your seed greatly, that it shall not be numbered for the multitude. You shall bear a son, and you shall call his name Ishmael, for I have heard your affliction. He shall be a wild man, his hand will be against every man, and every man's hand against him."

Hagar was comforted by the LORD's words and said, "You are a God of seeing; for she said, "Have I not even here in the wilderness looked after Him who sees me. I have seen the future of Him who sees me."

And Hagar bore Abram a son and Abram called the name of his son Ishmael. Abram was 86 years old when Hagar bore Ishmael.

When Abram was 99 years old, the Lord appeared unto him and said, "I am the Almighty God, walk before Me and be thou perfect. I will make My covenant, My solemn oath between Me and you, and I will multiply you exceedingly."

Abram was overcome with the Spirit of God. Like an invisible searchlight, the glory of God shone about him. Instantly, he felt a myriad of emotions, honored, unworthy, cleansed, and grateful, to name a few. When God's glory shines about an individual in this way, the soul knows immediately what to do; prostate yourself before the Almighty. Abram fell on his face immediately before God.

God continued speaking, "As for ME, behold My solemn pledge is with you, and you shall be the Father of many nations. Nor shall your name be called Abram (high father), but your name shall be called Abraham (father of a multitude); for I have made you the father of many nations. And I shall make you exceedingly fruitful, and I will make nations of you, and kings shall come from you.

And I will establish My covenant between Me and you and your descendants after you throughout their generations for an everlasting covenant and to be a God to you and your children after you.

And I will give to you and to your descendants after you the land in which you are a stranger, all the land of Canaan for an everlasting possession; and I will be their God."

God commands Abraham to circumcise himself and all his descendants. He commands him to circumcise all his newborn male descendants on the eighth day after their birth.

And God said unto Abraham, "As for Sarai your wife, you shall not call her name Sarai, but Sarah (princess) her name shall be. And I will bless her, and give you a son also of her. Yes. I will bless her, and she shall be a mother of nations; kings of peoples shall come from her."

Abraham fell on his face and laughed, and said to himself, "Shall a child be born to a man who is 100 years old? And shall Sarah, who is 90 years old, bear a son? And he said to God, "O that Ishmael might live before You!"

God said, "Sarah, your wife shall indeed bear you a son. You shall call his name Isaac (laughter), and I will establish My covenant with him for an everlasting covenant and his descendants after him.

As for Ishmael, I have heard and heeded you. Behold, I will bless him, make him fruitful, and will multiply him exceedingly; he shall be the father of twelve princes and I will make him a great nation.

But My covenant, My promise and pledge, I will establish with Isaac, whom Sarah shall bear to you at this season next year." The Spirit of God lifted off Abraham and God finished speaking to him.

And Abraham arose and did all that the LORD commanded him. He circumcised himself and all those within his house. Everyone in the service of Abraham was circumcised as the LORD commanded.

Sodom

Abraham had traveled to the plains of Mamre. And it came to pass that as Abraham sat in the door of his tent, in the heat of the day, that three men suddenly appeared standing right by him. It was Jesus and two other angels. Abraham runs to meet them. He bows down before them. Abraham says, "My Lord, if now I have found favor in your sight, please don't pass away from me, your servant. Let a little water be fetched, and wash your feet and rest yourselves under the tree. I will fetch a morsel of bread and comfort your hearts. After that, you can pass on."

They say unto him, "Do as you have spoken."

Abraham quickly got up and ran into his tent and told Sarah, "Quickly, make three measures of fine meal, knead it and make cakes upon the hearth. Abraham ran unto the heard and fetched a young calf, gave it to a young man, and he dressed it. Abraham took butter, milk, and the calf which he had dressed and set it before them.

And they said to Abraham, "Where is Sarah, your wife?"

Abraham answers, "There, in the tent."

The Lord speaks to Abraham, "I will return unto you in nine months and Sarah shall have a son."

Sarah was standing behind him, in the tent door.

Abraham and Sarah were well stricken in age. Sarah had gone through the change of life, which ordinarily meant it would be impossible for her to have a child. For this reason, when Sarah heard this she laughed within herself and said, "After I have grown old, shall I have pleasure, my lord being old also?"

And the LORD said unto Abraham, "Wherefore did Sarah laugh? She said, "Shall I of a surety bear a child, which am old?"

Is anything too hard for the LORD? At the time appointed I will return unto thee, according to the time of life, and Sarah shall have a son."

Sarah was afraid and denied it. She said, "I did not laugh." The LORD said, "No. You did laugh."

The three men arose and looked toward Sodom. Abraham went with them to lead them toward Sodom.

And the LORD said, "Shall I hide from Abraham that thing which I do; seeing that Abraham shall surely become a great and mighty nation, and all the nations of the earth shall be blessed in him? For I know him, that he will command his children and his household after him, and they shall keep the way of the LORD, to do justice and judgment; that the LORD may bring upon Abraham that which He hath spoken of him."

The LORD said unto Abraham, "Because the cry of Sodom and Gomorrah is great, and because their sin is very grievous; I will go down now, and see whether they have done altogether according to the cry of it, which is come unto Me; and if not, I will know."

And the men turned their faces from thence, and went toward Sodom, but Abraham stood yet before the LORD. Abraham drew near unto the Lord and said, "LORD, will You destroy the righteous with the wicked? Suppose there are fifty righteous people in the city, will You spare the city for the sake of fifty righteous people? LORD it is far from You to do this, to slay the righteous with the wicked. LORD, for You to punish the righteous with the wicked is not like you. Shall not the judge of all the earth do right?"

The LORD answered Abraham and said, "If I find in Sodom fifty righteous within the city, then I will spare the city for the righteous sake."

Abraham answered and said, "Behold now, I have taken upon me to speak unto the Lord, which am but dust and ashes:

Perchance there shall lack five of the fifty righteous: will You destroy all the city for lack of five?"

And the LORD said, "If I find there forty and five, I will not destroy it."

And he spake unto Him yet again and said, "Perhaps there shall be forty found there?"

And the Lord said, "I will not do it for forty's sake."

And he said unto Him, "Oh let not the Lord be angry, and I will speak: Peradventure there shall thirty be found there?"

And the LORD said, "I will not do it, if I find thirty there."

And he said, "Behold now, I have taken upon me to speak unto the Lord: Perchance there shall be twenty found there?"

The LORD said, "I will not destroy it for twenty's sake."

And he said, "Oh let not the Lord be angry, and I will speak yet but this once: Peradventure ten shall be found there?"

The LORD said, "I will not destroy it for ten's sake."

And the LORD went His way, as soon as He had left communing with Abraham: and Abraham returned unto his place.

The two angels go to Sodom to investigate. Abraham has interceded on their behalf and now they only need to find ten righteous people and God will save the city.

The two angels approach Sodom. Abraham's nephew, Lot, was sitting at the gate of the city. When he saw the two angels, he ran and bowed down before them.

And he said, "Behold, now my lords, turn in, I pray you, into your servant's house, and tarry all night, and wash your feet. Then ye shall rise up early, and go your ways."

And they said, "Nay, but we will abide in the street all night."

Lot pleads and begs them. He will not give up. He is so persistent that the angels agree to come to his house. Lot prepares a feast for them and bakes unleavened bread. Lot, his family, and the angels, disguised as men, all eat.

Before Lot and his family can turn in for the night, there is a knock at the door. The men of the city, both old and young, have come to Lot's house. They have completely surrounded Lot's house. It is an unruly mob. They cry out to Lot, "Lot, open up. Where are the two men that were with you earlier? Send them out, that we may have sex with them."

Lot comes out and shuts the door behind him. He tries his best to appease the crowd. Desperately he implores them, "Please brethren, don't do this wicked thing. Look, I have two daughters who are virgins. They have never been with a man. Let me please bring them out to you. Take them and do as you will, but please leave these men alone. They are my guests. As guests staying under my roof, it is my obligation to provide their protection. If you must do something, take my daughters."

The homosexuals are outraged, "Get out of the way! We don't want the women, we want the men."

Another homosexual turns to the crowd and says with indignation, "This man came as a stranger to stay in our city. Now he wants to judge us and our way of life. Who does he think he is?" Their evil gay pride has reached its zenith. Angrily he turns to Lot and says, "Now we are going to do worse to you, than we were going to do them." The rest of the crowd shouts, "Yes," agreeing with him and they lunge towards Lot.

They grab him and Lot beginning to fight them off, retreats against the door. Lot is horrified, afraid for his life and what they will do to him. The angels have heard enough. Quickly, they stride to the door, determined to put an end to this wickedness. They open the door and pull Lot inside. Lot's wife and daughter rush to embrace him. Embracing one another dearly, they all begin to weep, partly in relief and part fear. The men briefly step outside and momentarily close the door to shield those inside the house. The homosexuals look up at the angels. It is the last thing they will ever see.

The angels flash brighter than the noonday sun. They generate the light of a nuclear blast. The flash of light is so bright that it hurts the Sodomites eyes. They are disoriented and fall backwards. They learn, to their horror, that they are totally blind. They can't even find the door.

The angels come inside and say to Lot, "Don't you have family here in this city?"

Lot looks puzzled, wondering what is the purpose of the question. He is still shaken up from his near miss and he is afraid. He answers, "Yes."

The angel says, "Get your son-in-law, your sons, and daughters, and whosoever you have in this city. Bring them out for we will destroy this city, for the cry of their sin has come up great before the Lord, and the Lord has sent us to destroy it."

So Lot went out and spoke to his daughters husbands. He told them, "Get up. Get your belongings and get out of this city for the Lord will destroy this place."

Unfortunately, his son-in-laws never took him seriously. They thought Lot was teasing them. When the morning came, the angels began to rush Lot. "Arise, Get up and gather your wife and your two daughters before you are consumed in the wickedness of this city," they tell him.

Lot does not know what to do. He does not want to die, yet if he leaves without all his children. His son-in-laws would not let his other daughters or their children leave. He does not wish to abandon them. While Lot procrastinated, the angels laid hold upon his hand and his wife and two daughters. The Lord knowing Lot's inner conflict commanded the angels to drag them by force outside the city. The angels said, "Run. Escape for your lives. Don't look back and don't stay at all in this plain. Escape to the mountains, lest you be destroyed."

And Lot said unto them, "Oh, not so, my Lord: Behold now, I know that I have found grace in your sight, and you have shown me abundant mercy, which you have shown me in saving my life; and I cannot escape to the mountain, lest some evil take me, and I die. Behold now, this city is near to flee unto, and it is a little one: Oh, let me escape there (is it not a little one?) and my soul shall live."

And the angel said unto him, "See, I have accepted thee concerning this thing also, that I will not overthrow this city, for the words which you have spoken. Hurry and escape there, for I cannot do any thing till you get there." Therefore the name of the city was called Zoar.

Lot and his family traveled through the night to reach Zoar. About dawn, Lot and his family were entering Zoar. Suddenly there was the rumble of earth. God rained down fire and brimstone on the cities of Sodom and Gomorrah. Destruction had come, as the angels foretold. The screams of the dying echoed throughout the land. Lot's wife turned to look back in defiance of God's command, and she was instantly turned into a pillar of salt.

Abraham arose the next morning and looked out over the plains of Sodom and Gomorrah, and all the land of the valley and it was burning. The smoke arose from the burning valley like the smoke out of a great furnace. Everything in the valley was dead, because of the sins of the people of Sodom and Gomorrah.

As God had promised, nine months later Sarah gave birth to her son Isaac. He was circumcised on the eighth day, as the Lord commanded Abraham. The child grew and became the apple of Abraham's eye.

There came a time when God decided to test Abraham. God told him, "Take Your son, Isaac, and sacrifice him on top of Moriah and offer him to me as a burnt offering."

Abraham arose and did as the Lord commanded. He knew that God would bless his son Isaac. Now God had commanded him to sacrifice Isaac. Abraham was so convinced of God's promise that he believed God would perform it, even if God had to raise Isaac from the dead. He believed God, and it was accounted to him for righteousness.

Abraham took his son and some of his servants to Moriah. When he found the mountain that the LORD commanded him to sacrifice upon, he spoke to his servants. He said, "Wait here, the lad and myself shall return unto you."

As Isaac and his father climbed the mountain, Isaac noticed they did not have a ram. Isaac said to his father, "Father. I see the wood and firepot, but where is the lamb?"

Abraham answered him and said, "The Lord will provide."

When they came to the place where God told him, Abraham built an alter there. Then he laid the wood and bound Isaac his son and laid him on the altar of wood. Abraham stretched forth his hand and took hold of the knife to slay his son.

Suddenly, the Angel of the Lord called unto him from heaven. He said, "Abraham, Abraham!"

Abraham answered, "Here I am!"

The angel answered, "Do not lay your hand upon the lad, or do anything to him, for now I know that you fear me above all else, for you have not withheld your only son from me."

And the LORD said, "I have sworn by Myself (since there is none greater). Since you have done this, and have not withheld from Me or begrudged giving Me your son, your only son, that in blessing I will bless you. In multiplying I will multiply your descendants as the stars of the heavens and as the sand of the seashore.

"And your Seed shall possess the gate of His enemies. And in your Seed (Christ) shall all the nations of the earth be blessed, because you have heard and obeyed My voice."

After Sarah dies, Abraham remarries a woman name Keturah. She bore him sons named Zimran, Jokshan, Medan, Midian, Ishbak, and Shuah.

And Abraham gave all that he had to Isaac. To the sons of his concubines (Hagar and Keturah), Abraham gave gifts. While he was still living he sent them to the East country, away from Isaac his son of promise.

At the age of 175, Abraham died.

Chapter 12

Israel

Isaac had two sons called Esau and Jacob. Eventually, after a visitation from an angel, God changes Jacob's name to Israel. Jacob's sons and grandsons become known as the twelve tribes of Israel. One of Jacob's sons is named Joseph. Some of Joseph's brothers become insanely jealous of him and sell him into slavery. He is taken to Egypt and although a slave, God blesses him through a series of events to become an administrator for Pharaoh during a time of great famine. Jacob's brothers come to Egypt to buy grain. Unknowingly, they confront Joseph.

After a tearful reunion he persuades his brothers to bring their father and the rest of the family to Egypt. A total of 70 of Joseph's people come to Egypt. They remain there for 450 years. The Israelites become slaves in Egypt. God raises up a deliverer to deliver the Israelites from their hard bondage. His name is Moses. God uses Moses to work many signs and wonders to show Pharaoh that the Lord is their God. God judges Egypt with many plagues until Pharaoh consents to let the Israelites go. Moses leads his people out of Egypt. 70 Israelites went into Egypt and in 450 years the number grows to 600,000 men, not counting the women and children. Altogether, there were probably nearly three million of them.

As they get near the Red Sea, Pharaoh has a change of heart and decides to kill the Israelites. God splits the Red Sea and the Israelites walk across on dry ground. Pharaoh and his army try to cross the Red Sea, but God closes the sea upon them and they drown.

The Lord calls Moses to Mount Sinai. Moses is there for 40 days and nights. Moses was the meekest man upon the face of the earth. God spoke to Moses face to face. God takes his finger and write on stone tablets and gives him the Ten Commandments, gives His law.

Many people would consider some of the laws repressive and unusually harsh. However, God knows the heart of man. He knew the more temptation is present, the more men would yield to their temptation. Many times God calls His people sheep. That is not a compliment, for sheep are very ignorant beasts. They are easily misled and defenseless against wolves and other predators. So too is man easy prey for Satan and man is nearly defenseless against him. God knows that man will not fare well when temptations are abundant. Therefore God gives Moses some very strict laws with the most severe punishments. This will save the nation of Israel from extinction. Even though they will eventually be scattered around the world in various communities, their diet and customs keep them a distinct people and saves them from assimilation during their Diaspora.

God tells Moses that if Israel will serve Him, He will make Israel the mightiest nation on earth. He promises, if they obey His commandments, no nation will be able to stand before them. He promises, if they do not, He will deliver them to the will of their enemies.

Just as God would have rejoiced over them to bless them, He promised that He would rejoice over them to curse them. He promises them if they do not serve Him, He will scatter them all over the earth. God gives Moses His law. God gives the Israelites His law to will govern the Nation of Israel. The law is recorded in the first five books of the Bible. Moses takes whatever records and oral tradition he has and writes the book of Genesis. Moses also has the book of Job. The law covers civil, legal, religious, and dietary laws. (If the Europeans would have follow the sanitary and dietary laws of Moses, the bubonic and black plagues that killed over 60 million people over the span of an hundred years, would have never happened).

Moses is in the presence of the Lord on Mount Sinai for forty days. After forty days in the presence of God Moses' appearance was changed. Moses did not know it, but his skin was shining with the glory of God. The Israelites were afraid to come near him, so he put on a veil to cover his face. This was a temporary effect and after a number of days it wore off.

The Israelites were only a 14 days march away from Israel. Yet, 450 years of bondage in Egypt gave the children of Israel a slave mentality. They are always doubting and tempting God. The Lord says to Moses, "This people does always err in their hearts. The

Israelites offend God so that He swears in His anger, that the present generation of Israelites shall never enter into the promised land.

They are cursed to wander in the Sinai peninsula for 40 years. Only those twenty years old and younger are allowed to enter the promised land. God feeds the Israelites manna from heaven for forty years. He sends a cloud over them in the day to keep them cool and pillar of fire by night to keep them warm in the cool desert night.

After forty years, Moses is an hundred and twenty years old. God decides to take Moses to heaven. His replacement, Joshua, leads Israel into the promised land. God blesses them there and they prosper. Down through the centuries, He raises up many prophets and men of God who do great exploits. Their words and deeds are written in the 39 books that comprise the Old Testament.

God warned Israel that if they did not serve Him, He would scatter them among the nations. Israel reaches its height as a nation under the rule of King David and his son Solomon. After this, Israel sinks into sin. The prophets warn Israel that God will send His judgement and cause the nation and the people to be conquered.

Eventually Nebuchadnezzar, the king of Babylon invades Israel. He kills many Jews and scatters them around the world. This dispersion was called the Diaspora. Some Jews, he takes back to Babylon as slaves. King Nebuchadnezzar has a dream which deeply troubles him. He calls all his wise men before him and commands them to interpret the dream. Nebuchadnezzar tells them he has forgotten the dream. He reasons that if they have the power to interpret the dream, then they should be able to find out what it is. He commands them to interpret the dream or he will have them all killed. They protest at the unreasonableness of his decree to no avail.

The Prophet Daniel, who is one of the Jews in captivity in the palace. He would have been affected by the decree so he went into prayer. The Lord revealed to him the dream and the interpretation.

Daniel told King Nebuchadnezzar what occurred the night he had the vision. While the king was laying in his bed, he began to wonder about what the future holds, and what kingdoms would follow his. He fell asleep. While he slept, the Lord gave him a dream. In this dream, he saw an image. It had a head of gold. Its chest and arms were made of silver. Its belly and thighs were made of brass. Its legs were made of iron. Its toes were made of iron mixed with clay. A small stone that was cut out but not with man's hands, came and struck the toes of the image and it was destroyed. The stone became a great mountain that filled the whole earth.

Daniel interpreted the dream for Nebuchadnezzar. The statue represented different kingdoms that would come and rule the world. The head of gold represented the kingdom of Nebuchadnezzar. After his kingdom would come a second kingdom inferior to the first, as silver is inferior to gold. The second kingdom became the Medo-Persian Empire. The third kingdom of brass represented the Greek Empire of Alexander the Great. The fourth kingdom was made of iron. As iron breaks all these other metals, so does this kingdom. The fourth empire to rule the world was the Roman Empire. The fifth kingdom, which is yet to come, is the remnant of the Roman Empire. It will be an uneasy alliance of ten European nations that were once members of the Roman Empire. The stone that destroys the image is the Messiah. The Prophet Daniel prophesied of the kingdoms to come.

Down through the centuries, many prophets came that prophesy of a Messiah who would one day rule the earth from Israel. He will be a descendant of King David. He must suffer, but he will rule the nations with a rod of iron.

The deeds and words of these prophets are recorded in the Old Testament.

Although God said His Spirit will not always strive with men, there are some men who do receive the Spirit of the Lord. The omnipotent Spirit of the Lord can do anything. Sometimes the Spirit of God comes to reveal things. The Spirit of the Lord would come and anoint the prophets to do great exploits. There was no limit to what God's Spirit could do through His servants. Samson was anointed with the strength of thousands of men. Others parted the rivers, as Moses parted the Red Sea. Elijah, one of the most powerful of the prophets called down fire from heaven, split the Jordan River, outran the kings chariots and shut up the heavens that it would not rain. As God's Spirit would come upon these men, they could do supernatural things, including prophesy future events. Very few people were privileged to feel the Spirit of God. God only poured out His Spirit upon a few people, but He promised that would change one day.

God promised that the days would come when He would pour out His Spirit upon all flesh. He said the sons and daughters would prophesy. He said in that day He would pour out His Spirit upon the handmaidens. He also promised that He would speak to the Jews through people speaking with stammering lips and another tongue

(Isaiah 28:11). This prophecy was fulfilled on the day of Pentecost, when the disciples received the Holy Ghost and spoke in tongues.

God knew that mans heart was evil, even from the days of his youth. Israel had failed God as had the entire human race. Even though God had given them the Law, they were incapable of keeping it in their hearts. God had blessed and punished based on their obedience or disobedience. He had punished them until there was no point in punishing them anymore.

He allowed their cities to be burned with fire, the land became desolate, and strangers devoured the land in their presence. Even though they still kept the sabbaths, the appointed feast and the solemn assembly, God began to hate these appointed times. He instructed them to put away the evil of their doings. They were religious and had the forms of religious but they did not know God in their hearts. Isaiah the prophet, prophesied all these things to them as recorded in the book of Isaiah, the first chapter. Because of the evil in man's hearts there was need for God to do something. God began to institute plans for His new covenant.

Jeremiah 31:31   Behold, the days come, saith the LORD, that I will make a new covenant with the house of Israel, and with the house of Judah:

Jeremiah 31:32   Not according to the covenant that I made with their fathers in the day that I took them by the hand to bring them out of the land of Egypt; which my covenant they brake, although I was an husband unto them, saith the LORD:

Jeremiah 31:33   But this shall be the covenant that I will make with the house of Israel; After those days, saith the LORD, I will put my law in their inward parts, and write it in their hearts; and will be their God, and they shall be my people.

Jeremiah 31:34   And they shall teach no more every man his neighbour, and every man his brother, saying, Know the LORD: for they shall all know me, from the least of them unto the greatest of them, saith the LORD: for I will forgive their iniquity, and I will remember their sin no more.

Ezekiel 11:19   And I will give them one heart, and I will put a new spirit within you; and I will take the stony heart out of their flesh, and will give them an heart of flesh:

Ezekiel 36:26   A new heart also will I give you, and a new spirit will I put within you: and I will take away the stony heart out of your flesh, and I will give you an heart of flesh.

Ezekiel 36:27   And I will put my spirit within you, and cause you to walk in my statutes, and ye shall keep my judgments, and do them.

This new covenant would be ushered in with the coming of a new Messiah.

The Promised Messiah

The prophets begin to prophecy of a Messiah who would come. This Messiah would eventually rule the earth for a thousand years from Jerusalem. He will be both divine and human. He will have tremendous power and will rule the nations with a rod of iron.

Isaiah 7:14   Therefore the Lord himself shall give you a sign; Behold, a virgin shall conceive, and bear a son, and shall call his name Immanuel.

Isaiah 9:6   For unto us a child is born, unto us a son is given: and the government shall be upon his shoulder: and his name shall be called Wonderful, Counsellor, The mighty God, The everlasting Father, The Prince of Peace.

Many Jews, who perhaps respect Jesus as a great teacher and a good man, vehemently deny that He is the Son of God. They totally disagree with our doctrine of the Trinity, but fail to consider the meaning of these prophecies. The Messiah, who would be born, would be called God. He is the everlasting Father, because he with the Heavenly Father created everything. When man was created, it was said, "Let us make man in our own image." Angels were not a part of this conversation. This was the Father and the Son talking. Together they formed man.

Aside from prophecies that foretold of the Messiah's divinity, there were prophecies that foretold of His rejection by His own people, His imprisonment, His suffering, untimely and horrible death.

Psalms 118:22   The stone which the builders refused is become the head stone of the corner.

Isaiah 53:3-5   He is despised and rejected of men; a man of sorrows, and acquainted with grief: and we hid as it were our faces from him; he was despised, and we esteemed him not. {4} Surely he hath borne our griefs, and carried our sorrows: yet we did esteem him stricken, smitten of God, and afflicted. {5} But he was wounded for our transgressions, he was bruised for our iniquities: the chastisement of our peace was upon him; and with his stripes we are healed.

Isaiah 53:8   He was taken from prison and from judgment: and who shall declare his generation? for he was cut off out of the land of the living: for the transgression of my people was he stricken.

Psalms 22 gives a vivid picture of the crucifixion of Christ. King David prophesied of the Messiah's suffering. The first verse says, "My God, My God why has thou forsaken me?" These are the words He spoke on the cross. The psalmist continues to describe the mockery of those who see the Messiah being punished. It describes gentiles surrounding Him. He is thirsty and all His bones are out of joint. They pierce His hands and feet, they divide His clothes among them and cast lots for his vesture.

Isaiah 53:8, and Daniel 9:26 both mention that the Messiah would be cut off or killed. After He is killed, He goes to heaven. During this time He would be in heaven as the psalmist prophesied, sitting at the right hand of the Father.

Psalms 110:1   A Psalm of David. The LORD said unto my Lord, Sit thou at my right hand, until I make thine enemies thy footstool.

The Messiah would be priest for the people, making intercession for them as Isaiah prophesied in Isaiah 53:12. He would be a priest not from the tribe of Levi, but a priest after Melchizedek, who was so great that even the patriarch Abraham gave him a tenth of the spoils.

Psalms 110:4 The LORD hath sworn, and will not repent, Thou art a priest for ever after the order of Melchizedek.

With two such contrasting views of the Messiah given by the prophets, many of the Jews thought there would be two Messiahs (one of exaltation and the other of suffering). There are not two Messiahs, but two comings, a first and second of the one Messiah.

Probability of Prophecies

Many details of Jesus' birth, life, and death were prophesied hundreds of years before they were fulfilled. For this to be coincidence is all but impossible. In his book "Science Speaks," Peter Stoner applies the modern science of probability to just eight prophecies. He says, "...the chance that any man might have...fulfilled all eight prophecies is one in 10^{17}. That would be 1 in 100,000,000,000,000,000." (That's one hundred quadrillion). Stoner suggests that "we take 10^{17} silver dollars and lay them on the face of Texas. They will cover all of the state 2 feet deep.

Now mark one of these silver dollars and stir the whole mass thoroughly. Blindfold a man and tell him he can travel as far as he wishes, but he must pick up that one marked silver dollar. What chance would he have of getting the right one?" Stoner concluded, "Just the same chance that the prophets would have had of writing those prophecies and having them all come true in any one man, providing they wrote them in their own wisdom."

Chapter 13

A Child Is Born

In the days of King Herod there was a certain priest whose name was Zacharias, who was of the course of Abia. Zacharias wife's name was Elizabeth and she was a descendant of Aaron. They both were very righteous before the Lord and were blameless concerning all the statues and commandments of the Lord. However, she was barren and had no children. Now they both had become very old.

There came a time when Zacharias was in the temple executing his office, that something very strange happened. He was going about his office burning incense while the people were praying outside the inner room Zacharias was in. He looked and behold there was an angel on the right side of the altar of incense. Zacharias saw the angel and became greatly troubled and very afraid.

Then the angel opened his mouth, and spoke to Zacharias and said, "Fear not Zacharias for thy prayer is heard. For your wife Elizabeth shall bear you a son, and you shall call his name John. And he shall be great in the sight of the Lord, and you shall have joy and gladness and many shall rejoice at his birth."

For he shall be great in the sight of the Lord, and he shall neither drink wine nor strong drink, and he shall be filled with the Holy Ghost even from his mother's womb.

And many of the children of Israel shall he turn to the Lord their God. And He shall go before Him in the spirit and power of Elijah, to turn the hearts of the fathers to the children, and the disobedient to the wisdom of the just, and to prepare a people for the coming of the Lord."

Zacharias is stunned. For him, this is almost too good to be true. He questions the word of this holy angel and says, "How do I know that this is true, for I am an old man and my old age has weighed heavily on my wife?"

The angel says to him, "I am Gabriel that stand in the presence of God. I have been sent to bring you this good news. Now behold! You shall be dumb and will not be able to speak, until the day when all these things have come to pass. Because you did not believe my words, which shall be fulfilled in their season.

Meanwhile, the people were waiting for Zacharias, and were amazed that he lingered so long in the temple.

When he came out, he could not speak to them; and they perceived that he had seen a vision in the temple, for he motioned to them and remained speechless.

It came to pass that as soon as the days of his service were completed, that he departed and went to his own house. Afterward Elizabeth conceived; and she hid herself five months saying, "Thus the Lord has dealt with me, in the days when He looked on me, to take away my reproach among men."

Now in the sixth month, God, the Father, sent the angel Gabriel to a city of Galilee named Nazareth. He was sent to a virgin engaged to a man whose name was Joseph, of the house of David. The virgin's name was Mary.

Having come in, the angel said to her, "Rejoice, highly favored one, the Lord is with you; blessed are you among women!"

But when she saw him, she was troubled at his saying, and considered what manner of greeting this was.

Then the angel said to her, "Do not be afraid, Mary, for you have found favor with God. Behold, you will conceive in your womb and bring forth a Son, and shall call His name JESUS. He will be great, and will be called the Son of the Highest; and the Lord God will give Him the throne of His father David. He will reign over the house of Jacob forever, and of His kingdom, there will be no end."

Then Mary said to the angel, "How can this be, since I have never been with a man?"

The angel answered and said to her, "The Holy Spirit will come upon you. The power of the Highest will overshadow you; therefore, also, that Holy One who is to be born will be called the Son of God. Now indeed, Elizabeth your relative has also conceived a son in her old age; and this is now the sixth month for her who was called barren. For with God nothing will be impossible."

Then Mary said, "Behold, I am the maidservant of the Lord! Let it be to me according to your word." The angel departed from her.

A few days later, Mary arose and went into the hill country with haste, to a city of Judah, and went to the home of Zacharias and Elizabeth. Mary came in and greeted Elizabeth. When Elizabeth heard the greeting of Mary, the baby leaped in her womb; and

Elizabeth was filled with the Holy Spirit. She began to rejoice and praise God. She spoke out with a loud voice and said, "Blessed are you among women, and blessed is the fruit of your womb! But why has the Lord blessed me so that the mother of my Lord should come to me? For indeed, as soon as the voice of your greeting sounded in my ears, the baby leaped in my womb for joy. Blessed is she who believed, for there will be a fulfillment of those things which were told her from the Lord."

And Mary said: "My soul does magnify the Lord, and my spirit has rejoiced in God my Savior. For He has regarded the lowly state of His maidservant; for behold, henceforth all generations will call me blessed. For He who is mighty has done great things for me, and holy is His name.

And Mary remained with her about three months, then returned to her house.

Now, Elizabeth's full time came for her to be delivered, and she brought forth a son. When her neighbors and relatives heard how the Lord had shown great mercy to her, they rejoiced with her. Now so it was, on the eighth day, that they came to circumcise the child; and they would have called him by the name of his father, Zacharias.

His mother answered and said, "No; he shall be called John." But they said to her, "There is no one among your relatives who is called by this name."

So they made signs to his father; what he would have him called.

He asked for a writing tablet, and wrote, saying, "His name is John." They all marveled.

Immediately Zacharias' mouth was opened, his tongue loosed, and he spoke, praising God.

Then fear came upon all who dwelt around them; and all these sayings were discussed throughout all the hill country of Judea.

All those who heard them kept them in their hearts, saying, "What kind of child will this be?" And the hand of the Lord was with him.

Now his father Zacharias was filled with the Holy Spirit, and prophesied, saying:

Luke 1:68 "Blessed is the Lord God of Israel, for He has visited and redeemed His people, and has raised up a horn of salvation for us in the house of His servant David, as He spoke by the mouth of His holy prophets, who have been since the world began."

Zacharias goes over and takes his son in his arms and says, "And you child shall be called the prophet of the Highest. You will go before the face of the Lord to prepare His ways. You shall give knowledge of salvation to His people by the remission of their sins, to give light to those who sit in darkness and the shadow of death, to guide our feet into the way of peace."

So the child grew and became strong in spirit, and was in the deserts till the day of his manifestation to Israel.

Now Mary was espoused (a strong form of engagement) to Joseph. She told him of the visitation of Gabriel. She explained that she was pregnant without ever knowing a man and she had not been unfaithful to him. However, Joseph did not believe her and he was determined to divorce her. He was a just man, and he had determined to divorce her privately. While he meditated on these things, the angel of the Lord appeared unto him in a dream. The angel said, "Fear not Joseph, thou son of David. Do not be afraid to take unto yourself, Mary your wife. For that which is conceived in her is of the Holy Ghost.

She shall have a son, and thou shalt call his name JESUS: for He shall save His people from their sins. All of this has been done to fulfill the prophecy given by the Prophet Isaiah, "Behold a virgin shall be with child, and shall bring forth a son, and they shall call His name Emmanuel, which being interpreted is, God with us."

When Joseph awoke, he did as the angel commanded him. He took Mary as his wife and he did not have sex with her, until after she had brought forth her firstborn son.

And it came to pass in those days that a decree went out from Caesar Augustus that all the world should be registered, and every man had to return to the city of his birth to be counted. Joseph had to return to the city of his birth, Bethlehem. He took his wife Mary, who was now great with child.

Upon arriving in Bethlehem, they soon discovered that there was no room in any of the inns. The only place that Joseph could find for them was in a stable. That night, Mary gave birth to Jesus, and they laid Him in a manger. Jesus, the Son of God, was born, and he lay in a manger.

Meanwhile, the Lord had revealed to some wise men, it was now time for the King of the Jews to be born in Israel. They came to Jerusalem to see Herod. The wise men told him that they were seeking the King of the Jews. The wise men came from the East, bearing their gifts. These were men of means and they brought treasure with them. They brought enough men to safeguard their treasure and all Jerusalem was troubled because of their visit. When Herod heard these things he was greatly troubled. He called the chief priest and scribes and demanded of them where Christ should be born.

They explained to him, "In Bethlehem of Judaea, according to the Prophet Micah."

Micah 5:2 But thou, Bethlehem Ephratah, though thou be little among the thousands of Judah, yet out of thee shall he come forth unto me that is to be ruler in Israel; whose goings forth have been from of old, from everlasting.

Then Herod went to the wise men and diligently inquired of them when the star did first appear? They told him and he sent them to Bethlehem. Herod, a man full of the devil, was very afraid. He knew of the Jews longing for their Messiah. Satan instructed Herod, "If this is true, you cannot allow this Messiah to live. You do not want to lose your kingdom. Let them find the child for you, then kill it, before he becomes king and kills you."

He told them, "Go and search diligently for the young child, and when you have found Him, come and bring me word, that I may come and worship Him also."

They departed Jerusalem and while they were on their way, the star which they say in the East reappeared. It went before them and led them to where the young child was. When it came to the house where Jesus was, it stopped and stood directly over Him.

At last, their long journey was over. When they realized this, they were overjoyed. Anxiously they came into the house. They saw the young child with Mary his mother and fell down and worshipped him. Whenever one would visit a king, they would pay homage to him and bring worthy gifts of a king. They opened up their treasures and gave him gold frankincense and myrrh.

The wise men slept in Bethlehem that night and God warned them in a dream, not to return to Herod. When they awoke, they left for their own country by another route.

Anxiously Herod awaited the return of the wise men. When they did not return Satan spoke to Herod, "The wise men have made a fool of you!" Satan influences Herod and fills his heart with rage. The more Herod thinks about it, the angrier he gets.

Satan continues to agitate Herod. He says, "The arrival of the wise men with their company of men will convince all the Jews their Messiah has come. You know how much the Jews hate you. For hundreds of years they have waited for their Messiah. The sign of the wise men will be all these messiah-hungry Jews will need. If you do not do something quickly, it will be too late. Send your soldiers go to Bethlehem, and have every infant child killed. To be sure, have them kill every child, two years old and younger."

After they left, the LORD warned Joseph in a dream. He told him, "Arise and take the young child and his mother and flee into Egypt, and stay there until I bring you word. For Herod will seek the young child to destroy Him."

Joseph awoke and immediately took his wife and her son and fled into Egypt. Meanwhile, the soldiers came to Bethlehem and carried out Herod's orders. Unmercifully, they killed the children three years old and younger, to try to kill the Christ child. This murder of the innocents was foretold by Jeremiah.

Jeremiah 31:15 Thus saith the LORD; A voice was heard in Ramah, lamentation, and bitter weeping; Rahel weeping for her children refused to be comforted for her children, because they were not.

Joseph stayed in Egypt until Herod died. The Lord spoke to Joseph to come back to Israel. This was fulfillment of the prophecy, "Out of Egypt have I called my Son."

When Joseph heard that Archelaus ruled in his father's place, he was afraid to return to Bethlehem. God warned Joseph to go into Galilee. He came and dwelt in a city called Nazareth, that it might be fulfilled which was spoken by the prophets, "He shall be called a Nazarene."

And the child Jesus grew and waxed strong in strength and wisdom.

Baptism

John the Baptist was preaching in the wilderness. Many of his followers were there. Some people asked him, was he the Christ. He answered no. Some began to ask him, was he Elijah. He said no. Then they asked, "Who are you?" He replied, "I am the voice of one crying in the wilderness, prepare ye the way of the Lord. There is coming One after me, who is preferred before me. The latchet of His shoes I am not worthy to unloose. I baptize you with water, but He shall baptize you with the Holy Ghost and fire."

As John looked up, he saw Jesus standing in line to be baptized. When Jesus got to him, John said, "No Lord. I am not worthy."

Jesus said to him, "Suffer it to be so to fulfill all righteousness sake."

After John baptized Him, the Holy Spirit descended upon him in the shape of a dove. Then God spoke from heaven and said, "This is my beloved Son, in whom I am well pleased. Listen to Him."

After this, Jesus was led of the Spirit into the wilderness, to be tempted of the Devil. Jesus fasted forty days and forty nights. While He was fasting, He began to get hungry. After a while Satan came to Him and said, "If thou be the son of God, turn these stones into bread."

Jesus answered him and said, "It is written man shalt not live by bread alone but by every word that proceedeth forth out of the mouth of God."

Immediately, the Devil took Jesus to the temple in Jerusalem. He took Him to the highest point of the temple. Then Satan said to Him, "If You truly are the Son of God, cast yourself down: for it is written, He shall give his angels charge over You: and in their hands shall they bear You up, lest at any time you dash your foot against a stone."

And Jesus said unto him, "It is written that thou shalt not tempt the Lord thy God."

Satan now frustrated for the second time, takes Jesus to a very high mountain. There, Satan began to show Him a vision of all the kingdoms of the world, in all their glory. He saw the gold, the riches the fame and adulation of men and women.

Then Satan said, "All these things will I give to You, for it is given unto me to give to whom, I will. You can have all this, if You will fall down and worship me."

Jesus said unto Satan, "Go away Satan: for it is written, thou shalt worship the Lord thy God and Him only shall you serve."

Immediately Satan left Him. He had survived this test. God, the Father, was pleased and He sent angels to minister to Him.

Afterwards Jesus went to and dwelt in the city called Capernaum, by the sea of Galilee to fulfill the prophecy of Isaiah. Isaiah described the city of Capernaum and said in Isaiah 9:2 The people which sat in darkness saw great light; and to them which sat in the region and shadow of death light is sprung up.

Jesus was full of the Spirit and began to teach in the synagogues and His fame began to spread. From that time Jesus began to preach, "Repent for the kingdom of God is at hand." Many of the people began to glorify God because of Him, for He taught with authority and power and not as the scribes and Pharisees. After having great success in Capernaum, Jesus decided to return to Nazareth where he had been brought up and went to the synagogue. During the service they asked Him to read and from the book of Isaiah. He turned to the scripture and read,

Luke 4:18 The Spirit of the Lord is upon me, because he hath anointed me to preach the gospel to the poor; he hath sent me to heal the brokenhearted, to preach deliverance to the captives, and recovering of sight to the blind, to set at liberty them that are bruised,

Luke 4:19 To preach the acceptable year of the Lord.

After He finished reading, He closed the book and gave it to the minister. The Spirit of the Lord was upon Jesus and everyone's eyes were fastened upon Him. Then Jesus went and sat down. Every eye followed His every movement as they waited to see what He would do next. After He sat down with everyone in suspense, Jesus said, "Upon this day, you have witnessed this scripture being fulfilled in your ears."

All of them bore witness at the gracious words which proceeded out of His mouth. However, because of jealousy they could not accept that God could use someone that they have always known and their hearts began to harden.

Mark 6:3 Is not this the carpenter, the son of Mary, the brother of James, and Joses, and of Juda, and Simon? and are not his sisters here with us? And they were offended at him.

Jesus said to them, "You shall surely say unto me, "Physician, heal thyself. The miracles that we have heard that you performed in Capernaum, do here in your own country." But I say unto you, no prophet is accepted in his own country. But I tell you the truth, there were many widows in Israel during the days of Elijah, when the heavens were shut up that it did not rain for three years and six months, and great famine was throughout the land. Yet, Elijah was only sent to Zarephath, a city of Sidon, unto a woman that was a widow."

"During the days of Elisha, there were many lepers in Israel. None of them were cleansed except for Naaman the Syrian."

When they heard this things, they were filled with wrath. They rose up and this angry mob grabbed Him and began to escort Jesus outside the city. They were so full of anger, that they were determined to kill Him. They were pushing Jesus towards the cliff to throw Him down and kill Him. Jesus decided, He'd had enough of this, and He bowed His head in quiet resolution, and disappeared from there eyes. He was still there but the mob's perceptions were altered and they could no longer see Him. Smiling, He passed right through their midst and returned to Capernaum and began to teach them on the sabbath days.

One day Jesus went and began to preach by the sea of Galilee. A huge crowd gathered, and they each began to press closer and closer, desiring to touch Jesus. There was such a crowd that the people began to shove Him backwards. There were a group of men fishing near the shore, and two of them were brothers called Simon and Andrew. Jesus asked them if He could use their boat to preach from. They agreed and He went just a little off shore and preached. When He finished, He turned to Simon and Andrew and said to them, "Cast your nets on the other side of the boat."

Simon answered Him and said, "Lord, we have been fishing all night long and have not caught anything at all." Nevertheless, he cast his net on the other side. Immediately, they caught so many fish that the weight of them began to break the net. They called to their other brethren in the other boats to help them. After they finished catching all the fish, Simon went to Jesus.

He fell at His feet and said, "Depart from me Lord, for I am a sinful man.

Jesus said to him, "Fear not Simon, from henceforth you shall be a fisher of men."

After that Simon, whom Jesus surnamed Peter and his brother began to follow Him.

From there He went and saw two men James and John, the sons of Zebedee. They were mending their nets with their father. Jesus said to them, "Follow me." Immediately, they left their father and the ship and began to follow Him.

Jesus went about all Galilee, preaching and teaching the gospel of the kingdom in their synagogues. He healed all manner of sickness and diseases among the people and His fame spread throughout all Syria. They brought unto Him all manner of sick people. They brought those taken with the palsy, those possessed with devils, and those which were lunatics and He healed them. Then great multitudes of people followed Him from Galilee, from Decapolis, from Jerusalem, from Judea, and from beyond Jordan.

Jesus went about preaching the gospel. Many Jews resisted His preaching. They were religious, but knew not God. They were full of pride, trusting in there heritage instead of truly seeking God. They felt confident because they were the seed of Abraham. They had the law, but not the love of God in their hearts. They were careful to pay tithes but not careful to show mercy.

Matthew 23:15 Woe unto you, scribes and Pharisees, hypocrites! for ye compass sea and land to make one proselyte, and when he is made, ye make him twofold more the child of hell than yourselves.

Matthew 3:9 And think not to say within yourselves, We have Abraham to our father: for I say unto you, that God is able of these stones to raise up children unto Abraham.

Bartimaeus

The Spirit of the Lord impressed Jesus to go to Jericho. At this time, Jericho was seventy miles out of the way. Nevertheless, He obeyed and went to Jericho to be used by His heavenly Father. As Jesus travelled to Jericho on the Jericho Road, a crowd gathered around Him. There was a certain blind man named Bartimaeus, who was sitting outside the walls of Jericho. When he heard the noise of the crowd, he asked what was going on. Someone told him that Jesus was passing. When he heard that, he got excited! He almost could not believe it. This was too good to be true. This was what he had been dreaming of.

He had heard how Jesus was working many miracles. He was opening the blinded eyes, unstopping deaf ears, and healing the lame. He knew this was his one chance to be healed of his blindness! His reason gave way to desperation. If only he could get Jesus' attention. However, there was a noisy crowd around Jesus.

He began to cry out, "Jesus, thou son of David, have mercy on me." However, there was no reply. Jesus could not hear him over the crowd. Bartimaeus began to scream louder and louder, "Jesus! Jesus! Thou son of David, have mercy on me!"

Some of those near Bartimaeus tried to quiet him. They said, "Calm down. Calm down. You shame us by your outburst." Bartimaeus cried the more, "Jesus! Jesus! Thou son of David, have mercy on me!"

His friends said, "Control yourself. You are embarrassing us," and they tried to restrain him. But the more they tried to quiet him, the louder he got. They tried to grab him, but he kept pushing them away and he kept crying out, "Jesus! Have mercy on me, thou son of David!"

Finally, Jesus heard him and said, "Bring that man to me." When they brought Bartimaeus to him, Jesus said, "What would you have Me to do for you?"

Bartimaeus was so nervous, he was shaking and he could barely speak. His voice began to quiver and tears ran down his blinded eyes as he desperately pleaded, "Lord, I want to receive my sight." The crowd was moved by Bartimaeus' tears. Some had faith and others pitied him, believing he made an impossible request.

Jesus smiled with that special smile that seemed to wash away all lifes problems. Jesus said, "Go your way. Your faith has made you whole." Immediately his eyes were opened, and he was blind Bartimaeus no more. A slight jolt went through his eyes and he began to rub them. His eyes began to water and when he opened them he screamed, "I can see, I can see!" The people were all amazed and they glorified God who had given such power to men.

Amazing grace, how sweet the sound
that saved a wretch like me.
I once was lost, but now I'm found,
was blind, but now I see.

His Name is Legion

Jesus and His disciples got on a boat and sailed to the country of the Gadarenes. When they arrived at the shore, a demon possessed man came running at Jesus. This man was completely naked, his hair and nails had grown long like a wild beast. He lived in the tombs of dead men. Neither could any man bind him with chains. He would beat the chains and gouge himself until he was free. Sometimes the demons would give him supernatural strength, and he would break them.

This man came running to Jesus because Jesus had commanded the demons to come out of him. The demons began to speak through the man saying, "Jesus, thou Son of the most High God, what have we done to You? Leave us alone. Have you come to torment us before the time?

Jesus said, "What is your name?"

They said, "Legion, for we are many. Jesus, please we beg You, don't cast us into the bottomless pit. Cast us into the herd of swine feeding nearby."

Jesus said, "Go!"

Immediately the herd of swine began acting strangely. They began to squeal and run wildly. They ran to the edge of the cliff, jumped off, fell into the sea and drowned. The keepers of the herd of swine got so scared that they ran off towards town. When the townspeople came back, they saw the formerly possessed man clothed, in his right mind, and sitting at the feet of Jesus.

The Woman At The Well

Jesus and His disciples went to Samaria. He comes to the City of Sychar and goes to Jacob's well. Jesus was tired and He sent His disciples into the city to buy some meat. A woman of Samaria came to draw water from the well.

Jesus said, "Give me water to drink."

The woman was totally surprised and somewhat indignant. She said to Him, "How is it that You being a Jew, ask me for water? The Jews have no dealings with the Samaritans.

Jesus said, "If you knew the gift of God, and who it is that asks water from you, you would ask Me to give you living water."

The woman said to Him, "Sir, You have nothing to draw water with and the well is deep. Where can You get this living water from?"

Jesus said to her, "Whosoever drinks of this water shall thirst again, but whosoever drinks of the water that I shall give them shall never thirst again."

The woman said, "Sir give me this water, so that I will not thirst and I will not have to come here to draw water."

Jesus said to her, "Go call your husband."

She said, "I have no husband."

"You have answered truly, you have no husband, because you have had five husbands, and the man with whom you have now is not your husband. You spoke truly you have no husband," Jesus said.

The woman is amazed and somewhat frightened. She says to Jesus, "Sir, I perceive that You are a prophet. Our fathers worshipped in this mountain, and You say that in Jerusalem is the place where men ought to worship."

Jesus said, "Woman, the hour comes, when you shall neither in the mountain, nor in Jerusalem, worship the Father. You worship you know not what. We know what we worship, for salvation is of the Jews.

But the hour comes, and now is, when the true worshippers shall worship the Father in spirit and in truth, for the Fathers seeks such to worship Him. God is a Spirit, and they that worship Him must worship Him in spirit and in truth."

The woman says unto Him, "I know that Messiah is coming, which is called Christ. When He comes, He will tell us all things."

Jesus said, "I that speak unto you am he."

After He said this, the disciples came up and they were amazed that He spoke to the woman. However, none of them asked Him, "Why are you talking with her?"

The woman was so excited that she left her waterpot and went into the city. She told the men of the city, "Come see a man that told me everything that I ever did. Is not this the Christ?"

The men of the city went to the well to see Jesus.

Meanwhile, His disciples said, "Master, eat."

Jesus said, "I have meat to eat that you do not know of."

The disciples said to one another, "Has any man brought Him something to eat?"

Jesus said, "My meat is to do the will of Him that sent Me, and to finish His work."

Many of the Samaritans came unto Him. They asked Jesus to stay with them. Jesus stayed with them two days and ministered unto them. Many more believed on Him, because of His words.

The men said to the woman, "Now we believe, not because of your saying, for we have heard Him ourselves, and we know that He is indeed the Christ the Savior of the world."

Bethesda

Jesus returned unto Jerusalem. Now there was at Jerusalem by the sheep market a pool, called Bethesda. Around the pool was a great multitude of disabled people. Some were blind, crippled, and deformed, who all waited for the moving of the water.

At different times, God would send an angel to trouble the water. Whoever was first to step into the water was healed of whatever disease he had.

A certain man was there who had been sick for thirty-eight years. When Jesus saw him lying there, and knowing that he had been sick a long time asked him, "Will you be made whole?"

The impotent man said, "Sir, I have no man, when the water is troubled, to put me into the pool. While I am coming, another steps down before me."

Jesus said, "Rise, take up your bed and walk."

Immediately the man was made whole, and he took up his bed and walked. Now it was the Sabbath day. When the Jews saw him carrying his bed they said, "It is the Sabbath day. It is not lawful for you to carry your bed on the Sabbath day."

The man answered, "He that made me whole, said to me, "Take up your bed and walk."

Then they asked him, "Where is the man that told you to take up your bed and walk? Who is he?" The man did not know where Jesus was because there was a multitude of people in that place.

Later Jesus found the man in the temple, and said to him, "Look. Now you are healed. Sin no more, lest a worse thing comes upon you."

The man left and told the Jews, it was Jesus who healed him. The Jews were so angry that Jesus did these things on the Sabbath day that they began to persecute Him, and wanted to kill Him.

Jesus answered them, "My Father works unceasingly, and I must work too."

Therefore, the Jews sought the more to kill Him, because He not only had broken the sabbath, but said also that God was His Father, making Himself equal with God.

Jesus answered and said unto them, "Truly I say unto you, The Son can do nothing of Himself, but what He sees the Father do. Whatever the Father does, the Son does likewise. For the Father loves the Son, and shows Him all things that He, the Father will do.

And He will show Him greater works than these that you may marvel.

For the Father judges no man, but has committed all judgement unto the Son. That all men should honor the Son, even as they honor the Father. He that honors not the Son honors not the Father. He that honors not the Son, honors not the Father that sent him.

Truly I say unto you, the hour comes and now is when the dead shall hear the voice of the Son of God, and they that hear shall live.

Marvel not at this: for the hour is coming, in the which all that are in the graves shall hear His voice, And shall come forth; they that have done good, unto the resurrection of life; and they that have done evil, unto the resurrection of damnation.

I can of mine own self do nothing: as I hear, I judge: and my judgment is just; because I seek not mine own will, but the will of the Father which hath sent me.

A woman who was so moved by Jesus that she pronounced a blessing upon Jesus' mother, Mary. The woman said, "Blessed is the womb that bore you, and the paps from which you did suck."

Jesus not said, "Yea, but more blessed are they which hear the word of God and keep it."

Jesus received word that Peter's wife's mother was very sick with a fever. Jesus and his disciples went to Peter's house. When Jesus came in, Peter's mother-in-law was lying on the couch. Jesus went and touched her hand and immediately the fever left her. She arose and ministered unto them. Word began to spread that Jesus was there. The people of the village came and brought Him all that were diseased and those that had devils. He laid His hands on them and healed them all. Many of the demons came out screaming, "Leave us alone Jesus. We know who thou art. Thou art the Son of God."

But Jesus rebuked them saying "Hold your peace, and come out." Jesus ministered to the people all that night. When it was day, He departed unto a deserted place. The people were so blessed by Jesus, they went to Him and asked Him to stay with them. Jesus appreciated them but said, "I must go and minister to other cities as well, as God has sent me."

Lazarus and the Rich Man

Jesus told His disciples of the story of Lazarus and the rich man. This was a true story, which took place around the time of Moses.

There was a certain rich man who was clothed in purple and fine linen. He fared sumptuously every day. There was a certain beggar named Lazarus, who was laid at the rich man's gate. Lazarus was very sick and his body was full of sores. Lazarus was starving and would have loved to have eaten the crumbs which fell from the rich man's table.

And it came to pass that the rich man died, and Lazarus died also. The beggar, Lazarus, was carried by the angels into Abraham's bosom.

From hell, the rich man looked up in agony. He was experiencing all the torments of hell when he looked up and saw a familiar face on the other side. The rich man was trapped in hell but across from hell is Paradise or Abraham's bosom. The rich man sees Lazarus with Abraham. In agony the rich man cries out to Abraham.

He said, "Father Abraham! Send Lazarus to dip the tip of his finger in water and cool my tongue, for I am tormented in this flame."

Abraham answered, "Son, remember while you were alive, you sought after only earthly rewards and received them. Lazarus received only evil things. He is comforted, while you are tormented. Besides this, there is a great gulf that is fixed between us that we cannot go there. Neither can you pass over here."

The rich man said, "Father Abraham, I beg of you, send Lazarus to my fathers house that he may testify to them. I have five brothers and I do not wish for them to come to this dreadful place."

Abraham answered him and said, "They have Moses and the other prophets. Let them hear them."

The rich man said, "No! If one went unto them from the dead, they will repent."

Abraham said, "If they will not hear Moses and the other prophets, they will not be persuaded even though one rise from the dead."

Jesus Feeds the Multitude

As Jesus' fame spread, huge crowds followed Him where ever He went. Aside from His twelve innermost disciples, He had many others. He sent seventy disciples at one time to preach His gospel. They would go and prepare the way for Him. They would enter into cities and tell them Jesus was coming. They would testify of the miracles that He performed. When Jesus came into a city, the groundwork was laid and many of the people received him. Many of the people began to follow Him wherever He went.

Jesus went into the wilderness and a large crowd followed Him. His words were so moving that they stayed there to hear what He taught. They had not planned to stay so long and brought very little food. They did not know how long they would stay with Him. They were now with Him three days. Many of them were so anxious to hear Jesus, they just decided to fast.

Jesus looked on them and He had compassion for them. Mothers and fathers had brought their children. There was five thousand men, not counting the women and children. He said to His disciples, "I will not send them away fasting, otherwise they will not make it back. They will faint along the way. They have stayed with Me these three days and I wish to feed them."

One of the disciples said, "Shall we go and buy two hundred pennyworth ($40), of bread and feed them?"

Philip said, "Two hundred pennyworth of bread is not sufficient to feed this multitude, even if everyone only takes a little."

Another disciple says, "Where could we buy the bread?"

Jesus said, "I will feed them. Do we have any food?"

One little boy volunteered his lunch.

Andrew, Simon Peter's brother said, "There is a lad here, who has five barely loaves and two fishes. But what are they among so many?"

Jesus told His disciples, "Make the people sit down in groups of fifty."

All the people sat down upon the grass. Jesus took the food and blessed it. After He had given thanks, He began to break the bread. As He broke it, He created more. With every piece He broke, before the eyes of the disciples, more bread would grow. The disciples could hardly contain their joy. Everyone was so happy. Jesus gave them all the bread they needed. After He finished with the bread, He started on the fish. As easily as He broke the bread, He broke the fish. He multiplied the fish as well.

Everyone ate until they were filled. After everyone finished eating, Jesus told them to gather up the remains. The fragments that remained filled up twelve baskets. After eating, the meeting was over and they returned to their homes.

There were other times when Jesus fed the multitudes. He eventually stopped, however. He told the people, "You did not come to hear Me, but to eat the loaves and the fishes."

Jesus Mark 10:46   And they came to Jericho: and as he went out of Jericho with his disciples and a great number of people, blind Bartimaeus, the son of Timaeus, sat by the highway side begging.

Jesus sent His disciples out to minister to the people. Aside from the twelve, He appointed another seventy disciples. He commanded them to go out, two by two. He was training them for the time when he would be gone. He told them, "I give you power to heal the sick, cleanse the leper, and raise the dead. Freely you have received, so freely give. Do not go unto the cities of the Gentiles, but go unto the lost sheep of the house of Israel."

After a few days, the disciples came back rejoicing. They said, "Master. Even the devils are subject unto us in your name."

Jesus thought for a second, remembering the battle between the Father and Lucifer. Jesus smiled and said, "I beheld Satan when he like lightning was cast out of heaven. Behold! I give unto you power to tread on serpents and scorpions, and over all the power of the enemy. And nothing shall by any means hurt you. But without taking anything away from this, don't rejoice because I give you power to cast out devils. But rejoice because your names are written in heaven.

Issue of Blood

There was a certain woman which had an issue of blood. She hemorrhaged for years and had seen many doctors and tried many cures. She had spent much money, but she only grew worse. All hope seemed to be gone, until someone told her about Jesus.

She heard about all the miracles He performed. At first she believed if He prayed for her, she would be healed. However, as she heard more and more of the miracles which He did her faith continued to grow. Finally, her faith got to the point where she said within herself, "If I can but touch the hem of His garment, I will be healed."

When Jesus came by there was the usual crowd following Him. The woman went out to meet Him but He was surrounded by a great crowd. She kept pushing her way through to touch Him. She shoved and squirmed and squeezed her way closer to Him.

Finally, she got close to Him and reached out and touched Him. Immediately the power of God flowed from Jesus to her. She knew within herself that she was healed of the plague. For the first time in years, she was healthy and strong.

Suddenly Jesus stopped and said, "Who touched Me?"

The disciples could not believe it. They said, "Master, You see this crowd pressing You on every side and You asked, "Who touched Me?"

Jesus said, "Someone has touched me, for I perceive that virtue has gone out of me."

Now the woman knew that she had been found out. She came forward trembling and bowed before Him. She confessed all. When she told the crowd how she was healed, they glorified God.

Demon boy

There was a certain man who came to Jesus. He said, "Jesus will you please help me? My son is grievously vexed with a devil."

Jesus said, "Take him to My disciples."

The man said, "Lord, I already did. But they could not cast it out."

Jesus was angry with His disciples because they should have been able to cast the devil out. He said, "O faithless and perverse generation, how long shall I suffer with you. Bring the boy to me."

As the boy approached Jesus, the demon within him got afraid. The devil took control of the boy's body and he fell down writhing before Jesus. Jesus asked the father, "How long has he been like this?"

The man answered, "From a child. Sometimes the demon would take him and throw him in the fire." He said, "Lord can you help him?"

Jesus answered him and said, "If you believe. All things are possible to him that believes."

The father said, "Lord, I believe, but help me with my unbelief."

Then Jesus laid His hands on the boy and he was immediately healed and the demon was cast out.

Nicodemus

A certain man of the Pharisees, named Nicodemus came to talk with Jesus. He came at night so that he would not be seen. He said, "Rabbi, we know that You are a teacher from God for no man can do the miracles that You do, except God be with him."

Jesus said, "Truly, except a man be born again he cannot see the kingdom of God."

Nicodemus said unto Him, "How can a man be born when he is old. Can he enter the second time into his mother's womb, and be born?"

Jesus said to Him, "Truly I say unto you, except a man be born of the water and the Spirit, he cannot enter the kingdom of God. That which is born of the flesh is flesh, and that which is born of the Spirit is spirit. Do not be amazed that I have told you, you must be born again.

The wind blows where it wills. You can hear the sound of it, but you cannot tell where it comes from or where it is going. So is everyone that is born of the Spirit."

Nicodemus answered him, "How can these things be?"

Jesus said, "Are you a master of Israel, and yet you do not know these things? I am telling you the truth. We speak what We do know, and testify what We have seen and you do not receive Our witness. If I have told you earthly things, and you do not believe, how shall you believe if I tell you of heavenly things?

No man ascends up to heaven, but He that came down from heaven, even the Son of man which is in heaven. As Moses lifted up the serpent in the wilderness, even so must the Son of man be lifted up, that whoever believes in Him should not perish, but have eternal life.

For God so loved the world, that He have His only begotten Son, that whosoever believeth in Him should not perish, but have everlasting life.

For God sent not His Son into the world to condemn the world; but that the world through Him might be saved.

He that believes on Him is not condemned: but he that believes not is condemned already, because he hath not believed in the name of the only begotten Son of God.

And this is the condemnation, that light is come into the world, and men loved darkness rather than light, because their deeds were evil.

For every one that does evil hates the light, neither comes to the light, lest his deeds should be reproved.
But he that does truth comes to the light, that his deeds may be made manifest, that they are wrought in God.

A wicked and adulterous generation seeks after a sign. But no sign shall be given them other than the sign of the prophet earth. For as Jonah was three days and night in the belly of the whale, so shall the Son of Man be three days and night in the belly of the earth."

Lazarus

Mary and Martha sent Jesus a message concerning their brother. The message was, "Lord, he whom thou lovest is sick."

When Jesus heard that He said, "This sickness is not unto death, but for the glory of God, that the Son of man may be glorified."

However, Jesus abode in the same place two days. After that He said, "Let us go into Judaea again."

His disciples began to say, "Master, the last time we were there the Jews tried to stone You. Are you going there again?"

Jesus said, "Are there not twelve hours in a day? If any man walk in the day, he stumbles not because he sees the light of this world. But if a man walk in the night, he will stumble because there is no light."

After a while, the subject of Lazarus came up. Jesus said, "Lazarus, our friend, is sleep, but I go that I may wake him."

Then one of the disciples said, "Lord, if he's sleep, he is doing well."

They thought that Jesus was speaking of taking rest in sleep.

Then Jesus told them plainly, "Lazarus is dead, but I am glad for your sakes that I was not there so that you may believe. Nevertheless, let us go unto him."

Thomas who was called Didymus said, "Let us go, that we may die with him."

When they got to Bethany, they found out that Lazarus had already died and had been buried for four days.

When He got to Bethany, the town of Lazarus, one of his sisters came out to meet Him. It was Martha, for Mary was still in the house. She said, "Lord if You had been here, I know that my brother would not have died. But I know that even now whatever You ask God, He will do."

Then Jesus said to her, "Thy brother shall rise again."

She answered him, "I know that he shall rise again at the resurrection at the last day."

Jesus raised His voice in authority and said, "I am the resurrection, and the life: he that believeth in Me, though he were dead yet shall he live: and whosoever lives and believes in Me shall never die. Do you believe this?"

She said unto him, "Yes Lord, I believe that you are the Christ, the Son of God, which should come into the world."

Then she went into the house where her sister, Mary was still crying. There were many of the Jews there to comfort her. Martha told Mary, "The master is here and He calls for you."

As soon as she heard that she got up and went out to meet Him. When she got to Him she fell at His feet and said, "Lord if You would have been here, I know my brother would not have died."

When Jesus saw her weeping and the Jews who were with her weeping also, He was grieved in His spirit. Although He knew what He was about to do, their grief touched Him. It pained Him to see those He loved, weeping out of a broken heart because of the death of their loved one. One so full of compassion as He, could not help but be touched by their anguish.

Jesus said, "Where have you laid him?"

Jesus wept.

When they got to the tomb of Lazarus, it was a cave with a huge stone over it. Jesus said, "Remove the stone."

Martha, the sister of Lazarus, said, "Lord, by this time he stinks, for he has been dead for four days."

Jesus said unto her, "Said I not unto you that if you would believe, you would see the glory of God?"

Then they took away the stone from the cave. Jesus lifted up His eyes toward heaven and said, "Father, I thank you because you have heard Me. And I know that you always hear Me, but I said it for the sake of these standing here, that they may believe that You have sent Me."

After He finished speaking He said with a loud voice, "Lazarus, come forth!"

Immediately Lazarus came hopping to the mouth of the cave, for he was bound hand and foot. Jesus said, "Loose him and let him go."

Chapter 14

Jesus began to prepare His disciples for the time when He would be gone. He told them, " In my Father's house are many mansions. If it were not true, I would not have told you so. I am going to prepare a place for you, that where I am, you will be there also.

I will not leave you comfortless. But I will ask the Father that He will give you another Comforter, even the Holy Ghost. For He dwells with you, but He shall be in you. He is the Spirit of Truth, whom the world cannot receive."

His disciples began to look sad.

Jesus tried His best to comfort them. He informed them, "It is better for you that I go away. For if I don't go away, the Comforter will not come. He will lead you and guide you, and bring all things unto your remembrance, whatsoever I have said unto you. And whatsoever you shall ask the Father in My name, that will He do, that the Father may be glorified in the Son.

Triumphal Entry

Jesus has taken His disciples to the mount of Olives. From there He looks down at Jerusalem. He thinks of all the times when He tried by His Spirit to draw them unto Him. He says, "Jerusalem. Oh Jerusalem. How many times have I tried to gather you unto Myself as a hen gathers her chicks, but you would not. Therefore your house is left unto you desolate."

Many of the Jews did not receive Jesus. They did not want a religious Messiah, they wanted a political one. They were only concerned with this temporal world. They were in their own way as Godless as the Romans, which they hated. Many of them felt the only good Roman was a dead Roman. The zealots failed to understand in their attempts to be free of Roman tyranny, they had become as wicked in their own way as their enemies. If one empire was destroyed, Satan would use another. He did not want His message to be clouded with Jewish nationalism. Many of the Jews cared nothing for other nations.

Jesus was reaching out to save a world. His message was timeless. They had the law of God, but not His mercy or love. In their religious pride they had alienated themselves from the God which they claimed to worship. God is a spirit. They failed to understand that the true worshipers of God must worship Him in spirit and in truth.

He once told some of the Pharisee's, "Woe unto you scribes and Pharisees. You search the earth to find one convert, then you make him twice the child of hell you are."

Jesus turns and says to His disciples, "Go into that village and you shall find a donkey and its colt. Bring them both here. If anyone stops you and ask, "What are you doing?" Answer them and say, "The Lord has need of them." Then they will let you go."

The disciples go and come back with the donkey and its colt, just as Jesus told them. They put their coats on the donkey and its colt and Jesus gets on the donkey. They are now ready. Jesus had sent word that He was coming into Jerusalem. Many of His followers have gathered at the base of the mountain, waiting for Jesus to begin His journey through the eastern gate. They are anxiously awaiting for Him to enter Jerusalem. Jesus and His disciples begin the descent down the mountain.

The crowd that has gathered begins cheering for Jesus as He comes to meet them. They are shouting and waving. They are glorifying God for all the miracles that have occurred through Jesus' ministry. All this has been done to fulfill the prophecy of Zechariah.

Zechariah 9:9 Rejoice greatly, O daughter of Zion; shout, O daughter of Jerusalem: behold, thy King cometh unto thee: He is just, and having salvation; lowly, and riding upon an ass, and upon a colt the foal of an ass.

There is a crowd in front and in back of Him. Many of them have taken off their garments and laid them in His path. Some have cut branches off the trees and have laid them down in His path. It is a great multitude of people. The multitude shouts, "Hosanna to the son of David: Blessed is He that cometh in the name of the Lord; Hosanna in the highest." He climbs up the hill toward the eastern gate. He waits for the crowd to go before him. Cheering, they rush into the city. They enter the city through the eastern gate. In 1542 the eastern gate will be sealed shut to fulfill the prophecy of Ezekiel.

Ezekiel 44:2 Then said the LORD unto me; This gate shall be shut, it shall not be opened, and no man shall enter in by it; because the LORD, the God of Israel, hath entered in by it, therefore it shall be shut.

It will remain shut until Jesus returns to Jerusalem after the battle of Armageddon. From 1542 A.D. until this day, the eastern gate has remained shut. Despite all the changes that occurred in Jerusalem in the more than one thousand, five hundred years since this time, the eastern gate has remained sealed. In the early part of this century there was talk of the eastern gate being opened. Within a few days, World War I broke out and armies invaded Jerusalem. Despite their best efforts, the eastern gate has remained shut and will be so, until Jesus enters through it.

Jesus enters the city through the eastern gate.

There is so much noise that the whole city is in an uproar. They begin to come out of their homes and ask, "What is this?" Some of the Pharisees come to Jesus and said, "Master, rebuke your disciples." Jesus said, "I tell you that if these should hold their peace, then the very rocks would cry out."

Jesus continues until He gets to the temple. He sees the moneychangers cheating the people. He enters the temple and overturns their tables. He takes some reeds and whips the money-changers. He chastises them and says, "My house shall be called a house of prayer, but you have made it into a den of thieves.

But woe to you, scribes and Pharisees, hypocrites! For you shut up the kingdom of heaven against men; for you neither go in yourselves, nor do you allow those who are entering to go in.

Woe to you, scribes and Pharisees, hypocrites! For you devour widows' houses, and for a pretense make long prayers. Therefore you will receive greater condemnation. "Woe to you, scribes and Pharisees, hypocrites! For you travel land and sea to win one proselyte, and when he is won, you make him twice as much a son of hell as yourselves.

Woe to you, blind guides, who say, 'Whoever swears by the temple, it is nothing; but whoever swears by the gold of the temple, he is obliged to perform it.'

Fools and blind! For which is greater, the gold or the temple that sanctifies the gold?

And, 'Whoever swears by the altar, it is nothing; but whoever swears by the gift that is on it, he is obliged to perform it.'

Fools and blind! For which is greater, the gift or the altar that sanctifies the gift?

Blind guides, who strain out a gnat and swallow a camel!

"Woe to you, scribes and Pharisees, hypocrites! For you cleanse the outside of the cup and dish, but inside they are full of extortion and self-indulgence.

Blind Pharisee, first cleanse the inside of the cup and dish, that the outside of them may be clean also.

Woe to you, scribes and Pharisees, hypocrites! For you are like whitewashed tombs which indeed appear beautiful outwardly, but inside are full of dead men's bones and all uncleanness.

Even so you also outwardly appear righteous to men, but inside you are full of hypocrisy and lawlessness.

Woe to you, scribes and Pharisees, hypocrites! Because you build the tombs of the prophets and adorn the monuments of the righteous, "and say, 'If we had lived in the days of our fathers, we would not have been partakers with them in the blood of the prophets.'

Therefore you are witnesses against yourselves that you are sons of those who murdered the prophets.

Fill up, then, the measure of your fathers' guilt.

Serpents, brood of vipers! How can you escape the condemnation of hell?

Therefore, indeed, I send you prophets, wise men, and scribes: some of them you will kill and crucify, and some of them you will scourge in your synagogues and persecute from city to city, "that on you may come all the righteous blood shed on the earth, from the blood of righteous Abel to the blood of Zechariah, son of Berechiah, whom you murdered between the temple and the altar.

Assuredly, "See! Your house is left to you desolate."

Then Jesus went out and departed from the temple, and His disciples came to Him to show Him the buildings of the temple.

The disciples began to ask Jesus what would be the signs of His coming at the end of the world. He began to warn His disciples that first of all, "You shall be hated of all men for My name sake, but I shall preserve you. In your patience, you possess your souls. But when you see Jerusalem surrounded by armies, then know and understand that its desolation has come. Then let those which are in Judea flee into the mountains and let those which are inside the city, get out of it, and let none of those who are out of the country come into it.

For these are the days of vengeance, that all things that are written shall be fulfilled. Woe unto those who are pregnant and for those who have babies which they are nursing in those days! For great misery, distress, and anguish shall come upon the land. God shall pour out His indignation, and take retribution upon this people. Many shall fall by the edge of the sword and be led away captive unto all nations, and Jerusalem shall be trodden down by the Gentiles until the times of the Gentiles be fulfilled and completed."

After the Triumphal Entry into Jerusalem of Jesus, Satan is quite worried. The number of Jesus' followers seems to be increasing daily. Satan believes that Jesus will soon be crowned King of Israel and the Millennial Reign will begin. Satan knows he will be vanquished before the Millennial Reign. He cannot afford to let that happen. He figures his only chance is to use his power to influence the high priest to have Jesus killed. If Jesus is killed, he believes he will have broken the prophecies of God. He cannot control, but he can tempt and influence men. Satan tempts the priest and Pharisees to be jealous of Jesus. They have consistently fallen into Satan's trap and they are now desperate to stop Jesus before all the people believe in Him.

Satan now decides to use his trump card, Judas.

Judas has always been full of the devil. He has become increasingly dissatisfied with the life of a disciple. He was the treasurer of Jesus' ministry. For years he has stolen money out of the treasury, and he was unwilling to change. Because evil is never satisfied in the face of righteousness, he is miserable. He decides to get out while he can and make the best of it. Satan persuades Judas to betray Jesus. He makes a deal with the high priest to betray Jesus.

The Last Supper

Jesus has gathered His disciples for one last meal before His crucifixion in a certain room in Jerusalem. The mood is somber. The disciples can see that something is definitely wrong with Jesus. Yet, He seems unwilling to talk about it. He is deeply troubled, but He will not discuss the nature of His problem. They have never seen Him so sad. The disciples realize that if anyone can get it out of Jesus, it is John, the beloved. John was a teenager and he looked up to Jesus as a father. John was like a son to Him. Jesus could talk to John when He could not talk to anyone else. Peter whispers to John, "John. You ask Him what's wrong. He'll tell you."

John gets up and goes over to Jesus. He lays his head on Jesus' shoulder and asks him, "Master. What's wrong? Tell us, what is it?"

This is one of the hardest things that He has ever had to do. He has been dreading telling His disciples this. Yet, they must know. There is no more time left. Jesus tells them, "This very night, I will be delivered into the hands of the chief priests and Pharisees." They are stunned. He tells them one of them will betray Him. Some of them ask who. They begin to ask, "Lord is it I?"

Jesus takes a piece of bread and says, "He whom I give to sop, the same is he who will betray Me." Jesus goes and gives the bread to Judas.

Jesus looks at him. He knows that Judas has already made a deal with the Pharisees to betray Him. He has tried to reach Judas for three and a half years. He has shown him love and trust. He even allowed Judas to be the treasurer. How did he repay His trust? by stealing the money. He has tried everything and Judas has prepared to betray Him. He can no longer stomach the sight of this hypocrite, this chameleon who pretends to be a saint while he is the basest of sinners. Judas has already made up His mind to betray Jesus. There is no point in Judas' charade going on any longer. Jesus says to him, "Whatever it is you are about to do, do it quickly."

Judas looks into Jesus' eyes. One glance tells all. Judas knows that he has been found out. He is somewhat surprised by this confrontation. He surrenders his will to the forces that are driving him. It is not shame he feels now, only anger. Judas surrenders to his anger, not knowing he is giving in to Satan. He goes out to betray Jesus.

Only Jesus and Judas understand what is going on. Some of the disciples think Jesus sent Judas on some errand.

Jesus speaks to Peter and says, "Simon, Simon. Satan desires to have you that he may sift you as wheat. But I have prayed for you that your faith won't fail you. And when you are converted, strengthen your brethren."
He proceeds to tell them, that they will all deny Him that night.

Peter says, "Lord, though all these others deny you, I will never deny you!"

Jesus looks at Peter and says very frankly, "Peter before the rooster crows twice, you shall deny Me three times."

Peter denies Jesus charge and swears vehemently he will never deny Jesus. He says, "Lord although I may die with you, I will never deny you."

The other disciples say the same thing. Jesus knows there is no point in saying anything else. They will not believe until it happens to them.

He takes them to the Mount of Olives. Jesus knows that it is Satan's plan to kill not only Him, but His disciples as well. He asks them, "Do we have any swords?"
They say, "We have four."
He answers, "It is enough."

Jesus takes His disciples to a garden called Gethsemane, just outside Jerusalem. He leaves eight of His disciples near the edge of the garden. He tells them to wait there while He takes Peter, James, and John deeper in the garden. He tells them to watch and "pray here." He says to them, "Pray that ye enter not into temptation." He turns and goes further into the garden.

He goes into the deepest part of the garden alone. He must be alone to commune with the Father. The weight of the world is upon His shoulders and He is tired. He is more alone than any man has ever been. No one on this planet truly understands Him. Nor do they understand what He is about to do. All of history, all of humanity and all of creation, is dependant upon what He must do next. Yet, the agony that He must endure, is almost beyond comprehension. His suffering will be nigh endurable. He finds a big rock and kneels down to pray.

"Father if it be possible, let this bitter cup pass from me." Perhaps there is another way, another possibility that He has not explored, that will spare Him of the incredible agony which He is to endure. He prays and prays to His Father. He must have strength if He is to make it. Finally, He gets up to check on the three disciples. He knows they are not praying. If they were praying, He would feel their prayers helping His. Sure enough they are fast asleep. He wakes them up and says, "Can you not pray with me one hour?"

He looks at them and realizes that their spirits are truly willing but their flesh is weak.

He goes back and prays again. He prays and God sends an angel to strengthen him. He feels so much better. He has found the strength He needed. He submits Himself to His Heavenly Father and says, "Not My will but let Thy will be done."

He arises. He has the victory. He is prepared for whatever He must face. It is time. Even now the soldiers are approaching. He goes to His disciples. They hear Him coming and wake up and try to pray.

Jesus tells them, "Sleep on now, and take your rest; for now is hour of the power of darkness."

Immediately Judas enters the garden followed by a band of soldiers. They have torches, lanterns, clubs and swords. The disciples jump up. Peter pulls out his sword ready to fight to the death. The other disciples prepare to defend themselves. Judas kisses Jesus on the cheek. Jesus says, "Judas. Do you betray the Son of man with a kiss. In the commotion the soldiers miss the signal.

Jesus says, "Am I a thief or a robber that you come here with clubs and swords? Whom seek ye?"

They said, "We seek Jesus."

Jesus says, "I am He!" The sheer power of His voice momentarily seems to push them backwards. They seem confused and don't quit know what to do. Although it is necessary for Him to go to the cross, He will go as the Son of God. He asks them again, "Whom seek ye?"

Again they answer rather timidly, "We seek Jesus."

Jesus tells them in a voice that almost seems to be controlling them, "If you seek Me, let these go."

At that moment, Peter decides he has heard enough. Apparently Jesus has decided to go peaceably with the soldiers to spare their lives. With a cry of unbridled fury, he charges the soldiers to defend his best friend. He swings his sword at the head of one of the soldiers whose name was Malchus. Peter strikes him with the sword on the side of head. Malchus screams clutching the side of his head as the blood spews out. Peter has cut off his ear!

Before anything further can happen, Jesus commands Peter, "Put up thy sword in thy sheath." Peter stops and looks at Jesus. Peter is still angry and confused. He does not know what to do. Jesus looks

Peter in the eyes. Jesus' hand is stretched toward Peter to stop him. Jesus speaks with great authority, "All they that live by the sword, shall die by the sword. Peter, don't you know that even now I could ask my Father and He would send Me more than twelve legions of angels to save me. But how then would the scriptures be fulfilled? This must be.

The cup that My Father has given Me shall I not drink it?" Jesus turns to the soldiers and says, "Allow me to do this. He then picks up the severed ear of Malchus and places it back on the soldier's head. Miraculously, the flesh comes back together and the soldier's ear is completely healed. Neither the disciples nor the soldiers understands Jesus' actions. It was His desire to heal one last time, to work one last miracle before His time on earth was over.

They take Jesus away to the home of the high priest and Peter follows them afar off. The rest of the disciples had fled for their lives. Peter went inside the house to see what they would do with Jesus. The house was very large and some of the people made a fire in the middle of the courtyard. Peter sat among them, trying to see what would become of Jesus.

It was cold that night and some of the people are warming themselves by the fire. One of the maids, a relative of Caiaphas, confronts Peter. She says, "You are one of the disciples."

Peter is warming himself by the fire. He is standing near some of the men. He denies it and says, "I am not. Woman I don't know what you are talking about."

One of them is a relative of Malchus, the soldier whom Peter had struck earlier. He recognizes Peter and says, "You are one of them. Didn't I see you in the garden?"

He denies it and say's, "Man I don't know what you are talking about. I am not." Peter ignores him and continues watching the trial of Jesus.

The high priest has assembled many members of the council (Sanhedrin) to try Jesus. They secretly assembled this chosen group at night, so none of Jesus' friends would be invited. Nicodemus, one of Jesus friends in the council, was not invited. They knew not to invite him, because once before he had spoken up for Jesus, and warned them they may be fighting against God. The high priest hoped to get a speedy trial and conviction before news got out. They brought their witness to testify.

The chief priest and the whole council (Sanhedrin) sought to get witnesses to condemn Him. Many bare false witness and were unconvincing to the council. Satan realizes the trial is not going well. If he doesn't do something, Jesus may be acquitted. He prompts two men who have actually heard Jesus speak to come forward. The two men came forward and said, "This Fellow said, 'I am able to tear down the Temple of God and to build it up again in three days.'"

The high priest stood up and said, "Have you no answer to this accusation. What about this that these men testify against You?"

But Jesus kept silent. Satan whispered in the ear of the high priest, "Make Him swear by God, that He is not the Christ." The high priest said to Him, "I call upon you to swear by the living God, and tell us whether You are the Christ, the Son of God."

Jesus said to him, "You have stated the fact. More than that, I tell you that in the future you will see the Son of man seated at the right hand of the Almighty, and coming on the clouds of the sky."

The high priest tore his clothes and shouted, "He has uttered blasphemy! What further evidence do we need? What do you think now?" They answered, "Put Him to death!"

They begin to beat Jesus. They spit in His face. One of the men blindfold Jesus. They begin to beat him and smite him on the face saying, "Prophesy, Jesus. Tell us who hit you." The men do not know they are doing these things at the unction of Satan. He stands back, invisible to human eyes, smiling at his handiwork. Satan looks over and sees Peter watching all this. He unctions one of the men, to speak out to Peter, "You are one of his disciples."

Peter denies it saying, "I know him not." The rooster crows, but Peter pays no attention. He moves away from them and is seated at the table.

Then, another young woman stares at Peter for some time. She is watching him earnestly. Finally, she says, "I know I have seen you with Him. We know you are one of them for your speech betrays you, for you are obviously a Galilean."

Peter is afraid and so desperate not to be found out, that he begins to swear in such a foul manner that no one would believe that he is one of the disciples. Immediately the rooster crows the second time. Jesus looks up across the room at Peter. As their eyes meet, Peter remembers the words that Jesus told him that night, "Before the rooster crows, twice you will deny me three times." He is so ashamed that he cannot bear to be in Jesus sight. He rushes out of the room, as a floodgate of tears burst from his eyes.

Peter has denied the man who was closer than his brother. Do you know what it is like to see your hopes and dreams crushed before you? Do you know what it is like to feel the worst pain in the world? It is not a pain in the head or foot, but the pain inside a broken heart? Do you know what it is like to be in such pain in your tortured heart that minutes seem like hours, and hours feel like days? If you do, you understand the pain that Peter feels. He tries to hold back the tears, but he may as well try to hold back the rain. Finally, he finds a solitary place and wails like a wounded beast and weeps bitter tears.

Crucifixion

Judas has a change of heart and goes to the chief priest and elders. He returns the money and says, "I have sinned by betraying innocent blood."

They answer him, "What is that to us. You see to it."

Judas throws down the pieces of silver in the temple and goes and hangs himself.

The chief priest take up the money and say, "It is not lawful for us to put the money back in the treasury, because it is the price of blood."

They decide to buy the potters field to bury strangers in it, and it was called the field of blood. This was a fulfillment of Zechariah's prophecy.

Zechariah 11:12 And I said unto them, If ye think good, give me my price; and if not, forbear. So they weighed for my price thirty pieces of silver.
Zechariah 11:13 And the LORD said unto me, Cast it unto the potter: a goodly price that I was prised at of them. And I took the thirty pieces of silver, and cast them to the potter in the house of the LORD.

The chief priest and elders have tried Jesus and bring Him before Pilate for execution. They would have done it themselves, except the Roman's did not allow the Jews to execute prisoners. They explain the charges they have brought against Him. They accuse Him of blasphemy before Pilate. Jesus never says a word.

Pilate knows the Jews have brought Jesus before him for jealousy. He asks Jesus, "Are you King of the Jews?"

Jesus answers, "It is as you say."

Pilate tells the Jews, "I find no fault in Him."

The Pharisees are enraged. They say, "This man says He is the King of the Jews. He stirs up the people and says that He is their king. If you let Him go, you are not Caesar's friend."

Pilate's eyes bulge in surprise. That is the last thing he wants to be accused of, is treason to Caesar. One of the priest mention that Jesus is a Galilean. Pilate is relieved when he hears this. He says, "Since he is a Galilean, send Him to Herod."

Jesus is sent to Herod. The Jews accuse Jesus before Herod and Jesus never says a word. Herod had longed to see Jesus for some time. He wanted to see Jesus perform some type of miracle or trick. When Jesus would not co-operate, Herod ordered Him to be beaten and sent back to Pilate. Satan's plans to have Jesus crucified are not working. He signals for all his demons to help him.

From every corner of the earth, Satan's foul demons come. They fly with great haste to Jerusalem. Satan thinks, if he does not stop Jesus it will not be long before the people crown Jesus as their Messiah and King.

Once this happens, Christ will rule the world from Jerusalem. Satan does not fully understand the plan of God. He thinks the Millennial reign is about to begin. Satan knows when this happens, his time will be over. The devil is desperate. He has worked hard to try to stop Jesus' efforts to win Jerusalem. Now Satan thinks he has the upper hand. He has used Caiaphas the high priest and Judas to perfection. Now Jesus is on trial and Pilate is trying to let Jesus go. Pilate's wife has warned him not to have anything to do with Jesus. She was troubled in a dream about him. Satan curses and reminds himself, that's why he especially hates women. It is their willingness to listen to their spirit. Some call it intuition.

Satan knows it is now or never. He has signaled for all his demons. They have come to help incite the people to have Jesus crucified.

Pilate has a plan. Jesus has been beaten twice the previous night. Perhaps if he shows Jesus to the crowd, they will have compassion on Him. Pilate has Jesus brought before the crowd. He hoped that they would have compassion on Jesus and ask for Him to be freed. If he could see in the spirit world, he would have seen swarms of demons whispering in the ears of the crowd, "Crucify Him! Crucify Him!"

Pilate tells them because it is a time of celebration, he is bound by law to release one condemned prisoner to them. Jesus will be that prisoner.

They shout, "No! Give us Barrabas!

Pilate says, "No I'll give you Jesus."

However, the more he tries, the louder and louder they shout, "Give us Barrabas!"

Reluctantly, Pilate sentences Jesus to death by crucifixion. He motions to his servants for them to bring water. He knows he is condemning an innocent man to death. He washes his hands in front of the crowd, symbolizing that he was not accepting the blood of Jesus on his hands. The crowd replied, "His blood be upon us and our children."

Pilate orders his men to take Jesus away to be crucified. The soldiers gather in the hall called the Praetorium. They take off His clothes and put a scarlet robe upon Him. Every angel in heaven and every devil in existence have their eyes on the proceedings. Satan and his demons can hardly believe their apparent success. It appears that Jesus is actually going to be crucified. Cyphonnus, a particularly brash and cruel demon, cannot contain himself any longer. He cannot just sit back and watch. If the soldiers could have seen in the spirit realm, they would have seen him.

He walks through the walls of the cell. He appears in a glittering purple robe. He comes in smiling as he approaches an unsuspecting soldier. He possesses the cruelest soldier in the room. The possessed soldier goes out and gathers limbs from a bramble bush. The limbs have long thorns on them about an inch long. Cyphonnus inspires the man to make them into a crown of thorns. The other soldiers began to laugh and mock Jesus. The possessed soldier goes and gathers a big stick and walks up to Jesus. The soldier looks at Jesus and smiles. Then he hits Jesus on the head with the stick. Jesus not limited to normal human vision, looks up and sees Cyphonnus inside the man.

The soldiers take Jesus and ties Him to the whipping post. These soldiers were so brutal in their whippings, that special measures were adopted to handle the severe loss of blood from the prisoners. Around the base of the whipping post is a trench that was dug to drain the blood.

A soldier grabs hold of the whip. He unfurls it, and prepares to beat Jesus. His whip is called a cat of nine tails. It is a whip with nine leather lashes. In each lash was tied chunks of bone. When they would beat someone the bone would rip out chunks of flesh. The soldier begins to beat Jesus. As he gives the first lash, it immediately draws blood. The blood has hardly begun to flow down His back when the next lash is on its way. They continue to mock Him, as He is beaten.　As they beat Jesus with the whip, it would cut deep into His olive skin.　Again and again the unmerciful soldiers beat Him, and large wounds begin to open on His back.　The soldiers continue to strike as the blood flows down His back, and Jesus never says a word. This beating was foretold by the prophets.

Psalms 129:3　The plowers plowed upon my back: they made long their furrows.

Isaiah 53:5　But He was wounded for our transgressions, He was bruised for our iniquities: the chastisement of our peace was upon him; and with His stripes we are healed.

After the beating, one of the soldiers us takes a cloth and blindfolds Him.　The demons inspire this set of soldiers to do what the other soldiers did previously.　They begin to beat Him and say, "Prophesy Jesus, tell us who hit you.　Urged on by demons, they begin to spit upon him.　One of the soldiers runs up to Jesus and pulls Jesus' beard extremely hard.

Now they gather Jesus and takes Him outside to be crucified. These cruel hard soldiers viciously manhandle the kindest man the world has ever known.　These soldiers are so vicious they are like dogs.　They are products of all the cruelty that Satan has heaped on the world.　They are the vilest of sinners.　They are not worthy to touch the hem of His garment, yet they are preparing to crucify the Son of God.　It seems the cruelest of fates for one so righteous to die so ignominiously.

Down the streets of Jerusalem, Jesus carries His cross.　He is in agony and near exhaustion, as He struggles to bear His burden. The wooden cross is heavy on the back of Jesus, as He labors to carry it through His pain.　With each agonizing step, drops of sweat and blood mark His passing.　He strains with all His might, to carry His burden.　He will carry it for as long as possible.　It is not fear that drives Him, nor the beatings of the whip.　It is love that drives Him. With each step He takes, He thinks of His love for His Father, and Their love for the world.　He treasures every step and reminds himself, for this hour He came into the world.

Finally, He stumbles and falls.　There is a crowd that is following him.　Some of the women of Jerusalem see Jesus and feel sorry for Him.　They are weeping for Jesus.

Jesus hears the women weeping. He turns and looks at them. He feels sorry for them. He remembers that in just a few years, His prophecy about Titus will come to pass. The Roman General will beseige Jerusalem and kill them by the thousands. He looks up at them and says, "Daughters of Jerusalem, weep not for Me, but weep for yourselves and your children. For the days are soon coming when you shall say blessed are the barren, and the wombs that never bare and the paps that never gave suck."

His momentary respite is broken by the crack of the whip. The soldiers hit Jesus with the whip and He struggles to His feet with His cross. He struggles again and again in the heat of the Jerusalem sun. As the sweat runs down His back, its salt stings the cuts made from the whip. With each agonizing step, He treasures the path to the cross. Several times He stumbles, till He can walk no more. He collapses from exhaustion. The loss of blood and the dehydration He has suffered, has sapped His strength. He lays in the dusty streets with His cross on His back. He can go no further with His cross. Is there none who would bear this cross of wood for Him and save a dying world?

The soldiers see that Christ is at the point of exhaustion. They pick out someone in the crowd who looks willing. They order a black man, called Simon to bear His cross. Simon is from a city in Africa, called Cyrene. They have no idea of the honor they have bestowed upon him, to bear the cross of Christ. (Simon and His two son's Alexander and Rufus, will later become Christians). With Simon bearing the cross, they march to a hill called Calvary by some, Golgotha, or the place of the skull by others.

Atop Golgotha's hill they carry Jesus. They lay the cross down and take Jesus and lie Him on top. As they pound the nails in His hands, it seems as if they are pounding a steak in the heart of the earth. The sky begins to grow dark and even the limbs of trees seem to hang low.

They continue to drive the nails in His hands and feet, bursting arteries and veins. They lift the cross and Jesus is lifted up. With a sickening thud, the cross drops into the hole. Then someone nailed His accusation on His cross. THIS IS JESUS THE KING OF THE JEWS. Pilate had written this in Hebrew, Greek and Latin. When the Pharisees saw Pilate write this, they protested saying, "Don't say He is the king of the Jews. Write, He said He was the king of the Jews."

Pilate answered them and said, "I have written what I have written."

The soldiers parted His clothes among them, except His robe. It was exquisitely made and without a seam. They laid it down and gambled for it as David had prophesied. Then the soldiers sat down to watch Him die.

There were two thieves who were crucified with Him. One of them said, "If you be the Son of God, save Yourself and us also."

The other thief said, "Leave this just man alone. We deserve our fate, but He is innocent. Then he looked at Jesus and said, "Lord remember me when you come into Your kingdom."

Jesus looked at Him and smiled as only He could. Jesus had a way of smiling at you, that made you feel that He understood, and everything was going to be alright. His smile was more than a normal smile. His smile seemed to remind you that God had put good in the world, and that He had put good in you, if you let it come out. Like a blossoming flower in sunshine, His radiant smile seemed to make the good blossom in you. Jesus smiled through His pain for just a brief moment and said, "This day you shall be with Me in paradise."

Jesus looked and saw His mother standing nearby with Mary Magdalene and her sister. Near them was standing John, the beloved. Jesus said to Mary speaking of John, "Woman, behold thy son! Then He said to His disciple, "Man, behold thy mother!" From that day forward John took Mary into His own home.

Jesus says, "I thirst."

One of the soldiers takes a sponge soaked with vinegar and puts it on a stick. He then raises it up to Jesus.

Jesus smells the vinegar and turns His head refusing to drink.

Some of the people begin to mock Him. They begin to laugh and say, "He saved others, can He not save Himself."

They will not even let Him die in peace. This is the final indignity. What punishment does Jesus ask for His murderers? If He asked, their damnation would be the greatest of all. Does He prophesy they will be cast into the lake of fire? Does He curse them and their families for all eternity? No. He realizes they are as poor misguided children. He pities them and makes one last request of His Father. He says, "Father forgive them, for they know not what they do."

Hanging on the cross, He prepares to take the sins of the world upon Himself. He reaches through time, and takes hold of the sins of the world throughout time.

Think for a moment something you did or thought in your heart that was so wicked, that now you are ashamed to think about it. Maybe you try your best to shut it out, because you cringe at the thought of it. Even now, you feel guilty just thinking about that terrible sin. Imagine how it would be to feel the horror of all the wicked things, the sins, of your entire life. Imagine gathering them and feeling them for one moment in time. Can you imagine how horrible that would feel? You would feel so filthy, that you would feel that you could never be clean. I'm sure it would be enough to drive some men insane. Now multiply that by at least ten billion for all the people in the world who would born. This is what Jesus did on the cross.

Can you imagine how horrible it was to look upon all the sins of the world? It was more horrible than God, whose name is Holy, could bear to look upon. It was such a horrible sight that God, the Father, could not look upon His Son, and a strange darkness covered the earth. In this moment, He became a sin, and for the first time in all of existence, He was separated from His heavenly Father. He had taken on the ultimate spiritual curse; separation from God. He had taken His beating without uttering a word, but this was more than He could bear.

About the ninth hour Jesus cried with a loud voice, saying, "Eli, Eli, lama sabachthani?"

Which being interpreted means, My God! My God! Why hast thou forsaken Me. He was also trying to let those nearby understand, that the psalm of David had come to pass. Psalms 22 which starts out with those very same words. My God. My God. Why hast thou forsaken me. This was prophesied centuries earlier by David and gives a vivid picture of the crucifixion. In addition, the prophecy describes the piercing of His hands and His feet, and the casting of lots for His vesture.

At this moment, He truly became the Christ and He said, "It is finished." Then He cried out with a loud voice and said, "Father into your hands I commend my spirit!" and He gave up the ghost. Immediately an earthquake came and shook the land and the rocks did break.

A soldier cannot believe that Jesus had died so quickly. Normally a crucifixion last for days. To shorten the time, they normally break a prisoners legs. Jesus died sooner to fulfill the prophecy that said, they brake none of My bones. The disbelieving soldier takes his spear and pierces the side of Jesus. Blood and water comes out, signalling that His heart was pierced as well. It seemed that Jesus died when He concluded His prayer, as if He had power over His own life.

Not all the Roman soldiers are unaffected. One who has noticed all the strange things that have happened is very fearful. He fearfully looks up at Jesus and says, "Truly this man was the Son of God."

Immediately God sent an angel to the veil of the temple. The veil was a huge curtain that separated the holy of hollies from the people. The angel tore the curtain from the top down to signify that now God was abolishing the Levitical priesthood, and now He would pour out His Spirit upon all flesh.

Simultaneously from deep in hell, the demons scream in a cry of triumph, at the death of the Son of God.

Chapter 15

Sheol

There is a stranger that appears in Sheol. He has descended from earth. He stands near the edge of Sheol. He's looking at the great barrier that separates Sheol or Abraham's bosom as some call it from the hell the region of damned. This shield of force cannot be pierced from either side. It separates the two realms. Not even Satan, himself, has the power to cross the barrier. The stranger stands poised at the edge of the barrier.

A man goes to the stranger and says, "Greetings good brother. Welcome to Sheol. Because of your good works, you have been sent here, instead of the unholy place." He points to Geenna, the land of the demons and the damned.

The stranger does not answer. He stands gazing at the region of Hell.

The man continues, "What you see here is the great barrier that separates the two realms. They cannot come here. We cannot go there. It is impenetrable. Not even Satan's strongest demons can cross this barrier," the man continues.

The stranger still does not answer. He continues to peer at the realm of devils as though he desperately wishes to go to the doomed place.

The man who was once living says, "Come brother let me show you around. I came when my brother killed me. It was so long ago. I suppose it was thousands of years ago. My name is Abel. I was the first to come here."

The stranger turns and smiles and says to him, "I know."

Abel is in stunned silence. The stranger moves toward the barrier as if he means to cross it. Next, the stranger does the impossible. He takes a step and with a casual ease he leaps into the barrier.

As easily as one walks through mist, he moves through the impenetrable barrier. He crosses the great barrier, the Gulf of Despair, into the realm of demons. What is his purpose? He goes where none but doomed souls and fallen angels have gone before. He is standing at the impenetrable gates of hell.

There is a roar of laughter coming from the great hall of hell. Satan and his demons are in the great hall. Satan has caused a great celebration. Every devil is there in honor of their victory. They are rejoicing at the death of Jesus. Not since before their fall, have their spirits soared so high.

The devils think the Trinity is no more. With the death of Jesus, they think the power of the Trinity is cut by 1/3. They believe they have won a great victory with their war with the Godhead.

They are deliriously happy. Satan tells them, "With the death of Jesus, we will soon find a way to free our brothers which are chained in Tartaros. When we do this we will continue our war with the Father. They are blinded in their foul revelry, oblivious to the approach of the stranger.

He draws back his right arm and with great force he begins to beat on the gates of hell.

The echo of the deafening pounding reverberates throughout the kingdom of hell. He pounds once, then twice, then the third time. Three times the stranger pounds on the gates of Hell. One for the Father, two for the Son, three times for the Holy Ghost. The laughter from the great hall has ceased. The symbolism of the three knocks has not escaped Satan. They turn toward the sound of deafening pounding and hear approaching footsteps. The demons have become silent as fear grips them. The footsteps stop just outside the great doors of the hall. Every devil watches the doors in hushed silence. Suddenly, the doors to the great hall are knocked down.

Satan recognizes the presence of the stranger and says in deep guttural tone, "You."

The stranger reveals himself, he is Jesus the Son of God.

"Nooo!! This cannot be. We killed you," Satan screams in disbelief. Suddenly, Satan realizes they have Jesus outnumbered. "You are a fool to come here, where even angels fear to tread. We will destroy you," Satan says with the smile of a serpent on his face.

He orders his demons, "Kill him. With that cry, some of the devils rush to attack Jesus. The closest is Cyphonnus, the same devil who persuaded the Roman soldier to blindfold Jesus and smite Him. Cyphonnus reaches Jesus first and he raises his arm to smite Jesus as he did earlier.

Jesus grabs his arm in mid swing. He lifts his voice and defiantly and triumphantly says, "I," He momentarily pauses and hurls Cyphonnus over to the region of Tartaros, the place of eternal torment for demons.

The rest of the demons are beginning to get afraid because of the ease at which He dispatched Cyphonnus. Jesus continues, "AM.. NO.. ANGEL."

The earth begins to rumble. Some of the demons begin to cringe in fear and worse yet, there is a power building inside of Jesus. He says, "I AM..,

Jesus begins to glow with a blinding light.

Jesus continues his sentence,"THE SON..,"

He proudly proclaims this. Now He raises his voice to match the intensity of the power He radiates.

He finishes his proclamation, "OF GOD!"

The demons scream in abject horror as the force or righteousness and goodness flood the kingdom of hell. They writhe in pain as the goodness of God burns through their corrupted souls like thousands of fiery daggers. This force of love pierces their evil and vile souls. It pierces them and causes them to violently shake in pain. Unable to withstand this barrage of glory from the only begotten, they lose consciousness.

Meanwhile, across the Gulf of Despair, the people have gathered at the edge of the Gulf. They see something they have never seen before; the light of God radiating from the kingdom of hell.

As the battle ceases, Jesus goes over to the case which hold the jeweled keys. These keys symbolize the authority over hell and death. He breaks the case and takes the jeweled keys. He turns and leaves the hall.

A crowd has gathered near the edge of the Gulf of Despair. Abel has told as many of the citizens of the Sheol as he could about the mysterious stranger. The entire realm of Sheol has now gathered to see this startling event. There are millions of them, a number which no man could number. They see the Stranger return through the broken down gates of hell.

Abel says, "See, I told you."

They are in amazement as they see the stranger cross the Gulf of Despair. He comes over to them and crosses the barrier. They ask, "Who are you?"

He looks at them and said, "Do you not know Me. Shadrach, Meshech and Abednego, I was with you in the fiery furnace. Abraham, I ate in your tent. David, I am your son and your Lord. Daniel, you called me the Ancient of Days, Isaiah, you called me Wonderful, and Zechariah you called Me Messiah. I have been on earth and many of the things which you, the prophets, have prophesied of Me have come to pass. I had came to earth and fulfilled my mission."

"What was your mission My Lord?" one of them ask.

"Why? to be crucified and hung on a tree. I have become the Lamb which takes away the sins of the world, so that he that believeth in Me shall have eternal life."

Jesus explained to the spirits which had been imprisoned, all the things that the prophets had prophesied concerning Christ that have come to pass. At times, some of them had been disobedient. Some are there, even though they had no knowledge of the law of Moses. They were Gentiles from all over the earth. While they were alive, they were good people.

They were spiritually sensitive enough to listen to the voice of God speaking in their own conscience. Those in hell ignored the voice of their conscience until it became weaker and weaker. They did evil until they were no longer bothered by it. Jesus addresses all the multitudes of spirits in the land of Sheol. He explains to them God's plan of salvation. He shares with them His glorious gospel which will soon be spread unto all the earth.

Even though it is possible for those who have never heard the gospel to live according to their conscience, only a small percentage of the people do listen. The number of souls in hell far exceeds the number in Sheol. Broad is the gate that leads to destruction and many enter it. But straight is the gate and narrow is the way that leads to everlasting life, and few there be that find it.

In many cases, man was so sinful that God could not bear to have fellowship with him. For those without the Old Testament law, the primary means of God communicating with them was through their own conscience. When these people ignored their own conscience and went further in sin, God gave them over to a reprobate mind. As they forsook Him, God totally forsook them. His Spirit totally withdrew from them and demon spirits filled the void. This caused the people to sink into depravity.

Sin is the most deadly poison the world has ever known. Under the law when a person sinned, his sins could be only covered through an acceptable blood sacrifice. This sacrifice had to be without spot or blemish. It was not possible for the blood of goats and rams to totally remove sins, instead, it only covered them. This and their sin nature made it difficult for God to have fellowship with His creation.

Jesus became the lamb of God that was slain for the sins of the whole world. Only the power of the blood of the Infinite Son of God, could provide the infinite power necessary to be the one sacrifice for the near-infinite sins of the world. Through Jesus, the sins of the world can be washed away, and God can have fellowship with men, as each individual repents and receives Christ as their Lord and Savior. Now the prophecy of Joel can come to pass.

> **And it shall come to pass afterward, that I will pour out My spirit upon all flesh; and your sons and your daughters shall prophesy, your old men shall dream dreams, your young men shall see visions.**
>
> **Joel 2:28**

Jesus has become the mediator between man and God. Because He was God in the flesh, He understands the needs of men and the trials that they face. He lived on this earth for 33 years and was tempted just as we are tempted, yet He remained sinless. Jesus understands the pressures of this world, and He knows when man can resist and when He must have help from God. The Son will ascend to heaven and become the intercessor between God and man.

Now because of Jesus, His disciples will carry the gospel around the world. God will have more followers than ever before. This will make the world better on several accounts.

1. As God's law is preached, many will begin to obey His law. Kindness, love, and compassion will be preached. As men begin to hear the gospel message, it will bring peace on earth and good will to men.

Eventually, governments and society will change. The world will become a better place because of the gospel. It will never be perfect, until after the resurrection of the dead and Christ rules the earth from Jerusalem, until that time, it will be a better place as the gospel spreads.

When they hear the gospel, the Holy Spirit will try to convict a person of their sins. If they listen to the gentle pleading of the Spirit, they will be convicted of their sins. The purpose of this is to convince them to repent. Repent does not mean simply asking for forgiveness. It means you are godly sorrowful, and you purpose to completely turn from your sin, to God. It means that you intend not to sin anymore. For their sins to be washed away, they must receive Jesus the Messiah, as their Lord and Savior.

When they receive Christ, the Holy Spirit will take the blood of Christ and wash away their sins. At that point, a person is no longer sinful and at long last, God is able to have fellowship with him. The Holy Spirit changes their inward nature and they are born again. They will become a new creature. The Holy Spirit is able to have fellowship with them. He is able to lead them and guide them because their sins have been washed away. Although at the moment of conversion a person is immediately changed and saved from hell, they are not perfect.

Since God wishes to have a relationship with His children, they are not made perfect in one day. This is a process that takes place over the lifetime of the individual. A person must continually deny himself and yield himself to God. Satan will always try to ensnare him into sin again, but if he resists him, the devil will flee. If they should happen to stumble and fall, Christ will forgive and restore them, providing they sincerely repent, and wish to turn from their evil.

The story of the cross is the greatest story ever told. As the gospel is continually preached, more and more souls will be spared from the punishment of hell. As these spirits in Sheol remain faithful, they will one day live again in the resurrection. Jesus will take those from Sheol to heaven. One day, He will return to earth with them. Although they do not need bodies in heaven, they will need bodies to live and interact with men on the earth, that is why they will one day be resurrected.

Jesus preaches unto them for three days and nights. All of Sheol has rejoiced at the story of the cross. It is truly the greatest story ever told. They are all moved at the suffering of Christ. They are amazed that He who formed the world would die for it.

Because of His love for His Father, He humbled Himself and became obedient even unto the death of the cross. Wherefore God has highly exalted Him and given Him a name above every name. One day at the name of Jesus, every knee in creation shall bow, and every tongue must confess that Jesus is Lord to the glory of God the Father. On that day of the utter humiliation of Satan, when he, the king of pride is forced to confess the Lordship of Jesus, the rest of the universe will learn its final lesson. It is not those with a spirit too proud and stubborn to acknowledge God who will prevail, but the meek shall inherit the earth.

All of the spirits in Paradise worship and praise God at the wonderful story of the gospel. They know that God truly loves His creation. They are grateful for the tremendous price the Trinity paid to try and save an unrepentant world.

"For God so loved the world, that He gave His only begotten son, that whosoever believeth in Him should not perish but have everlasting life."

John 3:16

Resurrection

Joseph of Armethia went to Pilate and begged him for the body of Jesus. Joseph was a man of some influence, so Pilate released the body unto him. Jerusalem is almost solid rock. There had been no time to hew a grave for Jesus out of the solid rock. Joseph, who was a wealthy man, had Jesus buried in his own tomb.

Meanwhile the Pharisees went to Pilate and said, "Jesus, the deceiver, when He was alive said if He would be killed, He would rise again the third day. Now give us some soldiers to watch the tomb, so His disciples won't be able to steal away the body. Otherwise this mistake will be worse than the first."

Pilate said, "You have a watch. Now go and make it as sure as you can."

A Roman guard of twelve soldiers was dispatched to guard the tomb of Jesus. A guard is normally from 10 to 30 soldiers. Pilate really does not expect any trouble from Jesus' disciples. He just wants to satisfy the priests. However, he will spare no more soldiers than this. He is still resentful of his having to sentence Jesus to death. He knows the priest wished Jesus dead out of jealousy. However, his best efforts could not spare Jesus today. He feels a strange sense of foreboding. He knows something is about to happen, but what?

The soldiers arrive at the tomb of Jesus. They fixed a Roman Seal to the tomb. This meant that the stone could not be moved without breaking the seal, the symbol of Roman authority and power. Anyone who broke the seal would by in defiance of the Roman government and would face the severest of punishments.

The guards stand guard around the tomb with their weapons poised. In their right hands they carry the famous Roman pike. It is a spear with an iron head on a wooden shaft more than six feet in length. It can be hurled like a spear or used like a bayonet. For close quarters, they use their sword which hangs on their right side. The sword is three feet in length, and used for thrusting rather than slashing. On the left arm they have their shields. Hanging by means of a belt on their left shoulder is their daggers. They are prepared to defend the tomb of Jesus at all cost.

The penalty for deserting their post for any reason is death. The penalty for falling asleep on duty was equally severe. In the night they were well trained to take turns sleeping. There were to be some soldiers awake at all times, lest they all risked death.

Now it is the third day. God sent an angel from heaven. The Roman soldiers who were guarding the tomb looked up and suddenly they saw this twelve foot tall angel. His skin was like lighting. With an ease that defies description, he rolled away the stone. When the soldiers saw this, they became terrified and ran away like frightened children.

The next morning a group of women came to the tomb to properly dress the body. On the way, they realized they needed some men to roll away the stone. Mary told the others to go ahead and she would look for someone to help them. When the women got there, they saw the stone rolled away. They looked inside the tomb and saw two young men who said, "Why do you seek the living among the dead. Jesus is not here, but He is risen."

The women left, being very afraid. They went to tell some of the disciples that Jesus was not there.

The news reached Peter who was with another disciple at the time, that Jesus was not there. Immediately, they began to run as fast as they could to the tomb. Now the other disciple outran Peter to the tomb. When he got to the tomb, he stopped and stood outside the tomb. He was looking inside as if he was afraid to enter. He saw the stone was rolled away and it was empty.

Finally, Peter caught up with him. Peter ran inside the tomb and knelt down where they had lain Jesus. He saw the grave clothes and the napkin but there was no body. His mind was reeling. What did all this mean? What happened to the body? He got up and began to leave. As he left, he could not help but wonder what was going to happen next? As yet, Peter did not know the Scripture that said Jesus would rise from the dead. Then the disciples went away to their own homes.

Meanwhile, Mary Magdalene, whom Jesus had cast out seven devils, came to the tomb. She came to tell the women, she could not find anyone to help them move the stone. To her surprise, when she got to the tomb, everyone was gone and the tomb was empty. Obviously she thought, someone had stolen the body. This was more than she could bear. Suddenly she began to cry. She did not know what to think. It was bad enough that they had killed Jesus, but now they would not even let Him rest in peace. Where had they taken His body? Mary was sitting and crying outside the tomb. She continued to weep until she heard something, a sound coming from the tomb. Someone was in there. She decided to enter the tomb. When she went in, she saw two angels. They were sitting where Jesus' body had been lain: one at the head and one at the feet.

They said to her, "Woman why are you crying?"

She answered them and said, "They have taken away My Lord and I know not where they have lain him."

Then she sensed someone behind her and turned around. It was a man. He said, "Woman, why are you crying? Whom do you seek?"

She assumed He was the gardener. She said, "Sir, if you have taken Him from here, tell me where you have lain Him and I will take Him away."

Jesus said to her, "Mary."

She turned and looked up and said, "Master!" She rushed forward to greet Him with a hug and He held up His hand and said, "Touch me not; for I am not yet ascended to my Father: but go to My brethren and say to them, I ascend to My Father and your Father; and to My God and your God."

Mary went and told the disciples all that she had seen and heard.

Meanwhile, the soldiers have gathered their composure. They are afraid to go to Pilate. They would certainly be punished for deserting their post. They face certain court-martial and death. They decide to go to the only ones who can help them, the priest. They tell the priest everything.

The priest offer them money and tells them to say the disciples stole the body of Jesus away while they slept. They said if the news of this reaches Pilate, we will intercede in your behalf. "Don't worry, we will take care of everything," they say.

A few days later all the remaining eleven disciples were together, except Thomas. They were discussing all the things that had happened. The doors were shut and locked because they were afraid of the Jews. Suddenly, Jesus appeared in the middle of them. They were terrified supposing that He was a ghost. He told them, "Touch Me. Feel Me, for a spirit does not have flesh and bone as I have." He showed them the nail prints in His hands and His feet. Later when they told Thomas, he did not believe it.

Thomas was unmoved. He kept saying, "I don't believe it. It doesn't matter to me what any of you say. I don't care. I won't believe, unless I see the nail prints in His hands, if I put my fingers in those nail prints, and if I can put my fist in the wound in His side."

Eight days later, two disciples were walking up the road to Emanus. As they were walking another man came up and started walking with them. They were talking about all the things that had happened to Jesus.

The other man asked them, what they were talking about. They said, "Are you a stranger in Galilee that you know nothing of what has happened."

The strangers said, "Tell me what has happened."

They continued, "Haven't you heard of Jesus. How that Jesus, a prophet of God, whom we believed to be the messiah. He performed many miracles. He healed the blind and the lame, calmed the sea, and even raised Lazarus from the dead. He was crucified and ordered killed by the high priest. Now we are hearing strange things. Some of the women claim that He has risen from the dead."

They continued telling the stranger all about Jesus.

Then the stranger began to open up the Scriptures to them. He said, "Ye fools and slow of heart to believe all that the prophets have spoken. Ought not Christ have suffered these things and to enter into His glory?"

He told them, "Haven't you read in the Scriptures how they said that Christ must suffer. Didn't Daniel say that the Messiah would be cut off from the living but not for Himself? David prophesied that they would cast lots upon His robe and they would pierce His hands and His feet. Didn't Isaiah say He was wounded for our transgressions, He was bruised for our iniquities, the chastisement of our peace was upon Him and by His stripes we are healed?"

With these and many more prophecies made by the prophets, did He open up to them. He continued talking to them along the way.

When they finally got to the town, the stranger acted as if He was about to leave them. The two disciples said, "Brother come and stay with us. The hour is late. We insist."

When they sat down to eat, the stranger took the bread and broke it. When He broke the bread it seemed as if they had seen Him do it before. The disciples looked and suddenly their eyes were opened, and for the first time they truly recognized the stranger. He was Jesus! He looked at them and smiled with that special smile of His, and disappeared!

The two disciples were in shock. They turned to one another and said, "Did not our hearts burn within us as He opened up the

Scriptures. All that time, Jesus was with us and we did not know it. Hurry, we must run back and tell the others it is true! Jesus is alive!"

They ran out of the room and ran back to Jerusalem as fast as they could to tell the other disciples.

When they got back to Jerusalem, they found where the other disciples had gathered.

The disciples had gathered to discuss all the things that happened, starting with the experience of the women at the tomb. Suddenly, the two disciples burst in the room whom Jesus had appeared to. They told the disciples all that happened to them and how Jesus appeared along the way.

While they were speaking, Jesus suddenly appeared in the midst of them. He said, Peace be unto you. It was Jesus, in the flesh. He looked at Thomas and said, "Come here and look at My hands. Take your finger and place it in My hands and put your fist in My side: and be not faithless but believing."

Thomas said, "My Lord and my God."

Jesus said, "Thomas you believe because you have seen. Blessed are they that have not seen, and yet have believed.

For a period of forty days, Jesus appears to different disciples. Altogether, He was seen by five hundred people after His resurrection. He gathers His disciples on the Mount of Olives. He teaches them many things about the kingdom of God. John the Baptist had said, "I baptize with water but there was One coming after me who is preferred before me, who would baptize you with fire.

The disciples ask Jesus was He getting ready to restore the kingdom to Israel. Jesus tells them it is not meant for them to know the seasons which God has put in His own power.

Jesus tells His disciples to wait in Jerusalem to receive the promise of the Father which is the Holy Ghost. He said, "You shall receive power after that the Holy Ghost is come upon you and you shall be witness unto Me in Judea, Samaria, and unto the uttermost part of the earth."

The disciples were instructed not to leave Jerusalem, but wait and pray until they received the Holy Ghost.

Jesus continued encouraging them for their mission. He gave them the great commission. He told them, "Go forth into all the world, preaching the gospel to every creature, baptizing them in the name of the Father, the Son, and the Holy Ghost. And these signs shall follow them that believe. In my name shall they cast out devils.

They shall speak with new tongues. They shall take up serpents and if they drink any deadly thing, it shall not hurt them. They shall lay hands on the sick and they shall recover."

After He had spoken these things, Jesus began to ascend to heaven, and disappeared into the clouds.

The disciples were standing there watching when suddenly two men appeared to them in white. The men said, "You men of Galilee, why do you stand here gazing into the heavens. This same Jesus that you have seen go into heaven shall return in a like manner."

Pentecost

On the day of Pentecost the disciples were gathered together in one accord and one place. There were 120 disciples gathered in the upper room. While they were praying, there came a sound like a rushing mighty wind and it filled the house that they were in. The disciples' prayers were answered. They were all filled with the Holy Ghost and they began to speak in tongues as the Spirit gave them utterance. The disciples don't know what they are saying, but the power of God energizes them. It fills them with joy and they are awash in the glory of God. The Spirit moves them and floods every fiber of their being. They cannot contain their joy. The Spirit leads them outside and they begin to speak in tongues to the Jews outside the house.

Now there were Jews from all over the world, devout men from every nation. There were Jews and proselytes from Arabia, Crete, Rome, Asia, Libya, Egypt, Mesopotamia to name a few. As the Spirit impressed the disciples to go up to these Jews and proselytes, miraculously they spoke to them and gave them messages from God in their own languages. The people were amazed and wondered "What miracle was this?" What did this sign from God mean? How could the disciples be speaking to them in their own languages?

Some of the people mocked and said, "These men are drunk with new wine."

Peter stood up and addressed the crowd. You Jews and men of Jerusalem, these men are not drunk, for it is only the third hour (9 a.m). of the day. But instead this is that which was spoken of by the Prophet Joel.

Joel 2:28   And it shall come to pass afterward, that I will pour out my spirit upon all flesh; and your sons and your

daughters shall prophesy, your old men shall dream dreams, your young men shall see visions:

Peter continues preaching to them and explains how Jesus was the Messiah, whom the prophets prophesied of and why He was crucified, but rose again on the third day. Peter tells them that all of the disciples were eyewitnesses of the resurrection. He tells them that Jesus promised that if they prayed, they would receive the promise of the Father, which is the Holy Ghost. The Holy Ghost filled them and caused them to speak in tongues. That is why the disciples were able to speak in tongues and miraculously speak to the Jews in their own languages.

Peter finished his sermon to the Jews by saying, "Therefore, let all the house of Israel know assuredly, that God hath made that same Jesus, whom ye have crucified, both Lord and Christ."

When the Jews heard these words, they were pricked to the heart. The Holy Spirit convicted them. They said, "What must we do?"

Peter answered that they must repent and be baptized in the name of Jesus and they would receive forgiveness and remission for their sins and they would receive the gift of the Holy Ghost. Peter said, "For this promise is unto you, and to your children and all that are afar off, even as many as the Lord our God shall call."

Immediately about three thousand of the Jews came forward to receive Jesus and were baptized. They opened up their hearts and Jesus came in. They were born again and filled with the Spirit of God. The reality of their supernatural experience convinced them of its truth.

Peter and John were going into the temple to pray. There was a certain beggar who was lame from his mother's womb. He asked Peter and John for some money. Immediately the anointing of the Holy Ghost came upon Peter. Peter, sensing the Holy Ghost, began to yield to the Holy Ghost and follow the Spirit's instructions. The Spirit began to overflow and guide his words, thoughts, and actions. When a man is overcome by the Spirit of God, and the anointing of the Holy Ghost flows through every fibre of his being, it is the greatest feeling on earth. Nothing on earth compares to the sensation of the Holy Ghost flowing like liquid love and power through an individual. Peter was caught up in the flow of this cascade of power and it told Him exactly what to do.

Peter said to the man with an authority that comes not from earth, "Look on us."

Immediately the man obeyed Peter, expecting to receive some money.

With the words flowing carefully, yet powerfully, Peter said, "Silver and gold have I none, but such as I have give I unto thee. In the name of JESUS OF NAZARETH, rise up and walk!"

With the Spirit of God unctioning him, Peter grabbed the man by the hand and immediately the man's feet and ankle bones received strength. He jumped up and began to scream with great joy. With tears streaming down his face he shouted, "I can walk! I can walk!" He went into the temple leaping and praising God.

It was 483 years from the time of Daniel's vision of seventy weeks. In this vision a day represented one year. Daniel said after the 69th week, the Messiah would be cut off and not for Himself. 483 years had passed and indeed the Messiah had come and been cut off for the sins of His people. What Daniel did not know was that there is a time gap between the 69 and 70th week. During this time gap is the age of the church. The 70 weeks are a prophecy about Israel, therefore the church was not mentioned. After the church age begins the last week, which is the seven year Great Tribulation.

More and more Jews begin to receive Jesus as Messiah. The Jewish leaders are enraged. They begin to persecute the Christians. Stephen, a man full of faith and power, begins to preach about Jesus. Stephen was chosen to replace Judas by the other disciples. He works many signs and wonders before the eyes of the people. The Jews become so enraged at Stephen's continual preaching that they put him on trial for blasphemy. Stephen does not capitulate, but preaches to them about Jesus. Stephen preaches to them very eloquently at his trial. At the conclusion of his message, the Lord gives Stephen a vision of God sitting on His throne, with Jesus at His right hand. The Jews can't stand it anymore and they put their hands over their ears. They become so enraged with him that they take him outside the city and begin to stone him to death.

As they stone Stephen he says, "Lord Jesus, receive my spirit." He drops to his knees and says, "Lord, lay not this sin to their charge." Immediately after Stephen finishes saying this, a strange peace comes over him. He closes his eyes and sleeps the sleep of the righteous dead.

One of those watching the proceedings is a man named Saul of Tarsus. He does not participate in the stoning, but he is holding the coats of those who do stone Stephen to death.

Saul of Tarsus, gets actively involved in the persecution of the Christians. Under orders of the high priest, he searches out Christians and has them beaten, tortured, and imprisoned. He thinks he is doing God a service by trying to stamp out what he considers a blasphemous doctrine. In his blind arrogance, he has no idea that he is being used by the Devil. He causes many believers to be beaten for the gospel's sake. He makes havoc of the church, and practically all the Christians, except the disciples, leave Jerusalem.

The Jews continue their persecution of the Christians. As the Christians leave Jerusalem, they take the message of the gospel with them, wherever they go. Philip goes to Samaria and preaches Christ to them and turns the city upside down for Jesus.

Saul continues to grow in his hatred of the church. He threatens to have every Christian slaughtered. He goes to the high priest and gets letters from him. These letters authorize him to go the synagogues in Damascus and order the leaders to turn all the Christians over to him. No matter whether they are women or men, they are to be bound and brought back to Jerusalem.

Saul and a company of men travel to Damascus on the Damascus Road. When they get near to the city, Saul has a visitation. He has papers in his hand granting him authority to find and punish all Christians. Suddenly, there was a light that shone out of heaven. The light is so powerful that it strikes Saul and knocks him and his horse down. A voice speaks from the light and says, "Saul! Saul! Why do you persecute me?"

Saul is terrified. His mind is whirling. He cannot imagine who is the author of this voice. He has tried with everything he has to please God. In his zeal, he has even persecuted the disciples of Jesus. Finally, he asks the question, "Who is it Lord?"

The voice answers, "I am Jesus, whom you have persecuted! It is hard for you to kick against the pricks."

Saul asks him, "Lord, what would you have me to do?"

The Lord says unto him, "Arise and go into the city and it shall be told you what you must do."

The light begins to dim and the voice is gone. The men that were with Saul were speechless. They saw the light and heard the voice, but seeing no man, they were terribly afraid. As the light fades, Saul realizes that his sight is gone. He feels awful. God has punished him for wickedness. He did not know that all the time he was wrong. Jesus was the Messiah. Now he has punished him and struck him with blindness. This is not his imagination, but this was real. Paul is a broken, blind man now, and the soldiers lead him to Damascus.

Three days pass, and a certain disciple named Ananias is praying. The Lord appears to him in a vision. The Lord says, "Ananias."

Ananias says, "I am here Lord."

The Lord answers him and says, "Arise and go into the street called Straight and inquire in the house of Judah for one called Saul of Tarsus. He is praying, and he has seen a vision of a man named Ananias coming in and putting his hand on him, that he might receive his sight."

Ananias says, "Lord, I have heard of this man, and how he has persecuted many of Your people. He has authority from the chief priest to bind all that call on Your name."

The Lord said, "Go for he is a chosen vessel unto Me, and he shall be a witness for Me unto the gentiles, and governors, kings, and the children of Israel. For I will show him how he must suffer great things for My names sake."

Ananias went as the Lord told him and found Saul. Saul has been blind ever since his vision from the Lord. For three days he has been fasting and praying. Ananias found Saul and put his hands on him and said, "Brother Saul, the Lord, even Jesus, that appeared to you as you came to the city, has sent me that you might receive your sight, and be filled with the Holy Ghost."

Immediately the power of God swept over Saul. God filled him with the Holy Ghost and he began to speak in tongues. Immediately his eyes were opened, and his sight was restored. He arose and was baptized. Then Saul spent certain days with the disciples at Damascus. Then he began to preach that Jesus is the Son of God in the synagogues.

The Jews were amazed. They said, "How can this be? This is the same man which destroyed those who called on His name in Jerusalem. He came here to bind those who believed on Jesus bound to the chief priest."

Saul increased more in strength, and confounded the Jews which were at Damascus. He continued preaching and the Jews took counsel to kill him. They watched the gates of the city, day and night to kill him. Paul could not leave the city. The disciples put Saul in basket and let him down over the wall to escape to Jerusalem.

Saul comes to Jerusalem where initially the Christians shun him, expecting his conversion to be a ruse. This Jew among Jews submits himself to the disciples. He grows in wisdom and knowledge and becomes one of the greatest disciples. He becomes the Apostle to the Gentiles, carrying the gospel around the world. He helps build and establish many churches throughout the Roman Empire. Although persecuted for his beliefs, he is determined to let nothing stop him. Five times the Jews beat him with the lash, giving him thirty-nine stripes. Three times he is beaten with rods and three times he is shipwrecked. Not even prison dampens his spirit. Paul writes two-thirds of the New Testament and some of them written while he was in prison. Eventually Paul is beheaded in Rome at the command of Nero Caesar.

Jesus commanded His disciples to go into all the world and preach the gospel to every creature. His timing could not have been better. It was the fullness of time because of the *Pax Romana.* As Rome's armies went forth and conquered, their engineers built new roads. The armies also forced peace on the world. This provided the disciples of Jesus great latitude for the spread of the gospel. The time was right because this was after Alexander the Great's armies and greek philosophers had given the world a common language and culture. This made it much easier for the disciples as they traveled and preached to different nations. Unlike twentieth century missionaries, who must spend years in language study and cultural familiarization, the difference between language and culture in nations was minimal. Aside from all this, there was a great spiritual vacuum in the land. The reality of the new birth experience as well as the manifestations of the Holy Ghost, convinces thousands of the truth of the gospel.

Satan tries his best to stop the spread of the gospel, but it spreads like wildfire. He now knows he has a short time and now turns his wrath upon the people who have fathered Christianity, the Jews. Because they have rejected God by rejecting His Messiah, they have come outside of His divine protection. With great wrath, Satan begins his plans to destroy the Jews.

Chapter 16

The Destruction of Jerusalem

In 67 A.D. the Roman General, Titus, begins a 3 year siege of Jerusalem. It is a bitter war. Conditions are so bad within the city, that some even begin to eat their own dead. It is the time that Jesus prophesied of. In 70 A.D., Titus and his armies finally break through. When his armies finally enter Jerusalem, they go berserk. After three years of a difficult siege, they murder everything in sight. As Jesus had prophesied, they have no mercy, not even on pregnant women.

Although Titus wished to spare the temple, his soldiers destroyed it. They take rags soaked in oil and stick them in the cracks of the Temple walls. They set the rags on fire and as they heat up, the temple wall explodes. Not one stone is left upon another, just as Jesus had prophesied. Titus admits to killing 600,000 Jews. Josephus a Jewish historian says Titus killed 1,197,000 Jews. Many of them are crucified. Titus crucifies so many Jews that there are no trees left for miles around.

The remaining Jews are scattered around the world. Many of the Jews feel that God has abandoned them. This has happened because they knew not the time of their visitation. If they would have received Jesus as the Messiah, things would have been different. Satan knows that Israel is vital to God's ultimate plan. He hates Israel for bringing forth the Christ. If he can destroy Israel, he can destroy God's plan. In the centuries that follow, the Jews are persecuted all over the earth. When they are persecuted in one country they flee into another. Jerusalem is inhabited by Gentiles in fulfillment of Jesus' prophecy.

Luke 21:24   And they shall fall by the edge of the sword, and shall be led away captive into all nations: and Jerusalem

shall be trodden down of the Gentiles, until the times of the Gentiles be fulfilled.

If the Jews would have heeded the prophecy of Daniel, they would have known that it was time for the Messiah to come and for Him to be cut off. God gave Daniel a vision about the 70 weeks. We know now that each week represented seven years, by the partial fulfillment of the prophecy. In 49 years, seven weeks of years the temple and wall were built. 483 years from then, or sixty-two weeks, Messiah was due to be cut off.

Daniel 9:24-27   Seventy weeks are determined upon thy people and upon thy holy city, to finish the transgression, and to make an end of sins, and to make reconciliation for iniquity, and to bring in everlasting righteousness, and to seal up the vision and prophecy, and to anoint the most Holy.

25) Know therefore and understand, that from the going forth of the commandment to restore and to build Jerusalem unto the Messiah the Prince shall be seven weeks, and threescore and two weeks: the street shall be built again, and the wall, even in troublous times.

26) And after threescore and two weeks shall Messiah be cut off, but not for himself: and the people of the prince that shall come shall destroy the city and the sanctuary; and the end thereof shall be with a flood, and unto the end of the war desolations are determined.

27)   And he shall confirm the covenant with many for one week: and in the midst of the week he shall cause the sacrifice and the oblation to cease, and for the overspreading of abominations he shall make it desolate, even until the consummation, and that determined shall be poured upon the desolate.

What God did not reveal to Daniel, was that there was a time gap between the 69th and 70th week. Daniel's vision of weeks was a revelation of Israel. The church age takes place during the 69th and 70th week. The 70th week is the Great Tribulation.

The church continues to grow as the years pass. Despite continued times of persecution, the followers of Jesus continue to increase in number. The first official persecution of the church by the Roman Empire, started in A.D. 64, at the burning of Rome. The fire lasted for six days and seven nights, gutted ten of the fourteen districts of the city and caused untold suffering of the people. Nero blamed it upon the Christians. Christians were ordered to be burned at the stake at night to light the public garden. Some were thrown to wild beasts or mad dogs. Paul suffered martyrdom at the hands of Nero. Peter was said to have suffered the same fate.

The second persecution broke out in A.D. 95, during the reign of Domitian. Some Christians were martyred, some dispossessed of property and others were banished. It was during this time that John was exiled to the Isle of Patmos by Domitian. Here, John received the vision of the Revelation. Upon Domitian's death, John was freed from Patmos. He left and continued ministering in churches until his death. He died of natural causes. Even the death of the disciples did not stop the growth of the church. The disciples had trained faithful men to carry on in their absence. These leaders began to be known as bishops and church Fathers.

Though thousands of Christians were killed during the time of the persecution, they continue to spread the gospel. Some of them were fed to the lions in the Roman Arenas. The spectators began to marvel at the conviction of the Christians who were so convinced of their experience with God, they were willing to die for it.

Though Christians are persecuted throughout the Roman Empire, their numbers continue to grow. Christianity threatens to win the world. The reality of the new birth experience and the baptism of the Holy Ghost convinces many. Many people argue that Christianity should be accepted because it is morally superior to the Roman religion. The morally superior lives of Christians causes the spread of Christianity. Justin Martyr, one of the outstanding leaders in church about A.D. 150, observed:

There is no people, Greek or barbarian, or of any other race, by whatever appellation or manners they may be distinguished, however ignorant of arts or agriculture, whether they dwell in tents or wander about in covered wagons, among whom prayers and thanksgiving are not

offered in the name of the crucified Jesus to the Father and
Creator of all things.

Satan fights the Church from without and within. Not only is
there persecution of the Church, but there are constant battles with
heretical groups within it.

By the end of the second century, Church leaders declare that
revelation has ceased and decree an end to prophecy in the Church.
This was probably done due to excesses by certain church members
and heretical leaders. However, they threw out the baby with the
bath water. Because of the insistence of church leaders, the members
cease to seek for supernatural gifts. The signs, wonders and miracles
that accompanied the first century church cease to occur.

During the times of persecution, some of the Christians are
martyred for the cause of Christ. Unfortunately, many of these
martyrs are held in such high esteem, some mistakenly believe the
martyrs are capable of interceding on the behalf of the living. Prayers
are offered to God through these intercessors. They forgot the
teaching of Apostle Paul.

**1 Timothy 2:5   For there is one God, and one mediator
between God and men, the man Christ Jesus;**

Paul's statement was based upon the clear statement of Jesus to
ask the Father in the name of Jesus only.

As Christianity becomes more accepted, more pagans join it.
Unfortunately, standards become relaxed and some Christians, in an
effort to become more accommodating, incorporate some pagan
practices into the church. Christ clearly was not born in the winter,
yet His birthday is placed on a pagan holiday, the birthday of
Saturnacis. Jesus died during passover, but His death and resurrection
is celebrated on Easter, another pagan holiday. In the sixth century
the Church established the Feast of the Assumption of the Virgin into
heaven, and assigned to August 13, the date of the ancient festivals of
Isis and Artemis.

[4]Pagan festivals dear to the people, or necessary as cathartic

---

[4]Will Durant, *The Age of Faith*, (New York: Simon and
Shuster,1950)p.745

(continued...)

moratoriums on morality, reappeared as Christian feasts, and pagan vegetation rites were transformed into Christian liturgy. The people continued to light midsummer fires on St. John's Eve, and the celebration of Christ's resurrection took the pagan name of Eostre, the old Teutonic goddess of the spring. The Christian calendar of the saints replaced the Roman *fasti*; ancient divinities dear to the people were allowed to revive under the names of Christian saints; the Dea Victoria of the Basses-Alpes became St. Victoire, and Castor and Pollux were reborn as Sts. Cosmas and Damian.

Although neither Jesus, the disciples, or the early church gave any special designation to Mary, by the 18th century she is exalted as the Celestial Madonna, the Mother of God, the Queen of Heaven. It is said, that in the fourth century the Church finally conquered the Roman Empire, but it is just as true to say the Empire conquered the Church.

---

[4](...continued)

Muhammad

Galatians 1:8   But though we, or an angel from heaven, preach any other gospel unto you than that which we have preached unto you, let him be accursed.

For many years the Arabs have picked up on the Jewish theme of a coming Arab Messiah. Mohammed studies the Old Testament, the Apocrypha, and other heretical books such as <u>The Secrets of Enoch, The Testament of Abraham</u>. He cannot conceive that the God of the universe would allow His Son to die such an ignominious death. He accepts Jesus as a prophet, but not as the Son of God. Muhammad was taught this by his uncle, Waraqa ibn Nofal. He was alleged to have translated portions of the gospels in Arabic. Waraqa ibn Nofal was a Nestorian Christian.

Nestorius was patriarch of Constantinople from A.D. 428 to 431. In A.D. 431 the Council of Ephesus judged the Nestorian beliefs to be heretical. He and his followers were driven out of the Roman empire. They took refuge in Persia, Arabia, India, China, and Mongolia. Many of the Christians that Muhammad encountered were Nestorian Christians.

Muhammad wrote many accommodating things about Jesus. He said Jesus was blessed, He was a prophet and many other things. However, Jesus' true nature and mission, was unknown to Muhammad. Muhammad did not even believe that Jesus died on the cross. Muhammad taught that Jesus had the ability to change His appearance. He taught that when the Pharisees came to get Jesus, He changed into someone else and they crucified the wrong man. Muhammad chose to ignore all church and historical records that clearly proved Jesus was crucified. Jesus forewarned His disciples that He would be killed and rise again on the third day. He knew He was going to experience great pain and suffering. Still, He was determined to go to the cross. Notice what He said to His disciples.

John 12:27   Now is my soul troubled; and what shall I say? Father, save me from this hour: but for this cause came I unto this hour.

John 12:32   And I, if I be lifted up from the earth, will draw all men unto me.

This prophecy has certainly been fulfilled. Jesus was crucified and lifted up from the earth. He has drawn men of every nation, creed and color unto Him. By going obediently unto the cross, He became the Christ, and the most famous person in history.

Muhammad's wives and his death

Muhammad had a total of fifteen wives. We will deal with just a few them in this book. He was married to his first wife for twenty-five years before she died. During this time, she was his only wife.

Muhammad's first wife was Khadija, a rich widow of Mecca. She was believed to be a Nestorian Christian along with Muhammad's uncle. She died when Muhammad was fifty. He said he would never get over her loss, but married his second wife just two months after his first wife's death. Her name was Sauda, a widow. He then betrothed himself to 'Ayisha, the daughter of his best friend, Abu Bakr. At this time she was only seven years of age. He married her three years later. He was fifty three and she was only ten years old.

Some of Muhammad's supporters claim that some of Muhammad's wives were for political reasons, but this was not always the case. He acquired his ninth wife, Safiyya, a Jewess because of his own lust. Safiyya was the wife of Kinana, the Chief of the Jewish settlement Khaibar. Muhammad attacked this settlement which was on the way to Syria. The Jews surrendered the citadel on the condition that the people be free to leave the country, giving up all their wealth to the conquerors. The Muslims accused Kinana of keeping back part of his treasure and tortured him to death. His widow, Safiyya was fifteen years old at the time.

When one of Muhammad's followers saw Safiyya, he begged Muhammad to let him keep her for himself. When Muhammad saw her, he was struck by her beauty. He threw his mantle over her and took her into his harem. The wedding was celebrated by a feast.

Not long after the siege was lifted from Medina, Muhammad marched with three thousand men against the Quraiza Jews. The besieged Jews numbering more than two thousand, surrendered at last. The Jewish men were kept in one place, with their hands tied behind their backs. When asked what should be done with them, one of Muhammad's men named Sa'd (who had been wounded in the battle) said the men should be killed, the women and children sold into slavery, and the spoil divided among the Islamic Army. The followers of Mohammed let out a shrill of horror at the cruel and unmerciful punishment. Some of them began to protest. Muhammad stopped the debate. Muhammad told the people, "Truly the judgement of Sa'd is the judgement of the Lord, pronounced on high from above the seventh heaven."

Muhammad had the men to dig trenches near the marketplace. The next day Muhammad had the men brought by fives with their hands tied behind their backs. They were brought to the trenches and beheaded. It took all day, and part of the night, for them to butcher their helpless captives.

Zainab, a Jewess, lost her husband, father, and brother in this bloody battle, and she plotted to get revenge. She cooked a goat, steeped it in poison, and placed the dish before Muhammad for his evening meal. Accepting the gift, he took his favorite piece, the shoulder, and distributed portions to Abu Bakr and other friends. He took a bite and began to chew. Noticing something strange about the taste, he spit it out. "Hold," Muhammad cried out as he spat out the mouthful, "this shoulder has been poisoned." The man who had swallowed the meat soon died. Muhammad fell down in excruciating pain. He was seized with convulsions and fever. He never fully recovered from this poisoning and died suffering several years later. Zainab defended herself saying,

[5]**Thou hast inflicted grievous injuries on my people, and slain, as thou seest, my husband and my father. Therefore, said I within myself, If he be a prophet he will reject the gift, knowing that it is poisoned; but if only a pretender we shall be rid of our troubles.**

---

[5] Anis A. Shorrosh, *Islam Revealed*, (Nashville: Thomas Nelson Publishers,1988) p.68

Muhammad, had indeed accepted her gift, though he was poisoned, he did not eat enough to kill him then. He did suffer for years and the poison contributed to his death.

⁶Since then he had been subject to strange fevers and spells; in the dead of night, 'Ayisha reported, he would steal from the house, visit a graveyard, ask forgiveness of the dead, pray aloud for them, and congratulate them being dead.

His condition deteriorated over the next several years. He began to long for death. Once 'Ayisha complained of a headache. Muhammad asked her would she like to be put out of her misery and proceed him in death, so she could be buried alongside the Prophet of Allah. She knew how much he loved women and said, "If I did, by the time you left my grave, you would have found another wife to replace me."

After the death of his infant son, he was very depressed and his condition worsened.

⁷During a violent attack of fever, he called his wives together and said: "You see that I am very sick. I am not able to visit you in turn. If it be pleasing to you, I will remain in the house of 'Ayisha." They agreed.

After the fever had lasted nearly two weeks, his illness violently intensified on a Saturday night. Racked and restless, he tossed on his bed. Replying to one who tried to comfort him, Muhammad said, "There is not upon earth a believer sore afflicted, but the Lord causeth his sins to fall off from him even as the leaves from off the trees in autumn."

On Sunday he lay through the whole day in weakness. When he swooned, his wives gave him some medicine. Reviving, he asked what they had been doing to him. On being told, he said that they had given him medicine for another complaint, and he ordered them all to partake of the

---

⁶Will Durant, *The Age of Faith*, (New York: Simon and Schuster, 1950) p.173

⁷Anis A. Shorrosh, *Islam Revealed*, (Nashville: Thomas Nelson Publishers, 1988) p.71

medicine. So the women arose and poured the medicine in the presence of the dying prophet into each other's mouth.

Monday morning brought relief with some return of strength. Muhammad, leaning on an attendant, entered the mosque and sat on the ground for the service.

After a little conversation, he was helped back to the chamber of 'Ayisha. Exhausted, he lay down upon the bed. 'Ayisha, seeing him very low and weak, raised his head from the pillow as she sat by him on the ground, and placed his head on her bosom. His strength soon rapidly sank. He called for a pitcher of water and wetting his face from it, prayed, "O Lord, I beseech Thee, assist me in the agonies of death, come close, O Gabriel, to me." His last words in a whisper were, "Lord grant me pardon; Eternity, in Paradise! Pardon. The blessed companionship on high." He stretched himself gently, and the prophet of Arabia was no more. It was a little after midday on the eighth of June 632 A.D.

Obviously, Muhammad died believing that he still had sin in his life. What sins did he commit that were so great that died begging God for forgiveness? If he truly was a prophet of God, it would seem that God would have already forgiven him. None of the other prophets died begging God for forgiveness. They knew they were already forgiven. If he had been a true Christian, he would have known that he was going to heaven. Yet, he felt within his soul that he was not forgiven. He felt his sins were so great, he died begging God to grant forgiveness.

While Muhammad was alive, he wrote much of the Koran. When his health began to fail, his men gathered his words and comprised the Koran.

Although, they claimed it was free from faults, they knew that some of the Koran contradicted itself. So a verse was written to explain it. They said certain passages of the Koran are *mansukh*, or annulled by verses revealed chronologically later than themselves, which are called *nasikh*. This is taught in the Koran in The Cow 2:106

If we abrogate any verse or cause it to be forgotten We will replace it by a better one or one similar. Do you not know that Allah has power over all things?

God does not make mistakes. God does not contradict Himself, but man does.

Many people cite Islam's rapid spread as proof of it's Divine Authorship, however, there are other reasons. The religion of Islam was suited for the Arabs.

[8]The predominant characteristics of the ancient Arab were an almost inconceivable vain-glory and self-conceit. He was never weary of contemplating and boasting of his own perfections. Muhammad was precisely the Prophet to win such a race. The Arab gloried in his language; Muhammad declared that it was a Divine language--the decrees of God had been written in it from all eternity. The Arab gloried in the traditional practices and customs of the desert-- murder, predatory war, slavery, polygamy, concubinage. Muhammad impressed upon all these usages the seal of a Divine sanction. The Arab gloried in the holiness of Mecca. Muhammad affirmed it to the single portal whereby men could enter into Paradise. In a word, he took the Arab people just as he found them, and declared all that they did to be very good and sacred from change. The fancied revelation gratified the vanity of the Arabs, but it pro- nounced on them a sentence of perpetual barbarism. Such as they were when the Prophet lived, such are the Arabs now. Their condition is proof that Islam is incapable of elevating a people to a higher level.

There are many reasons that Islam spread so rapidly. Chief among the reasons, Muhammad promised victory for his followers. Any man who died fighting for Allah was promised to live in Paradise. Muhammad's view of Paradise was similar to the Viking's belief in Valhalla. Paradise was the Garden of Eden where men would be served by young virgins. When Muslims waged war on other peoples, they kept the spoils and the women as slaves and concubines (sex partners). Along with these incentives and their

---

[8] Anis A. Shorrosh, *Islam Revealed*, (Nashville: Thomas Nelson Publishers,1988) p.180

knowledge and mastery of desert warfare, caused the rapid spread of Islam.

Success or widespread acceptance is no indication of the favor of God. There have been many empires that have come and gone, several of them were evil. The Accadian Empire was an evil empire. Throughout history, there have been many evil empires, kingdoms and nations. We live in the time of man. Although God has an overall unchangeable divine plan for the world, He allows us to make our own choices, as long as they do not interfere with His ultimate plans. God's will is not automatically done on earth or in our individual lives. Jesus told us to pray so that His will be done on earth as it is in heaven. It is our responsibility to pray. If we do not, evil will reign in our lives.

If a Muslim believes in the Koran or Quran, he cannot contradict the Bible, for his Koran says the Bible is true.

And if thou (Muhammad) art in doubt concerning that which We reveal unto thee, then question those who read the Scripture (that was) before thee. Verily the Truth from thy Lord hath come unto thee. So be not thou of the waverers...

Muhammad later claimed when the Bible contradicted his beliefs, that the Jews and Christians perverted the Scriptures. When did this perversion occur? According to Muhammad, this must have occurred after God told him to consult the Scriptures. However, the discovery of the Dead Sea Scrolls proves that the Old Testament had not been tampered with at all. These scrolls contain all the books of the Old Testament, except the book of Esther. They prove that the Scriptures had not been tampered with. The most recent of them was written 500 years before Muhammad was born. Therefore Muhammad's claim that the Scriptures were perverted is untrue. The Muslim's claim that the Scriptures were accurate during the days of Muhammad and later changed, is totally untrue. In attempting to use the Bible to confirm his beliefs, it does the opposite and convicts them as false.

When Muhammad wrote the Koran, he made many mistakes. One of the most absurd mistakes in the Koran is found where the Koran says that Mary, the mother of Jesus is the sister of Aaron. It says this in Surat Maryam (Mary) 19:28

Oh sister of Aaron! Thy father was not a wicked man nor was thy mother a harlot.

Aaron lived 1,570 years before Mary the mother of Jesus. How did Muhammad make such a mistake? In Luke 1:5 it says, Elizabeth, the mother of John the Baptist, who was Mary's cousin, was of the daughters of Aaron, meaning a descendant of Aaron. However, Mary was a descendant of the tribe of Judah. Elizabeth was of the tribe of Levi. Apparently Muhammad could not adequately remember the details from the Apocrypha or the New Testament, and confused Mary for the daughter of Aamram, the sister of Moses and Aaron.

Foreign Words

Muslims believe that Arabic is the language of Allah. They believe that the Arabic Koran is perfect, exact representation of Allah's words. Only the Arabic version is the authorized version of the Koran. Surat 39:27,28 (The Hordes) claims that God has given the Koran in the Arabic tongue free from all faults. Yet, the Koran has foreign words. Is God's language so deficient that it needs help from foreign words?

[9] (1) "Pharaoh" comes from the Egyptian language and it means king or potentate. It is found 84 times in the Koran.

(2) "Adam" and "Eden" repeated 24 times, are Accadian words. The correct term for "Adam" in the Arabic would be *basharan* or *insan,* meaning mankind. "Eden" would be Arabic *janna,* or garden.

(3) "Abraham" comes from the Assyrian language, and would be more accurately represented by the Arabic *Abu Raheem.*

(4) *Haroot* and *Maroot* are Persian, not Arabic names of angels. Sirat should have been Altareeq, which means "the path." *Hoor* is the Persian word whose Arabic counterpart is *Tilmeeth,* meaning "a disciple." *Jinn* normally refers to good spirits or evil demons, and the Arabic word is *ruh. Firdaus* is a Persian word which means *Jannah* in Arabic and refers to the highest or seventh heaven.

(5) *Taboot, taghouth, zakat, malakout* are Syriac words.

---

[9] Anis A. Shorrosh, *Islam Revealed,* (Nashville: Thomas Nelson Publishers,1988) p.199

(6) *Heber, sakinah, maoon, turat, jehannim* come from the Hebrew language.

(7) Injil, which means "gospel" comes from the Greek language, and the correct word in Arabic is *bisharah*.

Contradictions in Science

Further proof that the Koran is not the Word of God are the incorrect scientific statements it makes. Most people of ancient times believed the earth to be disk-shaped and they envisioned the heaven to be a fixed roof over the earth. They believed the sun and stars to be relatively small compared to the earth. They thought the sun and moon, night and day chased each other across this roof which many called the lowest heaven. This is what most other leaders and religions thought. Muhammad made the same mistake. If God is the speaker in the Koran, then He certainly knows nothing about the Heavens.

Surat 21:32 (The Prophets) We spread the heaven like a canopy and provided it with strong support: yet of its signs they are heedless.

Surat 50:6 (Qaf) Do they not then look up to the heaven above them how We have made it and adorned it and it has no gaps?

Surat 16:79 Do they not see the birds that wing their flight in heavens vault..

Eavesdroppers are pursed by fiery comets.

Surat 37:6 (The Ranks) We have decked the lower heaven with constellations. They guard it against rebellious devils, so that they may not hear the words of those on high. Meteors are hurled at them from every side; then, driven away, they are consigned to an eternal scourge. Eavesdroppers are pursed by fiery comets.

Surat 72:9 (The Jinn) "We made our way to high heaven and found it filled with mighty wardens and fiery comets.

**We sat eavesdropping, but eavesdroppers find flaming darts
in wait for them.**

Obviously, Muhammad did not know the true nature of meteors
or comets. He did not know that millions of meteors strike the earth's
atmosphere every day, most of them burning up before they strike the
earth. Meteors strike every planet and moon in the solar system and
not just the earth. Meteors are space debris scattered throughout the
solar system. Whenever the meteors come close enough to a heavenly
body, the gravity pulls the meteor and it crashes on it. They are not
missiles to strike devils as Muhammad thought. There are some days
when you can look out and see the sun and the moon in the sky at the
same time. Yet Muhammad wrote,

**Surat 38:40 (Ya Sin) the sun is not allowed to overtake the
moon nor does the night outpace the day.**

Further proof that Muhammad, and not God, wrote the Koran,
can be found by reading the Pilgrimage chapter. Surat 62:25
Muhammad wrote "He holds the sky from falling down: this it shall
not do except by His own will."

We live at the bottom of a sea of air. This sea of air or
atmosphere extends above the earth for over a hundred thousand feet.
As fish swim in the ocean, birds and airplanes swim or fly through
this ocean of air. The air is heaviest near the bottom of this ocean
and it gets thinner as you go higher. The sky can never fall for it is
and always has been here.

In Surat al-Kauf (The Cave) 18:86 Muhammad wrote that DhU'l-
Qarneyn (Alexander the Great) went to the far west and saw the sun
setting in a spring of black mud.

**Till, when he reached the setting-place of the sun, he found
it setting in a muddy spring, and found a people thereabout:
We said: O DhU'l-Qarneyn! Either punish or show them
kindness.**

This statement alone proves the Koran is not the Word of God.
Who told Muhammad that the sun sets in a spring of black mud? He
claimed to receive revelations from the angel Gabriel. Certainly, the
true Gabriel knew the true nature and size of the sun. Nor was this

revelation given by Satan, or any of the fallen angels impersonating God's angels. They know about the true nature of the solar system as well. Since neither God nor Satan was behind this revelation, this causes one to wonder if Muhammad did not make it up. If this is the case, how much more did he make up?

Muhammad made other inaccurate statements. He said in Surat 67:5 (Sovereignty) that stars were lamps in the sky. He believed whenever a devil tried to enter heaven, these lamps became fiery darts or missiles that struck the devils and burned them.

Muhammad wrote..

Surat 16:14 (The Bee) He set firm mountains upon the earth lest it should move away with you;..

He also said in Surat 70 (the Steps or Ladder), the distance from earth to the edge of the seventh heaven is fifty thousand years. If a day's journey is 25 miles, then multiply 25, by 365, by 50,000 to figure what is the number of miles one could journey if possible, in 50,000 years. That equals 456,250,000 miles. That is not enough miles to take you out of the solar system. In fact, the planet Jupiter is 390,000,000 miles from earth. Saturn is 800,000,000 miles away from earth. Yet, Mohammed said that you could travel to the end of the seventh heaven or the edge of the universe in 50,000,000 years. Muhammad believed there are seven heavens, one on top of the other. He said the lowest heaven contains the constellations. Our galaxy alone is 100,000 light years across. Mohammed was talking about traveling on a camel. If you could travel at the speed of light, it would take you 100,000 years just to leave the galaxy. This is another statement that proves that the whoever inspired the Koran knew nothing about the solar system, the galaxy or the universe. God does not lie. If God inspired Muhammad, how do you explain these mistakes?

He said in Creator 35:42

It is Allah that keeps the heaven and earth from falling. If they should fall, none could hold them back but HE.

Obviously Muhammad wrote these passages based on his superstitious, primitive, misconceptions of heaven. It is not possible for Heaven or earth to fall in space. There is nothing for them to fall to.

The Koran claims to be the words of God in the Arabic tongue and free from all faults.

Surat 39:27,28 (The Hordes) We have given mankind in this Koran all manner of arguments, so that they may take heed. We have revealed it in the Arabic tongue, a Koran free from all faults, that they may guard themselves against evil.

Yet, we see the Koran does have faults. The authors of the Bible did not make these kinds of mistakes. Instead of a fixed roof with no gaps, the Bible correctly described the earth as a circle, suspended in space (hung on nothing), underneath moveable, flexible heavens.

Isaiah 40:22 It is He that sitteth upon the circle of the earth, and the inhabitants thereof are as grasshoppers; that stretcheth out the heavens as a curtain, and spreadeth them out as a tent to dwell in:

Proverbs 8:27 When He prepared the heavens, I was there: when He set a compass (circle) upon the face of the depth:

Job 26:7 He stretcheth out the north over the empty place, and hangeth the earth upon nothing.

Another difference between the Bible and the Koran is the Koran's command of ruthlessness to unbelievers.

Surat 48:29 (Victory) Muhammad is Allah's Apostle. Those who follow him are ruthless to the unbelievers but merciful to one another.

Muhammad promotes ruthless annihilation of peoples, claiming that God had commanded it.

Surat 17:16 (The Night Journey) When we resolve to annihilate a people, We first warn those of them that live in comfort. If they persist in sin, We rightly pass Our judgement and utterly destroy them.

Following the commands of Muhammad, the Muslims conquered Jerusalem by sword. When the Muslims conquered Jerusalem, they did not allow Jews or Christians to visit the Holy sites or demanded exorbitant fees for safe conduct to the sites. The Crusades were not an all-out war against Islam. Originally, it was an effort to force Muslims to allow Christians to visit and worship at the Holy places associated with Christ.

Originally, Muhammad preached tolerance to people of other faiths. However once his power was established it was a different story. He used his influence to establish what many call the religion of the sword. When the Muslims went forth and attacked the surrounding tribes and other nations, they gave them three options; accept Islam, pay tribute, or die by the sword (see the Repentance Surat verse 29).

Many Christians paid with their lives. Yet, most took the easy way out. As a result, many churches were turned into mosques to please the conquering Muslims. A shroud of spiritual darkness covered the Middle East, North Africa, and Spain. About one million Armenian Christians were savagely slaughtered by the Turkish Muslims at the beginning of the Twentieth Century.

Surat 8:16 (The Spoils) Believers, when you encounter the armies of the infidels do not turn your backs to them in flight. If anyone on that day turns his back to them, except it be for tactical reasons, or to join another band, he shall incur the wrath of Allah and Hell shall be his home and his fate.

Surat 8:39 Make war on them until idolatry is no more and Allah's religion reigns supreme.

This is totally different from what Jesus commanded His disciples. The battle for men's souls cannot be won by force. Jesus never commanded His servants to fight with the sword to win men's souls. As a matter of fact, the opposite is true.

John 18:36   Jesus answered, My kingdom is not of this world: if my kingdom were of this world, then would my

servants fight, that I should not be delivered to the Jews: but now is my kingdom not from hence.

Matthew 26:52 Then said Jesus unto him, Put up again thy sword into his place: for all they that take the sword shall perish with the sword.

Many have mistakenly believed that a relationship with God could be forced upon people. Men cannot approach God through merely keeping religious ordinances. Salvation cannot be forced upon anyone.

Revelation 3:20 Behold, I stand at the door, and knock: if any man hear my voice, and open the door, I will come in to him, and will sup with him, and He with me.

Matthew 15:8 This people draweth nigh unto me with their mouth, and honoureth me with their lips; but their heart is far from me.

Lip service is not enough. Many people have a form of religion, but they do not have a true relationship with God.
For further reading on this subject read the book Islam Revealed- A Christian Arab's View of Islam by Dr. Anis A Shorrosh; published by Thomas Nelson Publishers.

Matthew 24:24 For there shall arise false Christs, and false prophets, and shall show great signs and wonders; insomuch that, if it were possible, they shall deceive the very elect.

Chapter 17

In 1878, a man named Charles Darwin writes his book the "Origin of The Species." This book which expounds evolution changes the world. It teaches that all organism evolve into higher more complex organism. It teaches the "survival of the fittest." Darwin was not the first person to believe in evolution, but the idea had been around for centuries. Many ancient religions including Confucianism, Taoism, Buddhism, Hinduism and others, are evolutionary in nature. It is not long before Darwin's teachings reach the intellectual communities of the world. The chain of thought it produces "imperialism, laissez fair capitalism, and militarism and nazism." Many different nations assume they are more evolved than others.

According to evolution, it is only natural for the more evolved species to subjugate the weaker species and eventually replace them. Many European countries begin to become imperialistic and divide Africa, Asia, and India in the name of their countries. Millions are killed and tortured because of evolutionary-encouraged racism. The strong kill, pillage and maim, all because they believe in racial superiority as taught by evolution.

Karl Marx reads Darwin's book and is so fascinated by it that he wishes to dedicate his own book "Das Kapital," to him.

In the 1930's, a man comes to power in Germany. He becomes the most fanatical evolutionist of all. His name is Adolf Hitler. With his fanatical belief in evolution, Adolf Hitler convinces his whole nation that they are the most evolutionary evolved race of all. He tells them that their nation of "blond beasts" would rule the world for a thousand years. He teaches that Jews, blacks and other peoples were subhuman. Hitler believed that the Germans were intellectually and physically superior, to every people on the face of the earth.

Hitler's theory was embarrassed by two black men. Jesse Owens embarrassed him in the 36 Olympics in Munich. Hitler was so angry that he refused to present Jesse the gold medal. Another time was when Joe Louis fought Max Schmelling for the heavyweight boxing championship of the world. It only took Joe Louis 2:38 seconds to demolish the Fuheur's master race theory.

Hitler carries his evolutionary views to the extreme. He leads his nation into war. Hitler and his top aides are fascinated with the occult. This servant of the Devil mobilizes his entire nation for world conquest and the world is plunged into the World War II. Satan knows that if he can destroy the Jews, he will be able to defeat God's plan. It is not that they are superior or better than others, for many times they have failed to please God and have suffered for it. God promised Abraham that He would bless His seed.

This promise was extended to his descendants that pleased God. When Jacob (Abraham's grandson) finally passed his test, God put a blessing on him and changed his name to Israel. From his sons came the twelve tribes of Israel. God promised the Israelites that if they would serve God, He would bless them.

Moses gave the Jews a warning when He gave them God's law in Deuteronomy Chapter 28. God said that if they, (Israel), did not follow after God, He would scatter them among the nations. As He would have rejoiced over them to bless them, He promised He would rejoice over them to curse them and deliver them into the hands of their enemies. God promised that He would not totally forsake Israel, but He would gather them back into Israel in the latter times. Christ plans to return to earth as the Messiah and rule the earth from the nation of Israel. His rule will bring peace on the earth and it will last forever. This would of course bring the end of Satan's influence on earth. The prince of darkness will never settle for this. He knows if He destroys the Jews, He will forever destroy God's plans for eternity.

Satan fills Hitler with an insane hatred for the Jews. Many Europeans feel the Jews are the source of their economic problems. Hitler has a solution for the Jewish problem. Satan anoints Hitler's tongue to sway the masses of people. Hitler begins to round up the Jews. Their property and possessions are confiscated. Initially, some of the Jews are put in prison camps. From there, Hitler carries out the will of Satan. He begins to systematically exterminate the Jews. Some are shot. Some are killed by poisonous gas. Some are burned in the ovens in the prison camp of Auschwitz. Sometimes their ashes were used to help make asphalt. Never has a people suffered so inhumanely, so intensely, in such a brief period of time. Satan tries his best to exterminate the seed of Abraham, and defeat the plan of God.

Throughout the second world war, Hitler continues to exterminate the Jews. Most of the world is unaware of what he is doing. His crime is so horrible that no one would believe it. Before the war is over, Hitler has killed six million Jews. If not for the intervention of the United States, Hitler would have surely won the war. For America, WWII began December 7, 1941. The war in Europe ended in July 17, 1945. Hitler is never brought to justice for his crimes against humanity. He commits suicide rather than face the justice of man. However, there is no escape from the justice of God.

When the Americans finally liberate the survivors at Auschwitz, they cannot believe their eyes. They are horrified and sickened by the cruelty of the Germans. When the news of the Holocaust that killed six million Jews reaches the ears of the world, it is shocked.

Israel Reborn

Satan's plan has failed. Although millions have been killed, the Jews still survive. Many Jews are so sickened by the treatment of their fellow Jews at the hands of Hitler's Third Reich that they are now convinced that they will never be safe in any land but their own. The British had control over Palestine since 1922. In November of 1947 the British turn the troublesome region over to the newly formed United Nations. The U.N General Assembly announces a plan to partition Palestine into two states, one Arab and one Jewish. The Arabs reject it outright, and demand a single Arab state be created. They vow to exterminate any Jewish state that is created. On May 14, 1948, Israel once again becomes a nation. Some say Israel was born in the ovens of Auschwitz. Instead of Satan preventing Israel from coming forth, he has actually caused it.

Ezekiel 38:8   After many days thou shalt be visited: in the latter years thou shalt come into the land that is brought back from the sword, and is gathered out of many people, against the mountains of Israel, which have been always waste: but it is brought forth out of the nations, and they shall dwell safely all of them.

One day after Israel declared its statehood, they were attacked by five Arab armies. Egypt, Syria, Transjordan, Lebanon, and Iraq attacked from all sides. Israel resisted the attack, despite heavy losses. The fight lasted until a cease-fire was agreed upon until early 1949. Israel took over most of the land allocated by the U.N. for the Jewish and Arab states. The remaining portion, called the West Bank, was grabbed by Transjordan. Egypt took the tiny strip of land called the Gaza Strip. However, because the Arabs embraced Islam, they hate Israel and wish to destroy it.

"The Arab nations should sacrifice up to 10 million of their 50 million people, if necessary, to wipe out Israel...Israel to the Arab world is like a cancer to the human body, and the only way of remedy is to uproot it, just like a cancer."
--Saud ibn Abdul Aziz, King of Saudi Arabia, Associated Press, Jan 9, 1954

Many times Israel would be attacked by its Arab neighbors. In June of 1967 Egypt and Syria amassed troops on their borders. Egypt blocked Israeli shipping through the international Straits of Tiran. On June 5, 1967 Israel launched a preemptive strike against Egypt and Syria. Despite Israeli messages to Jordan to stay out of hostilities, Jordan invaded Jerusalem. Israel defeated the Arabs in bitter fighting in just six days. The Jews gained control of the East Jerusalem, the West Bank, Syria's Golan Heights, the Gaza Strip, and Sinai Peninsula. After the Six Day War, Israel signaled its desire to negotiate with the Arab states for genuine Arab-Israel peace.

In 1967, for the first time since Titus invaded Jerusalem, Jerusalem was back into Israeli hands. Jesus prophesied in 33 A.D. that Titus would lay siege to Jerusalem, the second Diaspora or scattering of the Jews, and the return of Jerusalem to the Jews.

Luke 21:24   And they shall fall by the edge of the sword, and shall be led away captive into all nations: and Jerusalem shall be trodden down of the Gentiles, until the times of the Gentiles be fulfilled.

When the Israelis soldiers approached the Holy City for the first time, they had tears in their eyes. Many of them wept when they touched the temple walls.

Many nations have pressured Israel to give Jerusalem back to the Palestinians. Many U.N. resolutions have been passed to pressure the Israelis to give back Jerusalem. It will never happen. The times of the gentiles have been fulfilled. God has given it back to the Jews. Not even all the power, of all the armies in the world, will ever be able to take it from Israel. The Prophet Zechariah foresaw these days, and prophesied that Jerusalem would be a burdensome stone to all nations.

God promised that He would bring the Jews back into Israel while the land was desolate. When Turkey had control of Palestine, they cut down all the trees in Palestine. Israel became desolate. When Israel became a nation, they began a massive reforestation project. They planted over 200,000,000 trees, including citrus fruit, banana, and others. Israel today is the fourth largest exporter of fruit. This is a fulfillment of prophecy.

Isaiah 27:6 He shall cause them that come of Jacob to take root: Israel shall blossom and bud, and fill the face of the world with fruit.

Israel has been transformed from a barren land, to a land flowing with milk and honey. They have fields of grain, wheat, and cotton. The Jews began a massive re-forestation project, planting 200,000,000 trees. I have been to some of the countries in the Middle East. It is amazing to see how barren they all are, except for Israel. When you compare it to the other countries that surround it, such as Jordan, Israel looks like the Garden of Eden.

When I went to Israel, I was amazed at the size of their fruit. The grapes were the biggest I had ever seen. The vegetables such as cabbage, and lettuce, others were the largest I had ever seen. This was not at a state fair, but at normal fruit and vegetable stands along the road. The cities are built up and the land is full of people. This is the fulfillment of Ezekiel's prophecy.

Ezekiel 36:35 And they shall say, This land that was desolate is become like the garden of Eden; and the waste and desolate and ruined cities are become fenced, and are inhabited.

By the time of Christ, Hebrew had become a dead language, used only by priest and Pharisees for religious purposes. God promised that He would cause the pure language to return to the Jews.

In Hebrew, it is not possible to swear. It is also probable that Hebrew was the original language of Adam. If this was the case, Noah would and his sons would have spoken this language until Babel. Noah's most spiritual son, was Shem. It was at Babel that God confused the tongues. Shem was alive during Babel and he would not have participated in their disobedience. Therefore, he probably would not have been subjected to the punishment. If his language was not changed, then his language was the original or pure language.

Zephaniah 3:9   For then will I turn to the people a pure language, that they may all call upon the name of the LORD, to serve Him with one consent.

God promised the Jews, He would bring them back to Israel for His name sake and not for theirs. They have failed God, as has most of mankind. As far as God is concerned, the mere fact that He has brought the Jews into Israel should be enough proof that He is God and His Word is true.

The Second Exodus

One of the most amazing things that the Bible prophesied of, is the return of the Soviet Jews to Israel. There are 4.8 million Jews in the Soviet Union. The Soviet Union is to the uttermost north of Israel.

Jeremiah 31:8   Behold, I will bring them from the north country, and gather them from the coasts of the earth, and with them the blind and the lame, the woman with child and her that travaileth with child together: a great company shall return thither.

Zechariah prophesied that this would happen after the Jews had been spread all over the world.

Zechariah 2:6   Ho, ho, come forth, and flee from the land of the north, saith the LORD: for I have spread you abroad as the four winds of the heaven, saith the LORD.

Like Pharaoh, the leaders of the Soviet Union for decades, would not let the Jews leave and return to their own land. However God prophesied there would be an Exodus of Jews from the north country, and the other lands where they had been driven. God promised they would return to the land that He gave to their fathers, the land of Israel.

Jeremiah 16:14-15 Therefore, behold, the days come, saith the LORD, that it shall no more be said, The LORD liveth, that brought up the children of Israel out of the land of Egypt;
{15} But, The LORD liveth, that brought up the children of Israel from the land of the north, and from all the lands whither He had driven them: and I will bring them again into their land that I gave unto their fathers.

Many people thought that nothing less than the destruction of Soviet Union would cause the Jews to be freed from it. God promised that He would bring them out. Because of Glasnost, restrictions are being lifted in Russia and Jews are being allowed to immigrate to Israel by the thousands. The Israeli and Russian governments have plans to immigrate over a million Jews in the next five years. The Jews are being persecuted in Russia and the other Eastern European countries. God is using the persecution to make them return to Israel. In Russia, the Jews have a saying. The optimistic Jew says, "In ten years we will all be in Israel. The pessimist answers, "We wont live that long." Bible prophecy is being fulfilled before our eyes.

What is the source of Glasnost? While much has been made of economic realities that have been forced upon the Soviets, there was another factor-- revival. Despite the religious persecution, the Church continued to flourish in the Soviet Union. Persecution always makes the Church pray. Prayers of hungry hearts are the seeds of Revival.

Setting The Stage

Few things are as confusing as trying to determine the exact sequence of events that the Bible prophesies. There are many different interpretations of these Bible prophecies. There is no question that they will be fulfilled, but we do not understand completely by what means and in what sequence. God could have told us exactly how these things would come about, but He did not.

Although much detail is given in some areas, in others, the information is sketchy. He knows exactly what He intends to do, but we do not. This causes confusion, and the confusion is deliberate. Our confusion is merely a side-effect. The confusion is meant for Satan.

Satan would not deliberately fulfill prophecy. God has magnified the validity of the Word of God above His name.

Psalms 138:2   I will worship toward thy holy temple, and praise thy name for thy lovingkindness and for thy truth: for thou hast magnified thy word above all thy name.

Jesus said heaven and earth would pass away before one jot or tittle of the Word of God would be unfulfilled, (Matt 5:18). If Satan can cause one prophecy to be unfulfilled, he would have caused God to become a liar, and defeated the Word of God. Satan knows his only hope for survival is to circumvent the Word of God. Satan does not knowingly cause prophecies to be fulfilled. If he had known he was causing the Word of God to be fulfilled, he never would have had Jesus crucified (1 Cor 2:8).

Satan never gives up. He still thinks he can cause changes in the plan of God. Although much of what God will do is stated in the prophecies, much is still shrouded in mystery. This is to insure the fulfillment of the prophecies. If we understood everything clearly, then so would Satan. God does not make Satan fulfill the Word of God, He tricks Satan into doing it. This is further proof of God's intellectual superiority.

For instance, Satan knew that God warned Israel that He would scatter them around the world. God promised in the last days, He would bring them back to the land of Israel. Satan tried to prevent this. Satan tried to exterminate them through Hitler. He failed, and because of his attempt, Israel was reborn. Yet, Satan has not given up, and has tried to destroy Israel through the Arabs. Satan laid the groundwork for this over 1400 years ago through Muhammad when he established the Muslim religion. As I proved in the previous chapter, the Koran was not inspired by God. It doesn't matter how many times a day you pray. If God is not pleased with your life, he will not hear you, especially if your hands are full of blood.

Isaiah 1:15   And when ye spread forth your hands, I will hide mine eyes from you: yea, when ye make many prayers, I will not hear: your hands are full of blood.

No one is guaranteed, that God will automatically hear them, no matter how much they pray.

Matthew 6:7 But when ye pray, use not vain repetitions, as the heathen do: for they think that they shall be heard for their much speaking.

Gulf Crisis

In 1991 there was a war in the Gulf. Saddam Hussein, the leader of Iraq, invaded Kuwait in August of 1990. He quickly over ran this tiny country and pillaged it. The U.S, the United Nations, and other Arab nations protested against his actions. He moved his troops toward Saudi Arabia and the world was convinced he was going to invade Saudi Arabia. The Saudis asked the United States to send troops. Saddam claimed he was invited into Kuwait. He announced he was pulling out of Kuwait. He moved some troops, but apparently changed his mind and decided to stay. He announced Kuwait was the 19th province of Baghdad.

The U.S coalition warned Saddam, his aggression would not stand. He was threatened with war. Nation, after nation tried to get him to withdraw from Kuwait. He was warned, his nation faced a vastly superior force which could annihilate his army and nation. Yet, he did not respect the power of the nations which were allied against him. Even though he acknowledged he was facing a superior force, he said that his god would save him. Most of the world could not believe that he would not give in. The proud and hasty Iraqis ignored the warnings and war has begun. The amazing thing about this, it was all prophesied beforehand the prophet Habakkuk, in the Bible.

Habakkuk 1:5-12 Behold ye among the heathen, and regard, and wonder marvellously: for I will work a work in your days, which ye will not believe, though it be told you.
{6} For, lo, I raise up the Chaldeans, that bitter and hasty nation, which shall march through the breadth of the land, to possess the dwellingplaces that are not theirs.
{7} They are terrible and dreadful: their judgment and their dignity shall proceed of themselves.
{8} Their horses also are swifter than the leopards, and are more fierce than the evening wolves: and their horsemen

shall spread themselves, and their horsemen shall come from far; they shall fly as the eagle that hasteth to eat.

{9} They shall come all for violence: their faces shall sup up as the east wind, and they shall gather the captivity as the sand.

{10} And they shall scoff at the kings, and the princes shall be a scorn unto them: they shall deride every strong hold; for they shall heap dust, and take it.

{11} Then shall his mind change, and he shall pass over, and offend, imputing this his power unto his god.

{12} Art thou not from everlasting, O LORD my God, mine Holy One? we shall not die. O LORD, thou hast ordained them for judgment; and, O mighty God, thou hast established them for correction.

During the Gulf War much of the Iraqi army was destroyed. Saddam has threatened to destroy Israel. Saddam has been compared to Hitler. In 9 of the 11 years he has been in power, he has been at war. During this time, Amnesty International reports he has killed over 500,000 of his own people. This modern day Hitler has threatened to destroy Israel with chemical weapons. On January 18, 1991, Iraq fired some of its scud missiles at the Israeli civil population. Later, Iraq fired more missiles. Miraculously no one was seriously hurt by either barrage of missiles.

Now the Gulf War is over. Here are some of the present and possible future repercussions of the Gulf War.

1. The war has already increased world concerns over the Israeli-Palestinian issue. The PLO, and most Palestinians living in the West Bank sided with Saddam Hussein in the Gulf War. Israel will certainly become more reluctant than ever to budge on the issue. The Bush Administration has been pressuring Israel to help solve this issue. Washington and Israel are greatly divided over this problem. At the time of this writing, the rift between Israel and Washington is greater than with any previous U.S. President in recent memory.

2. Many Arabs around the world are angry at the U.S and Israel for the Gulf War. The war will probably lead to greater anti-Western resentment, and closer ties with the Russians. Perhaps because of the breakup of the Soviet Union and their recent decline, they will try to reassert themselves as a true superpower. If the rapidly changing

political events of the recent years have taught us anything, they have taught us that nothing is certain and political fortunes of leaders and governments can change overnight. The tension will increase over the Palestinian issue until the Russians lead an Arab coalition in an invasion against Israel.

3. Already Israel has received batteries of American patriot missiles. These patriot missiles are designed to intercept and destroy enemy aircraft and missiles. These missiles help strengthen Israel's air defenses and will be of great use during World War III, if there own American sponsored anti-missile system, the *Israeli Arrow* is not ready by then.

Through Hitler's deeds, Israel was reborn. The very thing that Satan tried to prevent from happening, he caused to happen. This is because it was a mystery to him, how God intended for these things to come about.

Satan is still fighting, trying to circumvent God's plans. He would love to destroy Israel through Saddam or anyone else. In some countries he has believers killed. Satan is trying to destroy the political effectiveness of the church. He still believes he can change things, and he is trying to manipulate political events to fulfill his malefic agenda.

Just as there are political preparations that must be made before the Beast comes, there are spiritual preparations as well. Satan is preparing the world spiritually, for the coming of the beast.

Chapter 18

Satan knows his time is short. Just as he is preparing the world politically for his final assault, he is preparing things spiritually. If the spiritual conditions are not right, his plans will not work. Satan his deceived the world into glorifying sin and debauchery. Righteousness is a joke, and sin is in. Satan is getting from many people what he has always wanted, to be worshipped as God.

More and more people are worshipping Satan. Many rock stars are worshipping the devil. Some of them have put hidden messages worshiping Satan on their records. Many have done it, and the most recent to do it is Madonna. On Jan 10, 1991 at 10:11 a.m. on CNN Headline News, they ran the story about Madonna doing backward masking of Satanic messages on her latest album "Justify My Love."

A man in Florida who discovered it called CNN. They sent a crew out and they listened to the recording. When it was played backwards they heard Madonna's voice saying "hear us Satan." On five different songs they heard Madonna saying statements like hallelujah to Satan and similar blasphemous statements. When they got back to their studio, they bought their own copies of Madonna's record to make sure they were not listening to a doctored tape. They discovered the messages on their recordings as well and also discovered a satanic message on the "Like A Prayer" song also. When CNN called Madonna's record company and agent, there had no comment.

Why would anyone want to record hidden messages encouraging worship of Satan in their recordings unless they were a Satan worshipper? All across America, Satan worshippers and those that have participated in witchcraft have been growing in numbers. Although our government has had agents to infiltrate every group from the Klan to Soviet Spy rings and various terrorist groups, the FBI reports these groups are extremely difficult to penetrate. The witches always seem to be able to see through them.

Human and animal sacrifice are a normal part of their rituals. In state after state, human remains have been found that indicate these murdered victims were part of ritual sacrifices. They were horribly murdered. Some of the witches have come forward and testified of their gruesome practices. One woman who was in a witches coven testified she was instructed to become pregnant to have a child so they could sacrifice it in a ritual. She agreed and became pregnant. She never went to the hospital, so there were no records of the pregnancy. The coven took total care of her, and delivered her baby. The mother began to have second thoughts and told the coven that she wanted to keep her child. The witches ignored her and they sacrificed her baby.

Many young people developed an interest in satanism and witchcraft in part, due to certain rock and heavy metal groups. Some mistakenly believe they can receive power through witchcraft. Sadly, they do not understand the dangerous game they are playing. They do not understand Satan has no friends among humankind. They cannot use Satan without Satan using them. Some of the young people ended up committing murder, even murdering their own parents.

I saw some of these young people on a talk show who murdered their parents. They did the interview from their prison cells where they were serving life sentences. When asked why they committed their horrible crimes, they testified it was as if they were under control. They killed their parents without any remorse. They were aware of what they were doing, but it was as if a cloud that covered their heads. It seemed as if they were in a dream. They realized, but yet did not realize what they were doing. Satan did not save them from prosecution. When asked how they felt about Satan now, they said they felt betrayed by Satan.

In the summer of 1990 a young man in Warren, Mich a suburb of Detroit, said to his cousin about their friend, "Lets kill Steph." They got up and killed her in a ritual type slaying and severed her head from her body. They put her head in the freezer and called up some other friends and told them what they did. The friends came over in disbelief. The two girls saw the head in the freezer and took it to the police station. The young men were arrested without incident and initially showed no remorse for the girl's savage murder. If you participate in witchcraft, you risk demon possession and eternal damnation. While I was in high school I had an encounter with a girl who participated in witchcraft and became demon possessed.

A Demon's Nightmare

Joan, (not her real name), was someone I had known for several years. Other than being a little on the fast side, I had not noticed anything unusual about her. I had witnessed to her on several occasions and she told me she was an atheist. She told me she used to hate God. I asked her why, but she had no explanation. She used to break up every cross she could find. Her mother could not keep crosses in the house because she would destroy them. Her mother finally got a large metal crucifix. Joan told me she used to fantasize about melting it down. She would grit her teeth and say how she hated God.

I would say, "I thought you did not believe in Him. How can you hate what you believe does not exist?"

She answered, "I mean I used to hate Him, but I don't any more because He is not real."

I dismissed her talk as her attempts at being eccentric. I assumed she was blinded by Satan in her attempts to be different and that was it.

When she became a senior the next year, she decided to do a paper on demons in her Investigative Paper class. I was in college at the University of Michigan. She got in contact with me and wanted to use me as one of her sources for the paper. I came up to Pontiac Central High School for the interview.

As we were conducting the interview she asked me a startling question. A few days before, she had visited my home church with a mutual friend of ours. Nancy had told me that something strange had happened at the service but she did not have time to tell me everything. At that point she only told me that something wasn't quite right with Joan.

Joan asked me very seriously, "Why is it at your church, and I have only seen this at your church, whenever they sing or pray, the **demons** get nervous?"

I explained to her that we were Pentecostal. We believe that after a person receives salvation, or is born again there is another experience. This experience is called being filled with the Holy Ghost. As on the day of Pentecost, we believe that this experience is accompanied by the sign of speaking in tongues. I told her the other churches she had been to, did not believe in this experience, and therefore did not have the power to make the devils nervous. I explained we have the Holy Ghost and this gives us power over the devil. When we pray, we direct the power of God. When we praise God, because the Bible says God dwells in the praises of His people, more of His power comes in the place. All the while, I was giving this explanation, I realized there was no way she should have known this. Although this is something Pentecostal ministers believe, it was never spoken of. Her family was Lutheran, and would not believe such a pro-Pentecostal statement, even if she had heard it. However, she said, "the demon gets nervous." I thought, "How can you know how a demon feels unless you have one?"

Demons are contemptuous of men. They can see and hear one another, but we cannot hear or see them. They deceive most of mankind every day by planting evil thoughts in their heads. They rejoice in their ability to deceive mankind and take them to hell. I suppose to them, it seems like a sick game. I realized it would be just like the demon, to mock me by giving me such an obvious clue. Knowing the devils like I did, I realized the devils or demons think all humans are stupid.

I noticed that a sly smirk was on her face, as if she was up to something. Within myself, I begin to pray to God. I said, "Lord, I think this girl has a demon, and I want You to show me. Anoint one of my hands with Your power, and if the demon reacts to it, I will know that she is demon possessed."

Immediately, I felt the tingle of the invisible power of God begin to come on my left hand. Like unseen holy oil, the anointing continued growing on my hand. I continued talking to her as if I had not caught the demon's clue. There was no reaction on her face to indicate the demon sensed what was happening. I decided to wave the hand without the anointing in front of her first. I waved my right hand in a gesture in front of her face and she did nothing. Now I wanted to see if she would react to the anointing on my left hand. I waited a moment and waved my left hand exactly as I did the right.

Immediately, she gasped in terror and leaped backwards as if she saw death on my left hand! She backed up until she got to the wall. Her eyes were bulging and she continued gasping in abject terror. She would not take her eyes off my hand which was anointed with the power of God. Her face was white with horror. I was 18 years old, and face to face with a real demon. I was not afraid. For 5 years I had been praying for God to give me power over the devil to set his people free. Although I had seen God do it many for times for other minsters, this was my first sign that he had answered my prayer. I was smiling from ear to ear, because I knew I had power over the devil.

I was smiling triumphantly. I said, "What is the matter?" She said, "Nothing. Nothing," she said in a futile attempt to deny what had happened, and never taking her eyes off my hand. I knew I was in complete control of the situation. I said, "Come here. I want to pray for you."

Joan began to shake her head and said in a deep and guttural tone, "Nooo!" and ran down the hall. That was the last I had seen of her that day.

Repeatedly, I tried unsuccessfully to get her to let me pray for her. Despite what happened, I could not get her to believe she was demon possessed. Neither could I get her to admit that God was real. She had no explanation for what had happened. I figured she needed more convincing. One night while I was talking to her by phone, I was purposely agitating the demon to get it to manifest itself. I believed if I could only prove to her that she was possessed, she would seek deliverance and ask God for the gift of salvation through Jesus Christ.

I said, "I'll bet Satan felt like a fool when he had Jesus crucified and found out that he had done exactly what God intended. He crucified Jesus and fulfilled God's plans. Jesus became Christ and the disciples received the Holy Ghost. Then Satan had to contend with all the disciples running around doing the works of Jesus." I was laughing now and I said, "I know Satan felt like a fool." Joan made no response.

I continued, "I wonder how all the demons feel to know that they are doomed? They have absolutely no hope for forgiveness. I know they feel stupid. Can you imagine how dumb they feel to know they have blown it? They were in heaven, and were cast out. They have lived for thousands of years. Yet, I wonder how does it feel to know that their time is short? How do they feel knowing that Jesus will soon return and they will be cast into the lake of fire? I mean, although man may not realize what is going on, the devil knows that time is short. How terrible it must feel to know that you are doomed, and you have absolutely no hope for survival?" It was more than the demon could stand.

Joan had grown quieter and quieter. Now she began to laugh. Immediately, I knew my plan was working. The demon was taking control. Her voice had changed slightly. It had a mocking evil tone that always tried to make you feel like the demon knew something you didn't. It was not however, the deep voice that Hollywood makes you believe.

The demon said through her, "Fool. You fool." I told the demon he was the fool, he was doomed to eventually spend an eternity in hell. The demon began to curse me, and curse God. The demon began to threaten me. I threatened to cast him out. I said, "I'm going to cast you out of her, you foul devil, in the name of Jesus. God has given me power over you!"

I can't remember exactly what the demon said next. When I mentioned God again, it began to blaspheme more. The demon spoke about God in such a way that no human would ever consider. Its hatred of God was so real. The demon began to speak as if it was remembering its personal pain at the hands of the Almighty. It was obvious it was remembering God not as a concept, but as an ancient enemy. I marveled at the way the demon spoke. I knew this was real because no human could have conceived to blaspheme God in this manner. The scientist in me took over for a second. I began to think, "I am talking to one of the oldest beings in the universe. Imagine what glorious things it has witnessed." For a moment, I wondered if I could get it to tell me about heaven or creation.

I quickly dismissed the idea, remembering it's hatred of God was too great. I realized it was spiritually unhealthy to seek any kind of cooperation with a demon. I knew the demon hated all of mankind and because of its hatred, it would seek to destroy me if possible. I knew if I allowed my curiosity to get the best of me, I would be risking opening myself up inadvertently to the demon, to be deceived myself. I also realized that I could not believe anything a demon said, because they specialize in lying and deceiving. I realized that it was also possible that Satan had engineered this train of thought in my head, to trick me into opening myself up to him. If this was true, he would try to place some type of demonic spirit on me. I decided to banish all thoughts of cooperation with the demon for my own safety.

Suddenly, I noticed Joan was breathing as if she was coming out of a trance. She sounded as if she was very sick. I called her name softly like when you are trying to wake someone up. I called her several more times.

She said, as if she were about to faint, "I've got to go," and hung up the phone.

The next day, I caught the bus from Ann Arbor back to Pontiac. I went to the high school, anxious to talk to her about what happened.

When I repeated the story, she said, "You liar! You liar!" She looked terribly hurt and had tears in her eyes. She said, "How can you call yourself a Christian and tell lies like that?" She looked angry, hurt, and in total disbelief.

I said to myself, "Either this girl is a great Hollywood actress or the demon took her memory from her." I said, "All right devil. Fool me once, shame on you. Fool me twice shame on me."

Next week, I did the same thing and got the demon to talk. This time, I had a telephone recording device hooked up to my phone. It worked perfectly. I allowed many of my friends and associates to hear this tape. I came back to Pontiac the next day and confronted her. I asked her if she was still an atheist. She said yes. I asked her did she believe in demons? She said no. I said, "Well listen to this" and played the tape. While listening, a look of angry resolution came upon her. To my surprise, she said she knew it all the time. She also claimed she knew I was recording the conversation (I didn't believe that.) I told her she had to get delivered from this demon. I told her if she didn't get this demon cast out, it would destroy her. It was a strong possibility, it would drive her insane. If she died while possessed, she would certainly go to hell. I told her the demon would never leave on its own. I pleaded with her to get the demon cast out, but she refused. She claimed she didn't want the demon cast out, because she believed it gave her more power in her witchcraft. I could not accept this, so I still continued to pray for her.

A few weeks later, one of my classes at the University of Michigan was canceled. Coming back from class, I began to wonder what could I do with these two additional hours. I decided to go back to my dormitory, and go into my prayer closet and pray for Joan. I was on a personal crusade to save her, believing that I was probably her last hope to lead her to salvation. I knew the devil would never leave her on its own. I had tried everything I knew to do. I figured by terrorizing the demon, I could drive it out. Since reason had failed, I believed this was my last hope. I decided I was going to use my faith to the utmost to drive the demon out. I went to my room claiming this promise,

Matthew 9:29   .. According to your faith be it unto you.

I went in my closet and began to pray. I began by praising the Lord. Within a few moments, I felt the presence of the Lord. I said, "You foul devil that is living inside of Joan (not her real name), I take authority over you in the name of Jesus. I command you to lose your hold over her in the name of Jesus. There is no distance in prayer. I speak to you as if you are right here. These fifty miles mean nothing. I command you to come out of her now. You cannot ignore me. I have power over you. I know you are in class with her right now, but you must come out."

I continued to pray this way for about twenty minutes. Suddenly the phone began to ring. I wondered, "Who can that be? It must be a wrong number, because everyone that has my number knows that I'm always in class during this time." Then I went back to praying. The phone never stopped ringing. After a few minutes of continual ringing I said, "That phone is ringing like someone knows I'm in here. Then it dawned on me. I said, "Nah, it couldn't be." I stopped praying and said, "If the phone rings ten more times, I'll know it is her." I counted the rings, "One, two, three, four, five...nine, ten. I picked up the phone.

Before I could say hello, the voice on the other end shouted, **"STOP IT! STOP IT! STOP IT! LEAVE ME ALONE!"** It was Joan. Her voice changed to a pleading, "Leave me alone! Leave me alone! I'm not bothering you. Leave me alone!"

I never could persuade her to let me cast the devil out. She wanted to keep it. Although I had power to torment the demon, the Lord would not allow the demon to be cast out without her permission. Jesus said, when a demon is cast out, it always returns. If a person lets the demon back in, he will bring seven more demons with it more wicked than the first. The latter end would be worse than the beginning.

Since that time, I have had numerous experiences with demons. I have cast many demons out of people. My congregation has witnessed this many times. We have seen many supernatural events while we cast demons out. We have watched people squirm like snakes, make inhuman sounds, spit up blood, pieces of flesh, and other strange things. One girl jumped backwards over two rows of chairs, and walked up the wall. Many times people ask me am I scared when these things happen. The answer is no!

Usually when the Lord anoints me to cast out a devil, it feels like an angry Superman is on the inside. When the power of God rises up in you this way, it is literally the greatest feeling upon this earth. Nothing compares to it. There is such animosity between the demon and the Holy Ghost that it feels like a dog going after a cat. The Holy Ghost becomes indignant. Just as I feel the Holy

Spirit's power and righteous indignation, those who are possessed feel the demon's abject terror and pain. They scream with loud voices and convulse in pain as the demons come out. (I will be writing more about demons in a forthcoming book.)

Satan and his demons are real. Satanic worship and witchcraft are dangerous. If you open yourself up to demons, they will possess you. They will never leave you unless they are forcibly cast out. If you let the devil in, he will make you miserable. Many people are turning to these evil practices, seeking after power and blessings. If you receive Christ and get filled with His Holy Spirit, you will have power.

> **Luke 10:19   Behold, I give unto you power to tread on serpents and scorpions, and over all the power of the enemy: and nothing shall by any means hurt you.**

Not only will the Lord give you power but He will bless you if you serve Him.

> **Psalms 37:4   Delight thyself also in the LORD; and he shall give thee the desires of thine heart.**

Anyone who worships Satan should not be admired. Parents should not allow their children to buy records or listen to anyone who worships or encourages worship of Satan, no matter who they are. You should not admire these Hollywood whores and whoremongers who are contributing to the breakdown of our society.

> **Revelation 21:8   But the fearful, (those afraid to take a stand for Christ) and unbelieving, and the abominable, and murderers, and whoremongers, and sorcerers, and idolaters, and all liars, shall have their part in the lake which burneth with fire and brimstone: which is the second death.**

One Sunday morning while I was ministering, I saw a strange sight. I looked up and saw my father's face appear over the face of one the men in my church. Then he changed back to normal. Then he changed back to my father. This happened several times. Now my father had been dead for five years. Needless to say, to use this expression, this totally freaked me out. I said, "Lord! What is this? The Lord spoke to me and said, "This is the very same demon that was assigned to your father, day and night. He was assigned by Satan to torment your mother to try to discourage her, to keep her ministry form coming forth, and thereby stop your ministry from coming forth. As I watched this demon spirit, the Lord allowed me to see the power of the spirit. I could see the spirit was so powerful, that my father could not resist it. Oh, he could resist it sometimes, but because this was constant pressure from the demon, because he thought these were his own thoughts and emotions, he was bound to give in many times. The Lord also explained to me, that almost no one could resist that kind of pressure.

At this moment, a wound was healed in me concerning my father. I loved him, but I had never understood some of the evil things that he did. I unknowingly had still harbored some bad feelings toward him, because I believed the things he did was unexcusable. I thought about the many times as a boy I watched him make my mother cry, and I wished there was something I could do about it. Now I realized, he was an unwitting pawn of the devil, in this war between Satan and God.

The Lord also revealed to me that this demon spirit was going to begin to place some of its memories of my father upon this brother. The Lord also explained to me, "This is how the devil fools people into believing in reincarnation. He places the demonic memories of people from the demon's past and places them upon their present victims. When this happens, people think a past life intruding upon them. All this was something that I had never considered, and finally it explained some of my father's strange behavior.

My father was like two different people. He never drank or did drugs. At times, he was the perfect father. He loved and constantly played with his children. Yet, there were other times when he was unbelievably mean and inconsiderate. He did not drink alcohol or do drugs, so there was no explanation for his seeming split personality, other than he could be very mean. There was no sexual or physical abuse, just sometimes extreme cruelty. One of the worst things he did happened on a particular Christmas Day.

This particular day everything seemed to be fine. He and my mother had bought toys and clothes for all eight of the children. My mother had slaved all night, and prepared this big Christmas dinner. There were all types of dishes, cakes, pies, and a huge ham. It was more than enough to feed the ten of us. We were getting ready to eat. My mother took my father his food. He asked her where was his corn bread. I was standing next to her. She was taking the corn bread out of the stove.

He said, "How many times do I have to tell you to bring me my corn bread with my food?

He jumped up and tipped the kitchen table over. The food fell on the floor. The dishes broke. All my sisters started screaming and crying. My mother looked at the ham and said to herself, "Well. At least I can pick the ham up and wash it off, so we will have something to eat."

My father picked up the ham, took it outside, and fed it to dog. Then he left. We had nothing to eat. It was Christmas Day, and everything was closed. There was no place to buy anything to eat. My mother had to call my grandmother to come and bring us some food. She did not have much, but she brought what she had. Everybody went to bed that night, hungry and crying.

I do not wish to go into other things that he did here. I used to promise myself over and over again, that when I grew up, I would never treat my wife or children the way he did us.

Sometimes, when my mother would question him why he did these things, he used to say a curious thing. He would say, "I do what my 'mind' tells me to do." We used to ask him what did he mean.

He would repeat it. He said, "I do what my 'mind' tells me to do." We could not understand what he was talking about. He spoke of his mind as though it was different from him. What we did not know, this 'mind', was not his mind at all. It was this demon speaking in his mind, impersonating his thoughts, and emotionally driving him to do things which he normally would not have done. He did not recognize these thoughts were the devil. If he would have resisted, Satan would not have been able to influence him.

I remembered something that happened when I was a little boy. I am the oldest of eight children. I was in the sixth grade at the time. My father and mother were having a bitter argument. Although I had seen them have many arguments over the years, there was an extreme bitterness and hatred to this argument. It was not unusual for them to throw things against the wall in bitter arguments. I was deeply alarmed for this time, it seemed that they were could kill one another. Just a few days before my mother had told me, "If you see me and your father in a real bad argument, begin to pray." I began to pray, "Lord something is wrong. Show me what is wrong!"

The Lord opened my eyes and I saw something appear. It was a dark shadowy man that appeared. He was sitting in a chair directly across from me. The hair stood up on my skin as a cold chill went through my body. His legs were crossed and he began to smile with glee, as he watched my father and mother argue. I realized he was causing this argument and he was trying to make one of them kill the other. What kind of inhuman monsters are they that they could rejoice as they attempted to make one of parents kill each other and leave eight orphaned children? I felt all of our lives hung in the balance.

I leaned over to my sisters sitting next to me. I told them to pray because I had just seen a devil and he was making our parents argue. I told them, "Pray before something really bad happens. Really, really pray." We began to pray, and in a few minutes, the argument ceased.

I thought about all the misery that my family had endured over the years. I realized more than ever, more than 90% of the pain that I had experienced in my life was because of Satan. I thought about how many more families have been wrecked because of Satan and his demons. How many more men and women unknowingly yield to Satan and cause those they love, needless grief?

Now, this same demon that had tormented our family, was now on this brother in my church, trying to destroy him. I thought about all the misery the devils cause, how many billions of lives they ruin. Although I had said it many times, it never was more angry at Satan than that moment and I said, "I hate the devil."

I went to his wife and told her that I had seen the demon on her husband. I explained everything. I warned her that she was going to have to pray like she had never prayed before. I warned her that here husband was going to start doing some of the evil things that my father had done.

Almost overnight, this man had changed. He became very mean. Two days later, he came over my house and said a strange thing. Now my father had been a numbers runner for many years. He said, "I feel like I'm your Daddy. Give me a number. I want to play a number. Give me a number."

I was shocked! Even though I was mindful of what God had shown me, I could not believe it. He actually told me, he felt like he was my father! I was outraged. I said, "What is the matter with you? You know I don't give out numbers!"

He acted as if he had forgotten that. He said, "Oh yeah, that's right."

His condition worsened over the following weeks and months, and he went insane. He became a different person. Eventually after many prayers and a long ordeal, God delivered this brother. He never received treatment at a mental hospital or took any medication. God completely healed him. The brother later told me that while this was going on, although he had never met or seen my father, he began to take on his memories.

I have had many encounters with demons. I have cast demons out of many people. Demons are more real than you know. Some of their doings are subtle, others are blatant. Many people will dismiss talk of demons as ridiculous. They should heed the words of the serial killer who was called the Hillside Strangler. He killed over twenty people in California. He told his captors, "You think I'm crazy don't you? You don't know the power of Satan."

Another famous demon-possessed murderer was Charles Manson. He and his Manson family shocked the world with their grisly murder of actress Sharon Tate. One of his former followers, Susan Atkins wrote in her book about her initial meeting with Charles Manson. He had been a pimp with a fear of black people. He told her that he could postulate something in his mind and it would happen. She did not believe him. He said, "Watch this." He said, "I want someone to come up and give me a quarter."

A man came from down the street and told Manson, "I don't know why, but I feel that I should give you a quarter."

Manson did not know that when he thought he was using mental power, he was merely allowing himself to be possessed and used by demons. Susan Atkins listened to Manson talk and came under his spell. She thought that no one had ever spoke like him. Impressed by his talk and their free love, Atkins joined Manson's group of followers which they called the Manson family.

Manson heard the Beatles song of "Helter Skelter" and his paranoia of black people increased. He thought the Beatles were sending messages to him through their music. He became convinced there would be a great war between black people and white people, killing 1/3 of the population. During this time, Manson and his followers would hid out in the desert. He was convinced that the black people would kill all the white people in the world. Manson believed that once the blacks had conquered the world, they would be unable to run it. Manson believed, He and his band of misfits would emerge from the desert, 144,000 strong, and offer to show the black people how to run the world. He believed the black people would gladly accept his offer, and become the willing servants of Manson and his white followers. Manson took his followers to hide out in the desert. He expected to emerge after the war and take over whatever what was left.

Eventually, he decided the war was taking to long to occur. He thought black people were so stupid, that he had to show them how to do it. He decided to have his followers commit terrible murders and pretend like black people had done it. (Perhaps Satan thought he would use Manson to start a race riot.)

The Manson family broke in actress Sharon Tate's home and killed everyone in it. Sharon Tate was eight months pregnant at the time, but they had no mercy on her. They killed her and her unborn child. They wrote on the walls with her own blood, "Death to the pigs." They even carved out her vagina to further incite the police. Susan Atkins tasted the murdered actress' blood.

Somehow they were caught. Initially, many of Manson's girls agreed to testify against him. However when the trial came up and the girls faced him, it was a different story. Manson looked at them, (probably some of his demons flew to the girls) and they totally changed. They refused to co-operate with the prosecution. They shaved their heads bald and carved an X in their foreheads in protest. They were all found guilty. Manson is serving multiple life sentences for the crimes.

He has been interviewed many times by television hosts from prison. To most people, his talk sounds like the ravings of a madman. Unfortunately, there are many people who think otherwise. Today he gets over a pound of mail daily from admirers. They range from people asking Manson to give them direction, to asking for autographs. There was even one thirteen year old, who wrote Manson and told him, he could come and live with her, if he ever got out. How did Manson get so posessed? When Manson thought he was gaining new power, he was only opening himself up to be used by Satan.

The demons are using the New Age Movement, humanism, evolution, metaphysics and many other false doctrines, and religions, to prepare the world for Satan's last great thrust. When people allow themselves to go deeper and deeper in sin, they are yielding themselves to the devil. Satan does not always use his forces to do such obvious evil as ritual murders. However, the end result is the same, destruction of human souls.

Unfortunately, satanism and witchcraft are increasing. More and more ritual murders are being discovered across America.

Satanism will continue to increase and will reach its zenith under the antichrist. Eventually Satan will use his power to help the Beast deceive the world. He will anoint his mouth and use power to sway the masses. The Beast will deceive many and cause them to worship Satan and follow him into hell.

Just as the devil has prepared things politically, he is preparing the spiritual conditions for the most evil ruler of all time. Hitler was just the warm-up. This man will be the real thing. He will be the anti-Christ, or the Beast, but during his reign, most of the world will be deceived and think he is wonderful, as he leads them to Armageddon.

Chapter 19

1 Thessalonians 5:3   For when they shall say, Peace and safety; then sudden destruction cometh upon them, as travail upon a woman with child; and they shall not escape.

The Principal Players

1. The Beast
2. The kingdom of the Beast
3. Babylon the Great
4. Israel
5. Russia

The Man's A Beast

Who is the Beast? He is a man. According to Daniel 9:26, he is a descendant of the people who would come to destroy the city and temple. The Roman General Titus did this in 67 A.D. This would make the Beast a Roman. He will be the most wicked man in history. Through peace, he shall destroy many. He shall deceive wonderfully. His power and authority will come from Satan. He will seem invincible. Multitudes of people will worship him and openly worship Satan also.

Revelation 13:4   And they worshipped the dragon which gave power unto the beast: and they worshipped the beast, saying, Who is like unto the beast? who is able to make war with him?

He was once a ruler of the Roman Empire. At the time of the writing of the book of Revelation, he was dead. He will ascend out of hell and live again (Rev. 17:11)

Revelation 17:8 The beast that thou sawest was, and is not; and shall ascend out of the bottomless pit, and go into perdition: and they that dwell on the earth shall wonder, whose names were not written in the book of life from the foundation of the world, when they behold the beast that was, and is not, and yet is.

Revelation 17:11 And the beast that was, and is not, even he is the eighth, and is of the seven, and goeth into perdition.

As you can see, the Beast is a king who was alive, but dead at the time of this writing. He is a man whose foul deeds caused him to be condemned to hell. He will arise out of hell, and live again. He will worship the devil and many people will be aware of this and worship the devil with him. His number is 666.

Many 1st century Christians believed that the Beast would be Nero Caesar. Nero ordered Rome burned, then he blamed it on the Christians. He had Christians tied to stakes and doused in oil. Then they were set on fire to light the gardens. He had the Apostle Paul killed and the Apostle Peter. He was the first Caesar to officially persecute Christians. However, there is another reason why they believed Nero would one day become the Beast. In greek and aramaic languages, each letter has a numerical value. Nero is the only Caesar, whose name in both the greek and aramaic equal 666.

Whoever the Beast really is, doesn't matter. What matters is what he will do. He will be the most evil man in history. Yet, many will think he is a messiah. Some Bible scholars believe that the body the Beast will inhabit will be that of a Jew. According to these Bible scholars, the Jews receive the Beast or the anti-Christ as their messiah. The Jews will never accept a gentile as their Messiah, therefore they argue, the Beast must be a Jew. While this is plausible, there is not sufficient Biblical evidence for me to agree with their position.

The Beast will be a demonic workaholic, so consumed with destruction that he will not regard the desire of women. He will arise out of the pit of hell, gain power and lead the world to Armageddon. Who he was before, is really not that important. What is important is what he will do, and the fact that he is probably already here.

The Kingdom of The Beast

We know from Daniel and John the Revelator where the kingdom of the Beast comes from.

Daniel 9:26   And after threescore and two weeks shall Messiah be cut off, but not for himself: and the *people of the prince* that shall come shall destroy the city and the sanctuary; and the end thereof shall be with a flood, and unto the end of the war desolations are determined.

Here, Daniel prophesied that after the Messiah is killed, the City of Jerusalem and the temple would be destroyed. He accurately foretold of the devastation that would be caused by the Roman Army. If more Jews were aware of this scripture, they would realize that Jesus is the Christ. If they believe Daniel was a prophet, then they must believe that the Messiah had to be killed **before** the destruction of the temple, and the end of the war of the Jews.

According to Daniel, the anti-christ is a Roman and his kingdom is the remnant of the Roman Empire. In Nebuchadnezzar's dream, the LORD showed him of coming empires.

Nebuchadnezzar saw a statue of a man with a head of gold, his breast and arms were made of silver, his belly and thighs were made of brass, his legs were made of iron and his feet were made of iron and clay. There was a stone that appeared that was cut out, but not with the hands of man. It struck the statue on the toes and broke it in pieces. Not a trace of the statue was left. The gold, silver, brass, iron, and clay was completely obliterated. The stone became a mountain that filled the entire earth.

This statue represented different world empires. No kingdom has ever truly conquered the entire world, yet these succeeded in conquering the known world during their time. Although there were many empires besides these four, none have ever been considered to rule the world. Many have come close and made valiant attempts, but only these empires were considered to have ruled the world, since God gave Nebuchadnezzar this dream.

Nebuchadnezzar, himself, was the head of gold. The silver represented the Medo-Persian Empire that followed Nebuchadnezzar. The brass empire represented the Greek Empire. True to Daniel's prophecy, the Greeks conquered the world. The iron legs represented the Roman Empire, which was divided into east and west. Iron was used to describe this kingdom because of its strength. As iron breaks all things and subdues all things, so does this kingdom.

There is one empire yet to come. It is an uneasy mix of iron and clay. It is a remnant of the Roman Empire. It will be partly strong and partly divided. As iron and clay do not mix well, so it will be with these kingdoms. It will be a ten nation confederacy.

The Roman Empire is being reunited today, in the form of the European Economic Community. Like Daniel's vision, they are a loose confederation of nations. Their purpose is to integrate the economies of Europe. It was founded in 1957. The founding members, called the signatories of the TREATY OF ROME were, Belgium, France, Italy, Luxembourg, the Netherlands and West Germany. Its headquarters are in Brussels Belgium. The founders of the EEC (European Economic Community) hoped that the member countries would one day form a single political unit. The EEC allows other nations to be associate members. It presently has agreements with 64 African, Caribbean, and Pacific Nations. These nations have signed reciprocal trade agreements with the EEC. The EEC is well on its way to becoming the dominant economic power in the world.

The EEC is scheduled to unite in 1992. They have decided that all products must bear their seal. Any EEC nation or associate member must have the EEC seal on every product that will be sold in the EEC. In September of 1990, the EEC finished designing this seal, which every product must have. What did the EEC decide to call this seal? To my surprise, they don't call it a seal, a product code, but the EEC mark. Without this mark, the products will not be honored by the EEC. Is this the forerunner to the mark of the Beast? The irony is almost unbelievable.

The EEC has been working hard to harmonize the tax systems, social insurance, and the welfare programs of their countries. They have developed a common agricultural policy for the member nations. On October 29, the EEC agreed to go to one currency in 1994. They already have elected someone to be president of the EEC. One day, the EEC will unknowingly elect the Beast as leader or president of the EEC. Whether or not president will be his official title, I do not know.

Currently, there are twelve nations that are full members of the EEC. Other nations have applied for membership such as Turkey but were turned down. The EEC may allow other nations to join, but eventually it will end up with ten. Some of the individual nations could merge as East and West Germany did, to make the ten nations. Otherwise, they will withdraw, or be expelled. Daniel 7:8 tells us there will be a war within the group, and three nations will be destroyed by the Beast. It is not clear if the rebellion occurs while there are ten nations, or while there are thirteen and the rebellion reduces the number to ten.

MYSTERY BABYLON THE GREAT

The Beast will come in power due to the help of Mystery Babylon the Great. The Great Whore rules from a city that rules over the kings of the earth. The question is in what time period does this Scripture refer to. If it was during the time of the writing, then the city is clearly Rome. If it referred to today, then it would be New York city, home of the United Nations.

Babylon is described as a religious organization and economic center. Some people feel there are actually two Babylons, a religious one, and a political one.

Some Bible scholars believe that a new Babylon will be built on the site of the original one. Ancient Babylon is located in Iraq, twenty miles from Baghdad. Saddam Hussien has been trying to rebuild ancient Babylon. He has spent millions on the restoration of ancient Babylon, trying to restore it to its former glory. Saddam has tried to portray himself as the modern day version of Nebuchadnezzar, the ruler of ancient Babylon. There are billboards in Iraq that show Nebuchadnezzar standing over anceint Babylon reaching over across the centuries to shake hands with Saddam Hussien standing over Iraq. Saddam has tried to make the Arab world believe he is the next great Arab leader. Many Arabs did side with him in the Gulf War. Despite his humiliating defeat in the recent Gulf War, Saddam and his brutal regime have managed to survive to the surprise over much of the world.

With the rise of Iraq's military and political power in recent years, some believe that ancient Babylon will indeed rise again. I do not believe this is the case, however. John called it Mystery Babylon. A mystery is something that is not known. It is hidden and is anything but obvious. Therefore, it is highly unlikely that the obvious Babylon is Mystery Babylon. Because Babylon is a mystery, it may be a mystery to that city and the world until the end. Another reason I do not believe that Babylon will be rebuilt in Iraq, is because of the time factor.

I believe that Jesus is soon to return. During the Gulf War, much of Iraq was destroyed. Most of Iraq's infrastructure was destroyed. Baghdad has been bombed. For some time, Iraq will be busy rebuilding its roads, bridges, sewage and water treatment plants, power plants, oil refineries and recovering from the other forms of devastation caused by the war. While Saddam and his regime are evil enough to be the leaders of the Great Whore, Babylon the Great, it is highly unlikely that Babylon could be rebuilt in time, and replace such economically powerful cities such as New York, Tokyo, London or others in such a short time. If the Lord delays His coming and Iraq does rise to economic prominence that would be another story.

Is the Whore A Church?

Many Bible scholars have believed the headquarters of the religious organization that will aid the Beast, will be in Rome. Though the Great Whore presides and consist of many peoples, nations and tongues, its headquarters is located in a city that is surrounded by seven mountains. Rome is the only city, that has historically been identified as the city of seven mountains. Romans have bragged that it is the city that sits on seven mountains. During the Apostle John's time, it was the city that ruled over the world and the kings of the earth. If a world-wide religious organization that becomes the Great Whore is headquartered in Rome, the obvious choice here would be the Roman Catholic Church. The Roman Catholic Church is world-wide in scope, consisting of many peoples, nations and tongues.

Some would question, "If the Whore is drunk on the blood of the saints, how can it possibly be the Roman Catholic Church?" The answer, in centuries past, many Christians accused of heresy, have been killed under the direction of the Catholic Church.

They cite the pagan practices that infiltrated the church. They charge the prayers to different saints, the prayers to Mary are disguised forms of idolatry, which cause millions of souls to be lost. Mary is called the Queen of heaven, Mother of God, Blessed Virgin, and Holy Mother. These are all titles originally given to Semiramis, wife of Nimrod. They argue that the Catholic teaching that Mary is the queen of heaven is a new, disguised form, of the centuries old pagan practice of worshipping Semiramis. Because of these and other reasons, there are many who believe the Roman Catholic Church is the Great Whore. (Some Catholics think the Protestant Church is or will become the Great Whore).

It is possible that a new organization consisting of various denominations (Catholic and Protestant), and other non-christian religions, will form a new ecclesiastical body that will be head-quartered in Rome.

There is another interpretation that is gaining acceptance. Many people now believe that Mystery Babylon is New York City and the Great Whore is the United States of America. The amount of evidence for this interpretation is surprising. The original Babylon was the leader of the world. It was a place of great learning. Their technology was increasing. So much learning that God said in time, they will be able to do whatever they can imagine to do.

The Great Whore will be a great ally to the Western European powers that will become the kingdom of the Beast. Western Europe has no greater friend than the United States. Eventually there is a split between the nations of the Beast and the Great Whore. The U.S government certainly will not agree with all the heinous things that the kingdoms of the Beast will do. There would certainly be a split.

In the prophecies of the end, all the modern world powers are described, but one. Russia, Arab Nations, Israel, Europe and even Asian Nations. The accuracy is incredible, yet every world power is described except one; the U.S. It is unlikely that God would have left out a superpower such as the U.S.

Either the U.S. is destroyed, not a factor (becoming extremely isolationist) or we cannot find it. It is possible that the U.S is destroyed in the war that occurs when Russia invades Israel. 5/6 of the force that invades Israel is destroyed. During the start of the tribulation 1/4 of the worlds population dies. The U.S. comprises only 5% of the worlds population.

Perhaps we could not find the U.S. in the prophecies, because it was in the one place we were afraid to look. Let us look at the evidence for the United States being the Great Whore and Mystery Babylon.

Is The U.S Babylon?

The Bible prophesies concerning Babylon are very specific. Jeremiah prophesied of the destruction of Babylon in Jeremiah, chapters 50 and 51. Many of the prophesies were fulfilled. However, there was another Babylon that would be destroyed that did not fit the descriptions of ancient Babylon.

1. It is a land of many waters. The U.S is bounded by two oceans, Gulf of Mexico, and we have four major rivers, and the Great Lakes, the largest concentration of fresh water in the world. Ancient Babylon (Iraq) is mostly desert.

2. Future Babylon would be destroyed by a nation from its north. Ancient Babylon was destroyed by a Medo-Persian Empire from its east.

3. It is a nation with mixed people in it. The U.S. is a nation of immigrants (mixed people).

4. Future Babylon would mount itself into heaven. Is this a reference to the U.S. space program?

5. Future Babylon would be a people terrible from their beginning until the time of their judgement. The U.S has never lost a war. We are truly a people terrible from our beginnings.

6. Future Babylon will be one of the wealthiest nations and cities in the world. The U.S. is extremely wealthy.

7. Future Babylon would be one of the most prestigious cities in the world. Many of the wealthiest and most prestigious men in the world will live there. This certainly fits New York City. Many foreign leaders and businessmen have apartments in New York.

8. Future Babylon would become so desolate that no man will ever live there again. It will be so polluted that no one would even take a stone from there. Only nuclear bombs could destroy and poison a city in this manner.

The description of Babylon in Revelation 18 could very well be the economic capital of the U.S, New York, N.Y. The descriptions of Babylon fit New York perfectly.

1. It is the economic capital of Babylon and the world.
2. It is the greatest city on earth.
3. Many people around the world have been made rich through dealings in Babylon.

4. In Babylon you can buy everything, all types of merchandise including men can be bought. On the New York stock exchange, you can by everything in the world. When you buy a company, you are buying men.

5. It is known, among other things for its entertainment with trumpeters and musicians.

6. The Apostle John predicted that future Babylon would be destroyed in one hour. Before the coming of atomic bombs, it was not possible to destroy a city in one hour. The city of Rome burned for six days. Babylon will be destroyed with great fire and brimstone.

7. Babylon is proud and believes herself to be indestructible.

8. The City of Babylon will be seen from the sea by sailors who have traded with her and made themselves rich.

9. The **lamp** (King James version of the Bible incorrectly translates it candle) will no longer shine in the city of Babylon, (A reference to the Statue of Liberty?)

As previously stated, the Bible says the woman sits on seven mountains (Rev 17:9). Rome is the only city that has been known for being built on seven mountains. The question is does Babylon the Great rest on them literally and geographically or is it a descendant of Rome? The U.S does in a sense, rest on seven mountains or Rome. It does not rest geographically of course, but historically and philosophically. It was even founded by one of the kingdoms of ancient Rome (Britain). The Roman Empire changed the course of history and founded western civilization. Today, the United States is the leader of the western world. While the U.S does not rest on the seven mountains geographically, it does in many other ways.

Ancient Babylon participated in child sacrifice. The Babylon today participates in child sacrifice. Instead of stone altars, the altars are on operating tables. The high priests are doctors and the false god's name is personal freedom. Instead of a few hundred, today's Babylon has killed 27 million innocent babies, and the serpent is glad.

Jesus told His generation that He was holding them responsible for all the righteous blood that was spilled from Abel to Zechariah son of Barachias, who died just a few years before Jesus. That was four thousand years of persecuted righteous blood that they had to pay for. Even though they had not killed all those righteous men, the work of four thousand years was culminated in the coming of Christ. By rejecting Christ, they were rejecting God and the work of four thousand years of God and His servants. Because they did not accept the blessings, they had to take the curse. Therefore, God required the blood of the righteous men of that generation.

America was founded by Christians who wanted the freedom to worship God as they saw fit. Today, the U.S media protest whenever Israel has a skirmish with Arabs in the West Bank. Yet, Christians have been persecuted and killed in Arab countries and the government and the media look the other way. In Egypt, you cannot get a job if you have a Christian name. In 1987 in Diem in Sudan, 1,000 Christians were killed. [10]The *Baptist Record* newspaper on November 5, 1987, reported that dozens of pastors have been killed and many churches destroyed since Islamic law was imposed in 1983, when Sudan was officially declared an Islamic republic.

Christians had been persecuted in every Arab country. Many of them fled to Lebanon for safety as the last safe place for them in the Arab world. Since 1982, Muslims have been trying to eliminate Christians in Lebanon. The U.S government looked the other way while Assad's Syrian forces eliminated 1,000 Christians in Lebanon. This was done to get Assad's cooperation in the Gulf Crisis with Iraq.

Christian missionaries have been exterminated in many communist countries, in Europe, South America, Africa and Asia. Yet, this is of little concern to the U.S government or the media.

Undoubtedly America has not lived up to its spiritual responsibility. Separation of church and state is not God's plan. God said righteousness exalts a nation, but sin is a reproach to any people. We have made many nations rich. We have Americanized much of the world. We have taken them the god of mammon (money), but not the God of Israel. Through Hollywood, we have exported our standards of indecency around the world. Like Babylon of old, we have espoused human government at the expense of human souls.

This country was founded by people who came here to worship their God in freedom. The nations original colleges, Yale, Princeton, Harvard, and others, started out as Bible schools. American missionaries have helped evangelize the world. The Bible was the text book in most of our schools when the nation was founded. Yet, we let ungodly atheists tell us that the founding fathers of America did not mean for prayer and Bible reading to be done in our schools.

---

[10] Anis A. Shorrosh, *Islam Revealed*, (Nashville: Thomas Nelson Publishers,1988) p.171

Some will take my words to mean that I am un-American, but I am not. Nor do I think America is the Great Satan that some leaders have called it. I think America is the greatest country on earth. No country in the history of the world has been as kind, and as giving to other nations. I am proud to be an American for many reasons.

Currently, democracy is the best form of government on earth. For a democracy to work however, its people must be educated and informed to make the right decisions. In many cases the public is totally uninformed in areas of righteousness. Hence, they many times make the wrong decisions concerning righteousness.

Proverbs 14:34 Righteousness exalteth a nation: but sin is a reproach to any people.

Many people hold up the Constitution of the United States above the Bible. They use the Constitution to justify their "right" to commit all manner of sins. Although the government may say you have a right to sin, God does not. Those that do, will face His judgement.

America is the leader of the free world, but we have failed to use our position to lead nations to Christ. Jesus said, "To whom much is given, much is required." The Bible says in Psalms 9:17, "The wicked shall be turned into hell, and all the nations that forget God."

During the recent 100 year anniversary of the Statue of Liberty, many statements were made that seemed to deify the statue. Statements were made such as "For a hundred years she has watched over us and protected us." It is God that has watched over America and protected it, not a lifeless statue. I am sure that very few if anyone believes the Statue of Liberty is a goddess. Yet, it is blasphemous to suggest it, and wrong not to acknowledge God's blessings.

Last year I rejoiced with the world as the Berlin wall fell, the European countries were freed from communist rule. In Eastern Europe, they had a great spiritual revival that led to this. This was largely uncovered by the press. For a while it looked like China was going to have similar success. We watched the students protesting in Tenniman Square. The students decided they needed a symbol to inspire the masses. They made a copy of the Statue of Liberty and paraded it down the street on a float. I was horrified to hear what they called it, the Goddess of Liberty.

Instead of realizing that this was a blessing from God, and the prayers of millions of Chinese Christians being answered, they seemed to imply that the statue was bringing them liberty. Some of the American media were obviously moved that our symbol of liberty inspired the Chinese. When I heard it, I knew the students and their movement was in trouble.

At times God can be what we would call, very sensitive. For instance, they said the Titanic was the unsinkable ship, it sunk on it's maiden voyage. We took prayer out of the school, dope, rape, assault, murder came in. Muhammad Ali reveled in his reflexes, great speed, said he was the Greatest, a title that should be reserved only for God. Now his reflexes are gone and he suffers in his body with a debilitating disease.

Proverbs 16:18   Pride goeth before destruction, and an haughty spirit before a fall.

God said, His glory He will not share with another. When I heard them call the statue the goddess, a wave of fear swept over me, because I knew they had offended God. I said in fear for the students, "Lord are you going to desert them now, because they have offended you?"

Unfortunately, a few days later, my fears were confirmed. God withdrew His protection and the devil came in. Thousands were massacred, the movement was dead, and many of the student leaders were in prison.

The United States started out as a Bride of Christ. Now it has committed spiritual fornication and is unquestionably a great whore. Is it the Great Whore of Revelation? Is the "lamp" in Revelations 18:23 "that will not shine anymore" in Babylon, a reference to the Statue of Liberty? Only time will tell.

It will be fairly easy to determine exactly who is the Great Whore during the time of the Great Tribulation. The Great Whore will be the Beast's chief ally during this time. Its headquarters will be in the economic capital of the world. If you live in whatever city it happens to be, once the Tribulation starts, get out of it.

The Last Generation?

We already know that we are living in the last years. Ezekiel prophesied that the Jews would be brought back into the land of Israel during the last years (Ezekiel 38:8). This happened May 14, 1948.

When the disciples ask Jesus what would be the signs of His coming and the end of the world, He told them many things, as recorded in Matthew 24. He listed many terrible things that would come upon the world. He also said, "Now learn a parable of the fig tree."

Matthew 24:32-34   Now learn a parable of the fig tree; When his branch is yet tender, and putteth forth leaves, ye know that summer is nigh:
33)   So likewise ye, when ye shall see all these things, know that it is near, even at the doors.
34)   Verily I say unto you, This generation shall not pass, till all these things be fulfilled.

You know that when the leaves are tender that summer is nigh. In other words, He was talking about the budding or the rebirth of the fig tree. God had begun to refer to Israel as a fig tree in Hosea 9:10 and Joel 1:7. In other words, we should look for the budding of the fig tree or the rebirth of Israel as a sign of His soon return.

He went on to say that this generation shall not pass, until all these things be fulfilled. If He was referring to Israel's rebirth as the start of the generation, then all the signs must be fulfilled before the generation passes. If He was not talking about the rebirth of Israel as the last generation, then He was talking about the other signs. The signs such as the sun turning black, the moon turning to blood, and the abomination of desolation, as the last generation.

As a matter of fact, we know from Daniel that it is not a complete generation, but only seven years before the world ends once the tribulation starts. Therefore, it seems that He would have used 7 years instead of a generation, if He was referring to the signs as the last generation.

Now, Jesus said no man knows the day or the hour of His return. However, I believe He was talking about the rapture of the church, here and not His visible return at Armageddon. We know from Revelations and the book of Daniel, when the armies of the world are gathered in Armageddon, that Jesus will return. We know from the book of Daniel when the abomination of desolation happens, we have 3 1/2 years till Jesus return.

While it is true Jesus said, no man knows the day or the hour of His return, (the rapture), He also said that this generation shall not pass till all these things have been fulfilled. What is a generation? To us today, a generation is 25 to 30 years. That is why some people erroneously predicted that Jesus had to come by 1988. They made the mistake of using our generation, instead of a Bible generation. But what was a Biblical generation?

The Bible says from Abraham to Jesus was 42 generations. Bible scholars agree that it was 2,166 years from Abraham to Christ. To figure out how long a generation was we simply divide the years (2,166) by the number of generations (42).

$$2{,}166 / 42 = 51.57 \text{ years}$$

That means if He was referring to the fig tree as Israel becoming a nation, then Jesus would return before the generation passes. The generation began May 14, 1948. If you add 51.57 years to it, that means the generation ends December 7, 1999. December 7 is the anniversary of the Japanese bombing of Pearl Harbor.

If the rebirth of Israel started the generation, then the entire 7 year tribulation has to be over with before Jesus returns. Jesus returns at the battle of Armageddon. That would mean, the Great Tribulation would have to start by December 7, 1992 and be over with in seven years. Now before you run out and spend all your money, please read the rest of this chapter, because there are other possibilities.

I believe the rapture of the Church happens at the 7 trumpet, just after the Abomination of Desolation and just before the wrath of God is poured out upon the earth.

During the great tribulation, more than 1/2 of the worlds population dies. All the fish in the sea will die. God sends many plagues upon the earth and the sun turns black and the moon turns to blood. The Jewish Temple will have to be rebuilt, and they will begin the daily sacrifice. Many Israelis believe it is no longer a question of will the Jewish Temple be built, but when. Time magazine carried a story about the Jews preparing to build the temple. They already have made the priestly garments. Jews are raising money for the solid gold menorah. To discover which Jews are from the tribe of Levi, they have search historical records in Europe. They have found some of the Levites, took the name Cohen.

Eventually, they will find out who is eligible or select someone to be a high priest. Many Orthodox Jews are determined to build the temple, no matter who it offends. The disturbance that led to the Temple Mount slayings, was prompted by Palestinians beliefs (real or imagined), that some Jews were surveying to build the Temple on Muslim holy sites. This prompted a riot that led to the killing of 19 Palestinians. It is unfortunate that Jews and Arabs do not believe in the Love of Christ and do not learn to love one another. Hate only begets more hate. Eventually, the Temple will be rebuilt despite all obstacles. When that happens, you will know that time will be short.

The Thousand Year Days

The Bible says, that in six days, God made the earth and on the seventh day He rested.

2 Peter 3:8   But, beloved, be not ignorant of this one thing, that one day is with the Lord as a thousand years, and a thousand years as one day.

This could mean that God will finish His work with man on the sixth day or after six thousand years. When will the six thousand years be up? A Jewish rabbi by the name of Usher, calculated the year of creation to be 4,004 B.C. by using the genealogical records mentioned in the Bible. If he is correct, that would mean the six days end during the year 1996. It is possible that Usher was a little off on his calculations or God does not have to finish to one of His cosmic minutes. He may go a minute or two over the six thousand years or He may go to the second, I do not know.

After the time of man is up, Christ will rule the earth for a thousand years or one day. During this time, there is no record of God doing anything, as if He were resting. If it is indeed the seventh day, that would make it the Sabbath day. Jesus said that He was Lord of the Sabbath day (Matt. 12:8). The Prophet Hosea said something that seems to indicate that God will finish His work with man on the seventh day.

Hosea 6:2   After two days will He revive us: in the third day He will raise us up, and we shall live in His sight.

If Usher is correct, Hosea said this during the fourth day. Hosea said after more than two days have passed, He (God) would revive us, (Israel). This happened in 1948 during the sixth day. This happened more than two days or two thousand years from when Hosea prophesied this. He then went on to say, in the third day, He would raise them up (from the dead) and we shall live in His sight (during the millennium).

Psalms 90:4   For a thousand years in thy sight are but as yesterday when it is past, and as a watch in the night.

When you consider, according to Ezekiel, that we are living in the last years (Ezek 38:8), and if we are indeed close to the end of six thousand years, it is reasonable to assume that God will end His working with men after six thousand years or six days. That will mean the 7 year tribulation would be over and the millennial reign of Christ will begin at the end of the sixth day.

There are several genealogical tables mentioned in the Bible. Although the records may have been complete when originally recorded, the texts that now exists have gaps in the genealogical records. Some of them have gaps where names are left out and others are put in. For this reason, Bible scholars are in disagreement on the age of the Earth. The estimates range from 6,000 to as high as 50,000 years.

Even if Usher is incorrect with the six thousand years, no more than three thousand years (3 days) could pass from the time of Hosea's prophecy before Christ could return. Hosea prophesied this 2,749 years ago in 758 B.C. According to Hosea, the Messiah must come sometime between now, and the next 251 years before 3 days pass from his prophecy. The polictial situations are almost perfect now, it is doubtful that they will remain correct for much longer. Besides, how much more sinful does the world need to get before it is worthy of being destroyed by God?

The Rapture

If you look for the word rapture in the Bible, you will not find it. The event is described but the word rapture is not found. The word rapture means to be caught up or to snatch away. The rapture is described in 1 Cor. 15:42-55, I Thes. 4:13-18, and Rev. 7:9-12. The rapture occurs when Jesus comes to the clouds and shouts with a great sound.

The dead in Christ rise first, and those who are alive at the time are immediately changed. The mortal puts on immortality. The corruption puts on incorruption. This is necessary because the Bible accurately says that flesh and blood cannot inherit the kingdom of God. Our frail, fragile bodies cannot live in outer space. Therefore, He will change our bodies into a form like the angels that can survive the rigors of space.

There is great debate among Christians about the time of the rapture. Some believe it occurs at the beginning of the Tribulation. Others believe it occurs during the middle, and some believe it occurs at the end of the great tribulation. The people who hold these positions are called pre-tribulationist, mid-tribulationist, and post-tribulationist. Sometimes, Christians of varying positions on the rapture, ridicule one another for their beliefs.

I myself who was once a pre-tribulationist, have heard others say, "Perhaps some are going through the tribulation, but I'm going before the tribulation." We must remember that the rapture is like waiting for a delayed flight. While none of us want to miss the flight out of here, it is important to remember that we cannot leave, until the plane comes and is ready to depart. No matter how badly you want the rapture to come in the beginning of the tribulation, you cannot leave until the rapture comes.

Many American Christians, who have never experienced life-threatening persecution for their stand for Christ, find it incomprehensible that God would allow His people to go through any of the tribulation. They are ignorant of the persecution, torture, and murder of Christians and missionaries in foreign lands.

Are today's Christians better than the early Christians, who were fed to the lions in the Roman arenas? Are we better than the disciples who were killed for their beliefs? Certainly not. Most Christians today are more concerned about paying bills, and making charge payments, than winning souls to Christ. To not allow the Christians to be here at all during the tribulation is like declaring a war and allowing your army to go AWOL. How can the devil make war on the saints and kill them if they are not here? Some people claim, there will be a great revival during the tribulation, and many souls will be won to the Lord. However, the scriptural evidence is to the contrary. The Bible says that despite all the plagues that God pours upon the earth, men still won't repent.

Paul by inspiration of the Holy Ghost said that the rapture would occur at the last trumpet. There are seven trumpets that are sounded in the book of Revelation. The last trumpet occurs in Revelations just before the wrath of God is poured out upon the earth. The last trumpet is the seventh trumpet. This occurs just after the abomination of desolation and just before the pouring of the seven golden vials. These vials or bowls are full of different plagues. These plagues are the Lord's wrath, which will be poured out upon the earth.

The great tribulation begins when the anti-christ signs a treaty with many nations. The abomination of desolation occurs in the middle of the tribulation. Paul wrote that the Church's gathering unto the Lord (rapture) will not occur until after the abomination.

2 Thessalonians 2:2   That ye be not soon shaken in mind, or be troubled, neither by spirit, nor by word, nor by letter as from us, as that the day of Christ is at hand.

2 Thessalonians 2:3   Let no man deceive you by any means: for that day shall not come, except there come a falling away first, and that man of sin be revealed, the son of perdition;

2 Thessalonians 2:4   Who opposeth and exalteth himself above all that is called God, or that is worshipped; so that he as God sitteth in the temple of God, showing himself that he is God.

Obviously, the Apostle Paul was reminding the saints of his previous visit and conversation with them. He told them not to worry if someone sends a false letter or someone comes and preaches that Jesus' coming and gathering the saints (rapture) has occurred. He said that day would not occur until after a great falling away and the abomination of desolation occurs. The abomination of desolation occurs in the middle of the tribulation. This means the Jewish Temple must be rebuilt before the middle of the Tribulation. The rapture will not occur until after the abomination and just before the wrath of God is poured out upon the earth.

He will leave the Church down here to try to win as many souls as possible before the end. The anti-christ will make war on the saints and overcome them. Many will be killed. The saints are instructed to have faith and patience. It is important for those who are still alive during the tribulation, to remain spiritual. You cannot allow hatred and murder to enter your hearts. God will avenge the blood of His servants upon the earth. In His fierce anger, He will pour out His wrath on the planet. Because He has not appointed us to wrath, He will rapture us before He pours out His bowls of wrath upon the earth.

HOW SOON?

These are the signs that let us know that the time of the end is fast approaching. The number one sign that lets us know that Jesus is soon to return is Israel becoming a nation. 3,500 years ago, Ezekiel prophesied this would happen in the latter years. It is amazing that all these things have occurred since Israel became a nation.

1. Israel becoming a nation. Ezek 38
2. Jews returning to Israel from around the world. Jer 31:8
3. A great immigration of Jews from Russia. Jer 16:14-15, Zech 2:6
4. Jerusalem returning into Jewish hands. Luke 21:24
5. Jerusalem being a burdensome stone to all nations. Zech 12:13
6. Israel returning to a desolate land and making it prosperous. Ezek 36:35, Amos 9:14
7. Israel becoming a leading exporter of fruit. Isaiah 27:6
8. The Generation Gap. Matt 10:36
9. The world-wide drug problem. Revelation describes sorcies and socerers increasing. The greek word for sorcery used her is pharmakos, from which comes our word pharmacy or drugs.
10. Pestilences-terrible diseases with no cure (AIDS, cancer and other diseases) Matt 24:7
11. Increase in heart attacks. Luke 21:26
12. Increase in earthquakes. Matt 24:7
13. Evil men and seducers growing worse and worse. This would include increase in crime rates and other acts of violence. 2 Tim 2:13
14. The rise of Russia (Gog and Magog) as a major world power. Ezek 38

15. Russia's close ties with Arab nations. Eventually Russia will lead an Arab invasion into Israel. Ezek 38

16. Increase in wars and threatening rumors of wars. Matt 24:6

17. The Roman confederation of nations uniting-- The EEC. Rev 13:11

18. The EEC has already made its seal, the EEC mark. All products sold in the EEC starting in 1992 must have this mark-the forerunner to the mark of the Beast.

19. False religions, false Christ, and false prophets on the rise. Luke 24:24

20. Distress among the nations because of huge, almost unsolvable problems. Economic, political, drugs, crime, over population, landfill problems, and other environmental problems. Luke 21:25

21. Since the end of the Cold War and the invasion of Kuwait, there has been a great deal of talk about the new world order. The media and the President of the United States and other world leaders have made repeated statements about this. This new world order are the nations acting in harmony.

22. Jewish preparations to rebuild the Temple. They have made the priestly garments and are raising money to build the solid gold menorah. They have searched through historical records in Europe and found out that some of the Levites took the name Cohen. They are trying to discover who can be the high priest. Presently, it is believed the Dome of the Rock stands on the site of the Jewish Temple. If it is discovered that this Muslim shrine is not on the correct site, the Temple could be rebuilt. It is possible the shrine could be destroyed in a war. The Israeli Supreme Court has forbid the government to destroy the shrine. However, most Israelis feel it is not a question of if the Temple will be rebuilt, only when. The Temple must be built by the middle of the Great Tribulation if not before.

23. Scientific Adavancement. According to Dan 12:4 the end would only come after a period of scientific advancement when knowledge shall be increased. Over 99% of the worlds scientific knowledge was acquired in the last 200 years, with most of it occuring this century.

24. Alarming increase in Satan worship. As unbelievable as it seems, there are many people who secretly and some openly worship the devil.

Revelation 13:4   And they worshipped the dragon which gave power unto the beast: and they worshipped the beast,

saying, Who is like unto the beast? who is able to make war with him?

All these incredible and recent signs all lead to the soon coming of Jesus Christ. Before that happens, the world must go through the Great Tribulation. The following sections are theoretical chapters based upon the facts we have previously discussed, Bible prophecy and current political realities.

It is not possible for anyone to know for certain all the circumstances for the Bible prophecies to be fulfilled. The only way a person could know for certain is for God to reveal it to them. This will not happen, because if Satan found out, he would not cooperate to fulfill the prophecies. If Satan had known it was God's plan for Jesus to be crucified, he would not have done it (1 Corinthians 2:8). Therefore, we can only know for certain those things which the scriptures tell us. They provide a framework which we can theorize how these things will come about.

For instance, Revelations tells us that at the start of the Great Tribulation, a fourth of earths's population dies. There are many wars so that peace will be taken from the earth. There will be great famine, pestilence and death. Ezek 38 and 39 describe Gog (Russia) leading a confederacy of nations into Israel. Many people are relaxing since the breakup of the Soviet Union. Skeptics of Bible prophecy are doubting the Soviets will invade Israel.

The Bible never said the Soviet Union would invade Israel but Gog which is Russia. Over 1/2 the soldiers in the Soviet army were Russian. There are presently more than 10,000 nuclear missiles in the Russian Republic. The ease of tensions only lets us know that we are getting close to the time of the end. According to Ezekiel, the world will be unprepared for the Russian Invasion of Israel. The Bible warns us..

1 Thessalonians 5:3   For when they shall say, Peace and safety; then sudden destruction cometh upon them, as travail upon a woman with child; and they shall not escape.

Many people have not realized that Ezek. 38 & 39 describe two great wars, World War III and seven years later, Armageddon. We know that Ezek. 38 is not Armageddon because, verse 20 says the fish in the sea shake from the great earthquake. By the time Armageddon happens, all the fish in the sea will be dead. They die when the waters are turned to blood by the second vial being poured out.   World War III would provide cause the conditions described in Revelations chapter 6. This is an example of how the scriptures provide a framework of the coming events.

The scriptures do not tell us everything, but merely a framework. It is a mystery to **us**, exactly how all of these things will be fulfilled. There are different possibilities. As previously mentioned, there are only three possibilities for the United States.

1. The U.S. is destroyed before or during the first part of the Tribulation.
2. The U.S is very isolationist during the Tribulation and not a factor. 3. The U.S is Mystery Babylon.

In the following section I have taken the position that the U.S. is Mystery Babylon.   However, it could just as easily be an ecclesiastical body that presently is or will be, headquartered in Rome, and or Iraq. In the following chapters, I have given my estimation of how these things will come to pass, given the current world situation, political realities, and the Word of God.   How much is true? Whether some, most, or all is true, I do not know, but neither does Satan.

How close I will come to the exact sequence of events I don't know, but neither does anyone else but God. I have tried to get as close to the truth as possible. Only time will tell, how close I have come. I believe that time, will be very soon.

Chapter 20

1990's: The Days Of Noah

As it was in the days of Noah,

There are more than 30,000 cocaine babies being born in America per week. Some of these babies are born with parts of their brain destroyed. Many of them have violent mood swings with no control at all over their tempers. They will grow up to be very dangerous adults.

As it was in the days of Noah,

The number of children in the world that are sexually abused is growing. They generally grow up to be adults who abuse children. Many of these children grow up to commit heinous crimes.

As it was in the days of Noah

The number of people who are becoming drug addicts is increasing. People will do anything to get the drugs they crave. Prostitution, rape, murder, homosexuality stealing and whatever the seller demands are performed routinely to get the drugs. The drug problem is overburdening our courts, overcrowding our jails, and transforming once peaceful neighborhoods into war zones. Despite the war on drugs, the problem is only getting worse. Aside from these problems, you have racial and political unrest, in practically every nation. From Los Angeles to New York, to Belfast to Beirut, the whole earth is filled with violence.

The morals of society have deteriorated so that anything goes. Young people are killing people over a few dollars. Adultery, fornication and homosexuality is running rampant. Children are taught in sex education in schools that to have homosexual feelings and desires is normal. Everything is okay, except serving God. The ministry has become a joke to the world. The righteous are persecuted for their beliefs. Man has become so spiritually insensitive to God, he has no idea of the extent of His displeasure. Very few people even listen to him.

As it was in the days of Noah,

The earth has become hopelessly corrupt. As in the days of Noah, nothing can be done to save this generation. There is only one thing left to do with this generation. Destroy it.

As it was in the days of Noah,

The architects of society's downfall are having a meeting. Deep within the bowels of the earth, Satan, sends for the great horn. It is time for the gathering of demons.

20th Century Devil

From all over the earth, every manner of foul spirit comes. This repulsive gathering of demons is more vile than the mind can imagine. If a human was so cursed to behold this gathering of demons, he would sink into utter madness.

Satan, who is obviously agitated, asks his demons to report.

The first demon stands forth. He is head of the research and development department of disease. The demon says, "Because of all the world being under the curse, it allows us to manipulate God's creations. We have been able to continually create new and more deadly diseases. Our diseases such as cancer, heart disease, syphilis, and our new favorite AIDS kill millions every year.

We have been able to manipulate genes to form increasing deformities. With the increase of these diseases we are able to continually increase man's suffering. We have some new diseases on the horizon. I wish to report that we are making progress in accomplishing two of our main goals; number one, through their suffering, we make them doubt the justice of God. Number two; we kill as many of the despicable human worms as possible."

The next demon steps forth.

He says, "Man is constantly becoming more lustful through our efforts. The sexual revolution has progressed almost further than we deemed possible. In just a few decades, we have turned the tables. We changed sexual deviancy from outcast, to acceptable. Now those who believe in chastity and obeying God's commands are viewed as outcast. We have resurrected the gay pride, and arrogance of Sodom. More men and women are becoming homosexuals. We have influenced the schools where children are taught, despite all the evidence of nature that homosexuality is natural. As you know, this is abomination in the sight of God."

Satan responds, "Yes! Yes! In the Old Testament days, God had them stoned. Today we make movie stars, rock stars, and politicians of them. We have placed them in various positions in society to make their abomination acceptable. God hates it and I love it. I love anything He hates. Continue on."

The demon continues, "They have gained more and more political power. We have more and more of them traveling and molesting children. These children generally will grow up to be molesters themselves. Children are taught in schools that to have homosexual feelings is natural."

Another demon steps forward and bows before Satan. He says to him, "Lord of Darkness, this has been accomplished because of the successful implementation of plans that you gave me more than two centuries ago. Master you realized we needed to give modern man an alternative to faith in God. We inspired men to believe and propagate the false doctrine of evolution. You instructed me to see to it that it spread.

Through my machinations, I got it introduced into Harvard and Yale Universities. Once it became entrenched there, it spread to the universities around the world. We used it to influence young minds to continue to carry our false doctrine around the world. It now permeates every phase of science. We try our best to make sure the graduates who become judges, lawyers, politicians, businessmen and media representatives believe in evolution. When they do, this gives them an anti-Christian bias. They hire and promote people whose ideology agree with theirs. This has furthered our goals and now," the demon lifts his hands and says in triumph, "We have brought the spirit of anti-Christ into the land.

We have succeeded in filling organizations like the news media with people with an anti-Christian bias. The media is pro pornography. 76% of the media are against prayer in the schools. 86% of them believe in abortion, our 20th Century version of child sacrifice. More people have been arrested protesting abortion than were arrested during the civil rights movements. Yet, the media does not report these tens of thousands of arrests because of their bias. The media consistently under reports the strength, numbers, and effectiveness of the anti-abortionist movement. Over half a million Christians protested against abortion in Washington in 1990. Yet, we persuaded the media not to broadcast their success. None of the networks, or major newspapers showed the size of the crowd. We try to make the Christians look like dangerous fanatics who are a minority.

The American Civil Liberties Union calls abortion clinics to defend them when the Christians protest. They warn the clinics if they don't ask for the ACLU's help the ACLU will be forced to defend the abortion protesters. The ACLU defends the rights of klansmen, communists, murderers, nazis and others, yet they don't want to defend Christians.

We have filled the world with the spirit of Cain. Although they spend billions on themselves, they hate to give to God. Men can make millions playing sports, acting in pornographic films, and managing companies, yet if a preacher has a dime, we make people feel like he has robbed a nursing home. We publicize the failures of those in the ministry, but never their successes.

Satan asks, "And what of the church?"

A demon responds, "Mixed reports, Sir. Some are becoming more apostate. The average church in America has only 75 people. Because of the people having a spirit of Cain, they resist giving. The average church has great financial troubles. This puts great pressure on the leaders. Many preachers are cracking under the pressure of the job and they are leaving the ministry in droves.

In many churches, we try to water down the gospel. We try our best to infiltrate religious organizations and churches. From the time of Judas, we have been successful in placing hypocritical men to hinder the church's progress. We make the people doubt the Word, doubt their leaders, and doubt God.

Yet, there is a move of the Spirit in the land. The Spirit-filled churches give us the most trouble. We have heavy losses in Africa, Europe, South America, and Asia. Massive meetings are occurring where ten thousand souls come to be saved in a single service. In Seoul, South Korea, the world's largest church has over half 800,000 members attend every Sunday. As you know, they even have a prayer mountain, where their members receive prayer request from all over the world. We know the awful sounds of the prayers in tongues as these prayer warriors bind us up, and cast us out. In Africa, they are having massive meetings where more than one hundred thousand people come in every service. Some of the people walk for days to get to these miracle services."

The more this demon talks, the more Satan gets agitated. He says, "Yes, yes, I know all this! But what are we doing about it?"

The demon answers, "The same as always. We try to discourage them through their trials and tribulations. We tell them the usual lies. We try to get them so concerned about political, and material things, that they don't have time for the spiritual things. We try to keep them too busy to pray, read their Bibles, or go to church.

We try to negate their influence in the world. We try to make them look crazy through the media. We tell men, it is unmanly to be a Christian. We tell Jews, it is anti-Jewish to be a Christian.

Fear of persecution, keeps many from seeking after eternal life through Jesus. We try to make sure, that none of the churches successes ever make the news, only their failures. We try to make all the preachers look like charlatans and crooks. When we finally tempt a preacher to go astray, we magnify it, and tell people that all preachers are like that."

"Does it work?" Satan asks him.

"Most of the time," the demon answers him.

The next demon steps forth. His specialty is drugs. He says, "Master, the number of drug addicts has increased tremendously. This has made it easier for all the other spirits. People are doing anything to get the drugs they crave. They are selling their bodies, lying, stealing, raping, murdering, and generally all the good things that we love. For most people, the drugs have become their god. Master, only one of your genius could have discovered the potential of drugs. I must admit, when you first told us of the potential of these drugs, I for one, thought it was too good to be true.

As you know, when one takes drugs, his body fights the drug and builds up a tolerance to it. The stronger his immune system is, the more it will fight the drug. This does not affect their physical and psychological needs for the drugs, which remains overwhelming. They are faced with a dilemma of overwhelming cravings for the drugs, and because of the strength of their own bodies, the same amount of drugs will never be sufficient. It takes a higher dosage of drugs, to get the initial *high*.

Their drug habit will always increase, because their bodies fight against the drugs. We get many unsuspecting fools to take drugs by telling them, they are strong enough to resist getting hooked. The fools don't know that the stronger they are, the more they will get hooked. Those who are weak mentally, don't stand a chance. The drugs weaken the will and make users more susceptible to us. Nothing has contributed to the decline of modern civilization, as the growth of drug users in the world."

The next demon steps forth. His specialty is counterfeit religions. "Master, I wish to report great progress. The number of human fools who worship in our counterfeit religions are growing. In keeping with your directives, we impersonate the dead whenever possible and we also stage many other events to deceive the human worms.

Thanks to our efforts, we have caused some people to believe in reincarnation. We have done this by impressing our memories of past experiences with people upon them. Over the centuries, we have each known and deceived millions of mortals. Some mortals let us use them for years. Eventually, they all die. When we have led them to hell, we must seek new victims.

We find a suitable human fool who unknowingly yields his or her flesh to us. They listen to our suggestions, and yield to the temptation. As they become more yielded, they open the door of their spirits to us. We try to impress upon them, our memories of our past encounters, with people who we had possessed. When we impress our memories upon them, the idiots think it is a past life intruding upon them. Because the conditions must be so exact, this is difficult to do. However, we have had numerous successes, and we always try to make sure the humans publicize their faked reincarnated memories. When the memories are checked out, they bear up under investigation. Because these were real people, in real places, this makes many gullible fools believe in the fake reincarnations.

In addition to this, we have also been able to make many people believe they have seen UFO's. It is to our advantage to make people believe in advanced alien civilizations, who have grown beyond the primitive need for God. Most people are unaware that humans have not found one planet outside the solar system. They believe the stories of these Joe Blows who get on talk shows and say they were picked up by aliens in a deserted cornfield in Iowa or someplace. Supposedly, the aliens give them a message of peace to take to the world. The human idiots never realize if an alien civilization really wanted to make contact, they would land in Washington D.C. or fly over Times Square in broad daylight. Master, How can the humans be so dumb?"

Satan answers, "I don't know, but it sure makes our job a whole lot easier. Continue on."

The demon continues, "We have convinced many that they can enter heaven by their works, instead of the blood of the accursed Lamb. Though some of them foolishly pray daily, it is a total waste of their time, for they do not understand. God said no flesh would glory in His sight," the demon begins to chuckle. He stops snickering and says, "They are trying to gain entrance to heaven by their righteous works, but all man's righteousness is as filthy rags in His sight." All of the devils laugh at the irony of the situation.

Despite all the evil news, Satan is still troubled. The demons don't understand.

One of Satan's principal demons says, "Master, this is indeed good news. Is it not?"

Satan is outraged! He is in disbelief. He says, "You idiots! How can we be at ease? How can we take comfort when after six thousand years of struggle, the plans of God are still obviously being fulfilled? Despite all our machinations, the plans of God seem to be progressing. We must find a way.
There is nothing left to do but release him."

"You mean..?" the prince of Persia asks.

"Yes, it is time," Satan says.

The chief demons look at one another in disbelief. Finally the prince of Europe says, "But suppose that causes..". "Us to inadvertently fulfill the will of God?" Satan interrupts him. Satan answers, "What choice do we have?" Every man who we have used to try to defeat the plans of God has failed us. When we used Titus to kill all the Jews, he would not. He only killed 1 million, 6 hundred thousand. I wanted him to kill all of them. What did he do? He scattered the rest of them around the world and fulfilled the prophecy. And that Hitler..," Satan pauses and shakes his head in utter disgust.

Satan gets up and goes right up to the face of the prince of Persia. The demons know what is coming. Satan has raved about this four almost fifty years. He is going into his tirade again. Yet, they dare not anger Satan, so they act like they are hearing it for the first time.

"While that twerp was in prison, he secretly made a deal with me," Satan paces back and forth, raging and fuming.

He says, "He promised to worship me, if I would get him out of prison. I said I would put him in power, if he would serve me. He agreed. What did I do? I get him out. We give him wisdom."

The more Satan talks, the more agitated he becomes. The more agitated he gets, the faster and louder he talks. He continues, "We anoint his mouth, to make people believe him. I gave him armies. I gave him scientists who built rockets. I give him scientists who begin to build the atomic bomb. I tell him to secretly kill the Jews and he does."

He shouts in disbelief, "I give him the world. Do you hear me? If he would have waited, with his rockets and atomic bombs he would have ruled the world. I deliver the world within his grasp, and what does he do? He attacks England and Russia at the same time!" Satan says in disbelief. Satan acts as if he still can't believe that Hitler did that, even after 49 years. "Where is Hitler?" he asks.

One of the demons look out and says, "He is in the south quadrant of the lake of fire."

"Bring me one of the firebolts," Satan says.

They bring Satan one of the firebolts. Satan goes to the window and looks out over the lake of fire. Not even Satan can enter the lake of fire, lest he be burned by the spiritual fires as well. The only way he can reach him is through the firebolts. He finally spots Hitler burning in the lake of fire. Satan hollers out, "Hey Adolf! Hail Hitler!"

Hitler knows what is coming. He is already burning in the lake of fire. Although he is already in excruciating pain, the firebolt will only make it worse. He sees the fire bolt as it is hurled from the castle of hell. It arches high in the sky and then it flies toward him. Although he has never done it, he frantically tries to escape the firebolt. He only has a few seconds. The firebolt strikes him like lightning and Hitler screams to the top of his voice. This has gone on every day since Hitler arrived in hell.

One of the demons looks confused. He turns to another demon and says, "Didn't the master tell Hitler to invade Russia?"

Satan overhears him and goes over to the demon. Satan, who is never one for admitting mistakes or acknowledging failure, is furious. He is so furious, he goes over to punch the demon. He punches the demon so hard, his face literally caves in.

Satan watches the demon writhe in pain for a moment. Then he asks, "Where was I?"

Somebody says, "Hitler."

He continues, "Then that fool Hitler declares war on the United States. I told him to let the Japanese fight the U.S. buy itself. Wait till they destroy one another, then He could pick up the pieces. I wanted him to continue his conquest of Europe and the annihilation of the Jews. "

Satan is so angry he is now screaming his words. He screams, "I hand him the world and what does he do? He blows it! The U.S and Russia take the rocket and atomic scientist! Hitler is defeated. After that flop was defeated, I was so mad at him, I could not wait for him to start burning in hell. That is why I told him to commit suicide!" Satan's frustration has built up so that he could no longer contain it and he lets out a scream.

He continues his tirade, "The world finds out what he has done. The world is outraged, and they let the Jews go back into Israel. The ancient prophecies are fulfilled and Israel becomes a nation," he says as he sinks down in his chair disgusted.

Satan contemplates for a few moments. After a long pause Satan says, "We have the same problem with men that the Trinity has, their free will. Hitler was not able to listen to me all the time. Sometimes God put thoughts in his head. God tricked him, just liked He tricked the Japanese into bombing Pearl Harbor and bringing the United States into the war. The U.S saved England and Russia, and defeated Hitler and saved the Jews from extermination. On top of all that, as a result of the scientist I gave Hitler, Israel has rockets and nuclear weapons.

After 35 centuries we still can't find a man who can lead the world and annihilate the Jews. Everyone from Pharaoh to Hitler has failed us. Israel becomes more powerful everyday. More and more Jews are returning to Israel. If we don't do something now, it will be too late. Soon Israel will be so powerful that they will not be able to be destroyed. Christ plans to return to Israel, and from there rule the world. When He does, that will be the end of us. If Israel is not destroyed, then all we will have worked for will be in vain. I am convinced now that no normal man will be able to do it.

We need a man who is able to listen to us at all times. We will tell him everything he needs to know. Like Hitler, we will anoint his mouth to sway the masses. We will tell him every military secret so no nation can defeat him.

We need the man who is already dead and condemned to hell. He has burned for 19 centuries and he hates God. He is the one who has nothing to lose, and he will never serve God. We have trained him for two centuries. We have taught him all about human psychology and warfare, so he will have the wisdom to lead. We have imparted as much of our wisdom into him as possible. He is cruel and totally ruthless. He hates Jews and Christians.

I especially like him because his hatred of God is nearly as deep as ours. This makes him a wonderful blasphemer, a man after my own heart. We tried to avoid bringing him up, even after God gave us the power to release him from the pit. We tried

Hitler first and we only made things worse.   We must release him."

"But won't we be fulfilling the prophecy?" one of them asks.

"What choice do we have?" Satan says dejectedly.   "Our only hope is that we have done this ahead of schedule, and he will succeed, where others have failed. If we cannot have the world, then we will get him to destroy it. If not, at least we will kill a lot of Jews and Christians, and innocent people before we go. Besides, I would rather destroy the world, than make peace with God. Release him. Release Nero. Release the Beast."

World War III

The leaders of Russia begin to think an evil thought. As Iraq invaded Kuwait in a lightning fast strike and stole their wealth, the Russians decide to do the same thing to Israel. The Jews have returned to Israel from all over the world, and taken their wealth with them. The world is in a state of peace. No one will expect this lighting fast strike. The Soviets make a secret deal with many Arab and Muslim nations.

For many years, the Arabs and Muslims have longed to drive the Israelis out of Jerusalem and the West Bank. They wish to drive the Israelis out of Israel altogether. Gladly, they agree to be part of the invasion. Surprise is of the essence. The Soviets begin to stockpile the weapons and ammunition that they will need, in and about the Arab nations near Israel.

Some say the Soviets had planned to invade Israel in 1982. However, the invasion of the Israelis into Lebanon averted this catastrophe. When the Israelis invaded Lebanon, they found tons of Russian ammunition and weapons in underground caves. They found enough weapons to arm an army of nearly a million men. Aside from the weapons they found, they also found K-rations for this army. Since K-rations only have a shelf life of six months, it is believed that the Russians were planning an invasion of Israel within six months of the 1982 invasion of Lebanon.

The Iranians, Libyans, Ethiopians, Turkey, Germans, and Russians invade Israel. This combined army enters Northern Israel with a great air force. There are so many planes, it looks like a dark storm cloud has covered the land. It is an army of millions.

They come with all sorts of armor. Tanks, trucks, and even riding on horses. Israel looks hopelessly outnumbered. Sheba and Dedan, or Saudi Arabia do not take part in the invasion. England, Canada and the United States are horrified. This is exactly as Ezekiel prophesied in Ezekiel, chapter 38. Ezekiel also prophesied that the nations of the world would be aware of this prophecy.

This has already come to pass. Israelis, American, and British government officials are already fully aware of Ezekiel's prophecy. They have read Ezekiel 38 and books such as the "Late Great Planet Earth." Lectures have been given in the Pentagon and before Israelis officials on Ezekiel's prophecy. They all agree that Ezekiel gave an accurate portrayal of what would happen.

This invasion goes exactly as Ezekiel prophesied. It happens so fast, the merchants of Tarshish (British) and its offspring, the young lions, (Americans, Canadians, and Australians) can only protest. The Soviets and their allies prepare a lighting fast strike to try and overwhelm the Israelis, and destroy them. They never get the chance.

When this Russian confederacy invades Israel, the Lord of Hosts intervenes. He is angry and He is against this invading force. God's fury comes up in His face. He is extremely angry, and He is determined that this invasion force will not succeed. God calls for a sword against the invading armies. God makes other nations come to the aide of Israel.

The Israelis fight with everything they have. The Israelis are being annihilated. The Russians hoped to strike Israel before it could marshal all of its forces and use its nuclear weapons, but God does not let them. The Israelis let loose with everything they have and God sends a great shaking in the land of Israel.

God, the Father, reaches down and He shakes the entire earth. All the fish in the sea, and the fowls of the heaven, and the beast of the field shake at His presence. God sends such an earthquake that the mountains are thrown down and buildings collapse as their walls fall to the ground. The entire surface of the earth, shakes like a giant sheet when someone makes up their bed.

Zechariah 14:12 And this shall be the plague wherewith the LORD will smite all the people that have fought against Jerusalem; Their flesh shall consume away while they stand upon their feet, and their eyes shall consume away in their holes, and their tongue shall consume away in their mouth.

A rain of fire, brimstone, and even great hailstones, falls upon those who have come against Israel. Amazingly, the armies that have come against Israel are destroyed. The Russian army begins to turn back. They are being annihilated on the mountains of Syria and Lebanon.

Destruction begins to sweep across the planet. God causes five-sixths of the Russian force to be destroyed. Eighty-five percent of them are totally wiped out. They retreat to Siberia as Joel prophesied.

Joel 2:20   But I will remove far off from you the northern army, and will drive him into a land barren and desolate, with his face toward the east sea, and his hinder part toward the utmost sea, and his stink shall come up, and his ill savour shall come up, because He hath done great things.

There are so many dead bodies in Israel that the land is filled with the foul odor of the dead bodies. It stops the noses of the inhabitants. There are so many dead bodies it takes seven months to bury the dead. They hire men who pass through the land to bury the dead. There are so many weapons leftover from the battle, that they will burn the weapons for seven years for fuel.

The destruction is not limited to the Middle East, but it sweeps across the world. The balance of power is shifted. War begins to break out everywhere. Nation rises against nation, kingdom rises against kingdom. Because of the worldwide earthquakes, power lines are down, and buildings are destroyed. Most of the world's economies are destroyed. In some places, it will be months before electricity is restored. Some places will wait years. Many roads are destroyed. Pestilence, disease, and famine follow the wars. The world seems to have gone mad. Even wild animals begin to attack men. One fourth of the world's population dies. All these are the beginning of sorrows.

In the months that follow, the nations of the world become desperate. A confederacy of nations in Europe, most of whom are the remnants of the Roman Empire, rise in power. Now there a thirteen, but soon there will be only ten nations, for three will rebel and be destroyed. A man rises to power and influence in Europe. He has no kingdom of his own. Through flattery and persuasion, he gains more and more power. He is charming, brilliant and manipulative. His charisma is unbelievable. He persuades the European powers that the world has become too dangerous a place for them to stand idly by. Finally, the ten nations unite to confer their power to him.

These are desperate times. The world barely survives the devastation of World War III. They reason, it is too dangerous to have separate governments. The League of Nations failed to stop Hitler. After WWII, the world decided it needed something stronger than the League of Nations. It formed the United Nations in 1945. Yet, the world was almost destroyed by the invasion of Israel by the

Russians in World War III. Many people are crying out to take the United Nations one step further. The cry rings out for one world government, A NEW WORLD ORDER.

Leading the charge is the apostate church. It uses its vast power to rally the world behind the Beast. In the name of the brotherhood of man and for the sake of the world's survival, they urge their millions of followers to support the new leader. They argue that to delay, is to risk the ultimate destruction. They argue, the world will not survive the next nuclear war. For the sake of humanity, they heed the words of the Beast, who is the Anti-Christ. The arguments make sense to them. They do not know that the Great Dragon, Satan, himself, has put all his power behind the Beast. The forces of Satan anoint the Beast to sway the masses.

His speech is electrifying. The women find him charming, although he has no desire for them. The people of the world have never seen anyone like the Beast. His face is on the magazine covers, newspapers, and television. His charisma is unbelievable. Many think that God has brought him into the world at this time, to save the world. He is the consummate workaholic, a dedicated man striving to save the world. They do not know that he is the spawn of hell and through peace, he shall destroy many.

The ten nations give him the right to use military force when necessary to unite the world. He goes out and makes war on the nations who will not unite. He conquers every nation that rises against him. No one can stand before him. He is irresistible. He is the Beast.

He begins to unite the world. The nations of the world begin to agree with him. Many of the world's spiritual leaders encourage their followers to join the Beast. One of the most influential leaders is a man regarded as a prophet. He is able to perform many supernatural miracles before the eyes of the people. They are convinced he is a prophet from God. They do not know, his power comes from the Great Dragon, Satan, himself. The devil gives this false prophet great power to deceive the nations into following after the Beast.

As the Prophet Daniel saw in Daniel 9:27, he eventually signs a treaty with Israel, and other nations. He guarantees their security and their right to exist. He promises to protect them, at all cost. Israel does not know, they have signed a deal with the devil. When the treaty is signed, the Great Tribulation begins, and the world has seven years left.

The Beast begins his persecution of the Christians. The true Christians recognize the Beast and the false prophet for who they truly are. They will not follow after him and plead to an unbelieving world that the true Anti-Christ has finally come. The pleas fall on deaf ears. The world moves forward with its one world government.

As the society becomes more technologically advanced, they press for permanent identification with a mark on the palm of the hand or in the forehead. This will help keep track of all citizens and severely limit terrorism and crime. While voices are raised against it, the proponents argue it is the next logical step from drivers licence and social security numbers and credit history files. Eventually the system is adopted. Through a world-wide computer system, the Beast causes millions to take the mark of the Beast. It starts out as voluntary, but eventually it becomes mandatory.

Eventually everyone who does not have the mark of the Beast will be killed. The Beast tells people, "Those who will not take either the mark of the Beast, the number of his name or the name of the Beast will be tormented." Christians are blamed for many acts of sabotage and terrorism. They are accused as dangerous fanatics who are enemies of the New World order. Many are hunted down and beheaded.

Chapter 21

Abomination Of Desolation

The Beast has been shot. A sniper has shot him in the head. He has been mortally wounded. The world mourns the loss of the Beast. Many of the people of the world wonder how will the world go on without him. Miraculously, the Beast revives. He has a full recovery. The world rejoices at the news of his stunning recovery. He is more popular than ever. He announces to the world that he plans to make a visit to Israel. He wishes to come and visit the temple.

The Temple has become the symbol of the nation of Israel. To them, it is their greatest symbol of their special racial and spiritual heritage. To the Jews, it symbolizes the favor of God upon the nation. It is the source of renewed hope and faith in Judaism. The Jews knew the Messiah could not possibly come until after the temple was built. It is the holiest site in all of Israel. In ancient times, if anyone but the high priest entered the holiest of holies, they would be struck dead by God.

The Beast negotiates the details of his visit with the leaders of Israel. The Jews are excited about his visit to the rebuilt Jewish Temple. Most western leaders have been reluctant to visit the temple for fear of offending the Arabs. The Jews believe this visit will bring a new acceptance among the world leaders of the restored temple. Because of the recent attempt upon his life, he demands that he is allowed to bring a large security force with him. He will sail to Israel on one of his aircraft carriers. Reluctantly, the Israeli leaders agree.

Sailing on one of his nuclear aircraft carriers, the Beast enters the port of Haifa. He flies from the aircraft carrier via helicopter to his embassy. There, the Beast meets his false prophet. They finish going over the details for their visit to the temple.

Triumphantly, the Beast rides into Jerusalem. Security is tight.
The people gather and cheer him. The people of Israel are so happy
that he has come. He is the leader of the world, and he has signed a
peace treaty with Israel, guaranteeing its security. The Israelis think
they will have peace at last. It is the happiest day in Israel in many
years.

The people have lined up along his parade route. Dozens of
vehicles are in the motorcade. Directly behind the Beast's limousine
is the false prophet. Many believe that he is a prophet from God.
The people continue to wave as the Beast and his entourage pass by.

Tens of thousands have lined along the parade route. The Israelis
think this is a great day. The bands are playing in his honor. Finally,
his motorcade stops at the new temple. He gets out and waves to the
crowd. He has told the people that he is coming to worship. At the
steps of the temple some of the Israeli leaders are waiting, with some
of the priests and rabbis. He enters the temple with them. As he
enters, the priests are explaining the details and the history of the
temple. The Beast is smiling, he is ecstatic. The day he has longed
for, has finally come to pass. He tries to hide his impatience for as
long as he can. He finally says to the high priest, "I have a gift for
the temple. It is to be placed in the holy of holies."

He turns and signals to his men to bring in the gift. The high
priest and the other Jewish leaders try to explain to the Beast that this
cannot be permitted. The prime minister explains, "Your excellency,
we appreciate the gesture but our laws are very specific."

The Beast says, "Nonsense." He turns and signals to his men.

The huge object is brought in. It is in a crate that is 12 feet tall
and four feet wide.

The high priest says, "It is not permitted!" The high priest rushes
toward the Beast, pleading with him.

Suddenly, the Beast turns and slaps the high priest in the face,
knocking him down. The Israelis leaders do not know what to think.

The Beast looks at them and says, "I rule here." Dozens of the
Beast's bodyguards swarm into the temple. A wave of fear sweeps
over the Jewish leaders.

The Beast motions to his bodyguards to get the Jewish leaders
out of his way. The false prophet enters the temple. He and the
Beast look at each other and smile as if they possess some secret.

Triumphantly, the Beast turns and draws back the curtain that
separates the holiest of holies from the rest of the temple. The day
that he has waited for, for centuries, has finally come. This is the

abomination of desolation that Daniel, Jesus, and the Apostle Paul spoke of. He enters the holiest of hollies with a strange look upon his face. It is a mixture of evil glee, triumph, and boastfulness as if he is daring God to do something about it. He slowly looks around, savoring the moment. His men wait at the entrance with the crate. Some of his men are equipped with television cameras. The Beast has brought them here to record his triumph. He motions for them to bring in the object. They bring it in and open the crate. It is a statue of the Beast.

The Israelis begin to protest. "You cannot do this! This is sacrilege. You are blaspheming against God."

"He is the one, true god!" exclaims the false prophet.

"Your God is dead," shouts the Beast! "Or worse yet, He is impotent. Did He save your people when Hitler marched them to the ovens of Auschwitz!? I am the only true god that is left," he says. "If your God is alive," the Beast pauses and looks skyward. He opens his arms wide as if he is waiting for God to smite him. He spouts his foul blasphemy, "I stand in the holiest place. Strike me if you can! Jehovah, I challenge you. Your people need you. Strike me down now oh impotent One, if You can!"

Everyone in the room pauses as if waiting for some response from heaven. The Israelis hoping, and the Beast's followers hoping not. After a few moments it becomes apparent that nothing will happen and some of the Jews drop their heads in disappointment.

The Beast pauses and drops his hands. He turns to the Israelis and says, "See. I told you. Is not the true measure of a god, his ability to create? More specifically, to give life to the unliving. Watch, and I shall prove to you that I am god."

The false prophet stands in front of the image of the Beast. He raises his hands and stretches them toward the statue of the Beast. He commands the statue of the Beast to come to life. He says, "Live! Live! In the name of the one true God, I command this unliving image of stone to come alive."

There is a strange sound as slowly, the statue of the Beast begins to move. He turns his head toward the false prophet. Slowly he frees himself from the base. The statue is alive. It steps off the platform and walks before the Beast. It stops and waits for his next command. The Beast smiles with an evil glee. His triumph is complete. This event has been recorded by his television equipment and has been broadcast around the world through satellite.

He orders the high priest and some of the other Jewish leaders to be brought before him. His men grab them and bring them before the Beast. The Beast says to them, "I have passed the test. I have proven that I am god by giving my servant power to give life to this statue. Now fall down and worship me."

The high priest is obstinate. He says, "I do not know how you did this. Whether it is some sort of trick or by the power of Devil. But Jehovah is my God, and only Him will I serve. You said, He did not save us from Hitler, but He did. In Hitler's ovens the rebirth of Israel was formed. Hitler is dead and he will pay for his crimes and if you raise your hand against Israel, you will die and pay for your sins as well."

The Beast is enraged. He says, "He that will not bow down and worship my image will be killed by my image." The statue of the Beast reaches down and grabs the high priest by the throat. The statue lifts the priest in the air, like he is a rag doll. The high priest begins to gag, and struggles to free himself from the massive hands around his neck. His struggle only last moments before the statue breaks his neck. Then the statue hurls him against the wall, like an unwanted doll. The priest hits the wall with such force that his blood splatters against it.

The other Jews are brought before the image of the Beast. Those who will not worship the statue are killed by it. Some of the people worship the image of the Beast as god, for fear of the statue. Many will not, and are killed by it. Israel knows it has been betrayed. The nation is horrified by the actions of the Beast. The forces of the Beast invade Israel and occupy it. Israelis' defense forces (depleted because of the Russian invasion) are insufficient to drive back the invaders.

It is time to institute his final plan to ensure the nations of the world are loyal to him. He will try to use his political, economical and military might to try to make sure every man, woman, and boy on this planet worship him as god. He will expand his mark of the Beast and to make everyone take it before his time runs out. Everyone who does not take the mark of the Beast, or the number of his name or his name in their foreheads or in the palm of their hand, will be killed.

There is a rebellion of three nations in the kingdom of the Beast. The Anti-Christ goes with great wrath and destroys these three nations of the EEC. Now it is only ten nations. So many men have been killed by the wars, that now seven women take hold of one man.

The women know they have no chance of the man taking care of them. The women promise to take care of themselves, as long as the man will be theirs for a little while. It is terrible that the world has come to this. Yet, the world will not repent.

Radio signals on earth go wild. On the surface of the sun, sunspots, which are black spots on the sun, grow at an alarming rate. They affect radio transmissions on earth. The number of sunspots grow and they increase in size until the sun turns ebony black. Have you ever heard a world scream? The entire planet is in terror. The moon looses its brightness. It grows dimmer and dimmer. It begins to turn red in color. It is changing. God changes the atomic structure of the moon. It turns into blood.

The great day of the wrath of the Lord is near. The LORD calls an angel and tells him to go forth in the earth. His job is to seal the servants of God in their foreheads. Those who are sealed will be protected from future plagues that shall come upon the earth.

God sends four angels to each of the four corners of the earth. These corners were discovered in 1965 by researchers working under a grant from the U.S Navy at the John Hopkins Applied Physics Laboratory. They discovered that satellites were not able to achieve a true orbit because, they were pulled from their orbits by a slightly stronger gravitational pull, at four points around the globe. The Lord sends the angels to these four corners to affect the earth's weather.

The first angel goes to the first corner or high point between Ireland and the North pole. The second angel is sent to the next high point, between New Guinea northward to Japan.

The third corner is located between Africa and Antarctica, and the last angel is sent to the fourth corner located just west of South America.

God commands the angels to hold the wind that it blows not on the earth, sea, or any tree. For the first time in the earth's history there is no wind, no gentle breeze of any kind upon the planet.

The Lord calls another angel forth. God, the Father, gives him the great seal and tells him to go to earth and seal the servants of the Lord. The angel flies to the earth. He comes from the east and says to the four angels, "Do not hurt the earth, the sea, or the trees until the servants of God have been sealed in their foreheads." The angel goes and seals the servants of God in their foreheads.

Seven Golden Trumpets

God is getting ready to send His judgement upon the Earth. Men have worshipped the creature more than the Creator. He is getting ready to send forth signs so fantastic, that man will not be able to explain them away. There will be no scientific explanations for these happenings. They will not be dismissed as freaks of nature or strange coincidences. There will be no attributing these plagues to the blasphemous doctrines of evolution. The plagues that shall come upon the earth will be exactly as was prophesied by the prophets and the apostles of Jesus. There will be no question, that these are the judgements of God.

God sends the first angel forth. He takes out the first of the golden trumpets. When he blows the trumpet it causes hail and fire to fall to earth. This burning hail is mixed with blood. When it strikes the ground, it causes a third of the trees and all green grass to be burnt up.

Sometime later, God sends the second angel forth. He sounds his trumpet and a great burning mountain crashes into the ocean. A third of the creatures in the sea die, and a third of the water turns into blood. It causes gigantic tidal waves and a third of the ships, especially those near ports, are destroyed.

The third angel sounds his trumpet. It causes a star to fall from heaven. It is burning as if it were a lamp, and it falls upon a third part of the rivers and the fountains of waters. The name of the star is Wormwood, because it causes the waters to become wormwood. Many men die because of the poison waters.

The fourth angel sounds and the third of the sky is strangely covered. This strange covering hides a third of the sun, moon, and stars. It covers the light of day and the darkness of night.

Locust From Hell

The fifth angel sounds his trumpet. An angel flies to the earth who is glowing like a living star. He is given the key to the bottomless pit. He opens the bottomless pit, and a huge amount of smoke comes out, like the smoke of a great furnace. The light of the sun is darkened because of the smoke of the pit that fills the air.

Out of the pit comes locust-like creatures. These locust have been imprisoned for thousands of years. They have a king over them whose name is Abaddon. Abaddon means destroyer. They were once evil angels. They look like small horses. On their heads were crowns like gold. They have faces like the faces of men. They have hair like a woman and teeth like a lion. Men will swat at them, but discover to their horror, that they seem to be armor plated. Their covering is as tough as iron. Despite their weight, they can fly. Their unique configuration causes them to sound like chariots of horses running to battle.

They are commanded not to hurt the grass or any green thing or tree. They can only attack those men which do not have the seal of God in their foreheads.

These horrible looking locusts go forth and attack men. They do not have the power to kill, however, their bite causes excruciating pain. The pain last for five months. In those days, men shall seek death and will not be able to find it. Death shall be taken from the earth. No matter how mangled a body may become, a person will not be able to die.

The sixth angel sounds his trumpet and the four angels which are bound in the river Euphrates are released. For nearly six thousand years, these evil angels have been imprisoned. The four kings are released and they release the 200,000,000 demons inside them. They go to the east and begin to persuade Red China and some of the other Oriental nations to go to war.

The Chinese government only allows its citizens to have one child. If a couple has a second child, they are deducted a years wages. If they try to have anymore children, the government forces sterilization on the couple. Consequently, most couples prefer to have a son to carry on the family's name and to help work. Most couples abort the female babies. For the last ten years the ratio of boys to girls being born in China is 9 to 1. Most of these young men will have no chance of ever having a family. Most of them have no hope of ever knowing the love of a woman or having the love of their children. What kind of people will they become?

The murderous demons begin to persuade the leaders in the Orient to raise an army of 200,000,000 men. The leaders never know they are being manipulated by demons with a hatred for all of mankind. The demons tell them they must do something to stop the Beast. He is becoming too powerful. The Beast and his armies are destroying the world. It is conquer or eventually be conquered. It is the day of the Oriental. The days of the domination of the *round eyes* are over.

This massive army is mobilized. They go forth and begin to conquer. They are relentless. They march and slaughter the inhabitants of other countries. They have no idea they are being driven by demonic monsters who have an insane hatred for all mankind. Eventually, they will slaughter 1/3 of all the men on the earth.

The Two Witnesses

For nearly three and one-half years the two witnesses have prophesied. These two prophets wearing sackcloth and ashes have prophesied to the nations. They have warned them of the consequences of their sins. God gave them power to shut up heaven that it would not rain. They had power to turn water into blood and smite the earth with many types of plagues. They have punished nation after nation. At first they were thought to be crackpots. When the people of earth saw them perform miracles before their eyes, they had to believe it. Yet many would not accept them as prophets of God. People who think that God does not care about sin or that He is a vengeful and angry God, view the two witnesses as monsters. As the witnesses would preach against the people's sins, the people hated them.

Despite the signs and wonders the witnesses perform over a period of three and one half years, most people do not believe in them or respect them as messengers from God. As Pharaoh did not believe Moses, Jezebel did not believe Elijah, and the Pharisees did not believe in Jesus, the people of earth do not believe in the two witnesses. When the witnesses called plagues upon the nations, they sought to capture them. Whenever someone tried to capture them, an irresistible fire would come out of their mouths that totally destroyed their enemies. They have called down so many plagues upon the nations, they are the most hated men on the planet.

The Beast has never confronted them, but now it is time. The witnesses come to Jerusalem. The Beast is there and he goes out to meet them. The Beast that ascended out of the bottomless pit makes war with them. It is a ferocious battle. Finally, the Beast overcomes the witnesses and kills them. The people of earth hated the witnesses so much that they will not allow the bodies to be buried. Their bodies are left to rot in the streets of Jerusalem.

The people of earth are so happy they cannot believe it. Thousands come by to view the bodies. The pictures of their bodies are flashed around the world. They feel the Beast has given the world a great gift. Some of the people are so happy, they feel it is like Christmas. They mistakenly think their troubles are over. They begin to send gifts to one another all over the world. The bodies of the two witness lie in the streets for three days.

After three days, The Spirit of life enters the two witnesses and they stand upon their feet, and a great fear falls upon everyone who sees them.

Suddenly a voice from heaven says, "Come up here." The two witnesses ascend up to heaven in a cloud while everyone watches them. In that same hour a great earthquake strikes Jerusalem. It destroys 10% of the city. Seven thousand people die. The rest of the survivors are afraid and give glory to the God of heaven.

The Last Trumpet

It is now time for the seventh and final trumpet. This trumpet causes several things to happen. The seventh trumpet sounds and Jesus knows that the day and the hour has finally come. This is one thing the Father kept even from Him, the appointed time of the rapture. Instantly Jesus appears in the clouds above the earth. He has come back for His Church, the Bride of Christ. He has come back for His true Christians, those without spot or wrinkle. Those that are not ready will be left behind. He shouts with the voice of an archangel. He causes those who are dead, who were saved, to rise first. The mortal puts on immortality, the corruption puts on incorruption. The remaining true Christians who are alive are caught up to meet Him in the air. As miraculous as this change is, it happens in an indivisible amount of time.

Together they leave earth and go to heaven. The Lord has prepared a great feast for them. It is the marriage supper of the Lamb. They are all given white robes. They are from every nation, kindred, and tongue. There are so many of them, that the number of them is a number which no man could possibly number. God has wiped away every tear from their eyes. They will remain on heaven until the end of the seven year tribulation. The sounding of the last trumpet signals it is time for the wrath of God to strike the earth. Seven angels are called. They are given seven golden bowls (vials). It is now time for the seven bowls to be poured out upon the earth.

Tension increases between the Beast who rules in Israel and Egypt. Egypt decides to attack the Beast. He gathers his forces and launches a land, air, and amphibious attack. He attacks with many ships. His armies begin to overrun Egypt. As the Iraqis pillaged Kuwait in 1990, so does the Beast pillage Egypt.

The 7 Golden Vials

With the saints of God safely in heaven, God decides to pour out His wrath upon the earth. The true Christians have left. God left them here as long as He possibly could to try and reach as many as they could. Satan had wished to incite the world to exterminate all of them.

True Christians were a small minority among men. In some nations they were as rare as a pinch of salt. They were the salt of the earth, the spiritual preservative that kept mankind from turning completely rotten. They were not always visible, but their prayers were always working. They are gone, and the spiritual condition of earth quickly deteriorate. Every nation in the world, from Canada, to the United States, from Russia, to China and every other country, becomes increasingly wicked, with all the saints gone. With the righteous gone, the wicked are in charge of the world. The demons run amok in men. The cities of the world become increasing violent, more wicked, more vile, and more dangerous than ever before.

The saints of God look down upon the earth and they are sickened by what they see. They ask God, "How long Oh Lord, before you avenge us, for our blood that was shed on the earth? How long Oh Lord, before you judge the earth?"

God calls the angels with the Seven Golden Vials which contain the wrath of God. IT IS TIME.

The first vial is poured out upon the earth. It causes all the men and women, who have the mark of the Beast, to have a foul and loathsome sore. They are in excruciating pain because of the sores.

The second golden bowl is poured out upon the earth. The angel pours out the bowl upon the seas. The people are horrified as the ocean begins to turn red in color. It changes the oceans into blood. All marine life dies.

The third golden bowl is poured out upon the fountains of fresh water. All fresh water in the rivers and lakes becomes blood. The saints in heaven rejoice and praise God.

And I heard the angel of the waters saying: "You are righteous, O Lord, the One who is and who was and who is to be, because You have judged these things. For they have shed the blood of saints and prophets, and You have given them blood to drink. For it is their just due." And I heard another from the altar saying, "Even so, Lord God Almighty, true and righteous are Your judgments."

Despite all the happenings on earth, the Beast continues to deceive many. He blasphemes against God. He deceives some of the people into believing that these plagues are the result of bacteriological warfare, chemical weapons, and genetic warfare caused by their enemies. He produces phony documents and reports to confirm this. He gives logical explanations for every occurrence. He tells the world that these strange happenings are merely the actions of hostile governments and experiments gone mad. Anyone who actually believes the book of Revelations is coming to pass, is made to look like a fool. The people of earth decide to believe the Beast and many join him in his blasphemy. Despite all the warnings, they choose not to repent and worship God.

The angel who has the fourth bowl flies to the sun. As he approaches the sun, he flies past the space debris that burst into flames as it approaches the heat of the sun. As he flies closer and closer, the temperature rises. He seems uncaring as he flies to the heart of this nuclear furnace. And why should he care? He is impervious to the heat.

Although the temperature is near 10,000 degrees, it does not affect him at all. He lands on the surface of the sun. It is like standing in the midst of an atomic explosion. Yet, so mighty is this angel that he might as well be standing on rock. He is unmoved by the constant nuclear explosions. With his golden hands, he takes out the golden bowl. He hesitates for just a moment and empties its precious contents, pouring it out upon the sun. This causes the sun's temperature to increase. This causes erratic temperature changes in the sun. The sun begins to scorch men with fire. Despite all these things men still will not repent. Many attribute these things to natural phenomenon. They will not give God the glory.

The angel who has the fifth bowl, pours it out upon the kingdom of the Beast. It causes a strange darkness to cover his kingdom. It not only puts his kingdom in total darkness, but it puts them in excruciating pain. Many of them gnaw their teeth for the pain.

The angel who has the sixth bowl goes to the Euphrates River and pours it out. It causes the river to dry up to prepare the way for the Kings of the East.

Chapter 22

From his headquarters in Jerusalem, the Beast hears some troubling news. Egypt attacks the kingdom of the Beast. The Beast is enraged. He launches a full scale assault. He attacks Egypt by land sea and air. He completely overruns the Egyptians. He conquers all of Egypt. He loots the country.

He then makes a move near the Libyan and Ethiopian borders. He considers conquering them as well when he hears some more troubling news. An Oriental invading force of 200,000,000 men invading from the East and an army from the North is attacking. The Beast returns to Israel with great fury to destroy these great armies. He means to exterminate those who have moved against him.

The Beast is preparing to institute his diabolical plan. He has gathered his armies and they are preparing to invade Israel. It is Satan's final desperate plan to exterminate every Jew and destroy the plans of God. If there is no Israel left, then Christ can't rule the earth from Israel. He will have defeated the ultimate plans of the Almighty. That is Satan's last hope. Satan feels that if he can defeat God's plans, then he can defeat God. If he can't defeat God's plans, then he certainly can't defeat God. Satan has anointed the Beast as he anointed Hitler. Invisible, unseen spirits like frogs, come out of the Beast's mouth. His words inspire friends, and infuriate his enemies. He has persuaded most of the people of the world, to meet him in battle, in the land of Israel. He assembles his massive army. Never in history, has the world seen such an invasion force.

The Death of New York: The Fall of Babylon

The sins of Babylon have reached into heaven. God has decided it is time to judge Babylon. The tensions between the kingdoms of the Beast and the U.S have continually escalated. The anti-Americanism of leaders of the Beast's kingdom hate the U.S. God has put it in their hearts to agree and give their power unto the Beast. The United

States has continually protested against the increasing belligerent actions of the revived Roman Empire. The U.S has threatened to take action against the Beast and his forces. The Roman Empire decides to initiate a pre-emptive nuclear strike. God has put it in their hearts to fulfill His will.

Finally, God the Father sends the angel forth with the seventh and final vial. Resolutely, he pours it out upon the earth. A voice from heaven shouts, "IT IS DONE."

The Beast and his allies decide not to risk U.S. intervention. With their remaining nuclear missiles, they attack the United States. One of their primary targets is New York City. Suddenly without warning, the city is bombarded with nuclear missiles. In one hour, the greatest city in the world is destroyed. The magnificent New York skyline, with its manmade mountains are destroyed.

Because of the massive amounts of nuclear detonation, the radiation levels will remain dangerously high for centuries. The radiation level of the city is so high that no one will ever live there again. No one will even take a stone from New York.

From out in the sea, the sailors mourn over the destruction of this great city. The stock market is gone. No more will men buy gold, silver, ivory, commodities, or men. When companies were bought, its men or workers were bought. Everything in the world was bought and sold in New York. The wealthiest, and most powerful men on the earth lived there. The world will mourn its loss.

The leaders of the U.S were not taken by complete surprise. They initiate a retaliatory strike against their enemies. If the U.S is to die, it will go in a blaze of glory. From SAC bases, submarines, ships, airplanes and military bases around the world, the U.S fires its remaining nuclear arsenal. Millions die from the blasts. As the thousands of nuclear bombs go off around the earth, they begin to de-stabilize the planet. Nature is disrupted as the earth begins to shudder like a drunken man.

All across the planet, huge electrical storms begin. Lightning flashes strike the earth. The earth begins to rumble. It is an earthquake. Walls of buildings seem to liquify, as they come together, then finally fall. All creatures, both great and small on the earth, are horrified at this new plague. The people panic, and run in terror. They are trying to escape, but there is no where to run. In vain, they try to maintain their footing. Solid earth is as unstable as jello. The earth shakes like a sheet, when one makes up their bed. This is not just any earthquake. It is not centered in any particular city, state, or country. There has never been an earthquake like this, since men have been on the earth. The whole world is shaking.

Every creature on the planet is terrified. Every few seconds seem like an hour. Many run for cover, but few find it. The whole world is screaming. Most of the earth's people expect to die. Others expect it to soon end, not believing it could get any worse. Yet, the earthquake intensifies.

This earthquake is off the Richter scales. The earth continues to shake violently. Roads are destroyed. Buildings are leveled around the globe. Islands collapse into the sea. Whole mountain ranges are laid flat. Millions are buried alive by this terrible earthquake. Some are literally scared to death, and they die of heart attacks. Jerusalem is divided into three parts by the earthquake. It seems that this earthquake will never cease. Almost everyone feels they are about to die. Everyone on the earth is in a panic. After what seems like an eternity, the earth stops rumbling.

This worldwide upheaval affects the weather as well. The wind begins to howl and great hail stones, some weighing as much as 60 pounds, strike the earth. Many more people are killed by the hail. Men begin to blaspheme God because of the hail and the other plagues. Despite all this, man still will not repent.

Isaiah 24:1 Behold, the LORD maketh the earth empty, and maketh it waste, and turneth it upside down, and scattereth abroad the inhabitants thereof.

{2} And it shall be, as with the people, so with the priest; as with the servant, so with his master; as with the maid, so with her mistress; as with the buyer, so with the seller; as with the lender, so with the borrower; as with the taker of usury, so with the giver of usury to him.

{3} The land shall be utterly emptied, and utterly spoiled: for the LORD hath spoken this word.

{4} The earth mourneth and fadeth away, the world languisheth and fadeth away, the haughty people of the earth do languish.

{5} The earth also is defiled under the inhabitants thereof; because they have transgressed the laws, changed the ordinance, broken the everlasting covenant.

{6} Therefore hath the curse devoured the earth, and they that dwell therein are desolate: therefore the inhabitants of the earth are burned, and few men left.

Somehow many of the worlds armies survive the holocaust. Many had hid in bomb proof bunkers. They arise from the rubble and each force rises to confront the other to gain control of the world. The armies of the world are being gathered in Armageddon.

The Russians from the North, and the army of the Kings of the East, have moved against the Beast. It is a desperate gamble. Each army moves in its bid for world domination. In their insane lust for power, they will destroy the earth, if unchecked.

The Lord has shaken the entire earth. The inhabitants of the earth are scattered. Billions have died since the Tribulation began. More than two-thirds of earth's population has been wiped out is just seven years. Still, men will not turn to God.

ARMAGEDDON

Like a cloud that covers the land, the armies of the Beast invade Israel. Many of them are riding horses. With so many roads destroyed from the earthquakes, the armies took every horse they could find. Earthquakes have also destroyed many oil refineries and gasoline is in short supply. This shortage of gasoline has forced a return to horseback as a means of transportation. The armies of the Beast are riding thousands of horses.

The Israelis put up a valiant fight, but they are hopelessly outnumbered. They know that they are fighting for their very existence. Satan has anointed the Beast, and like Hitler, he has spread his anti-Jew message. Some of the Arab soldiers think that this is the Jihad, the holy war. Satan has deceived them into believing that it is the will of God to destroy every last Jew. They are trying to carry out the will of the devil.

The casualties mount. The Israeli Army is being wiped out. Israelis are dying by the thousands. Men, women, boys and girls are all being wiped out by the armies of the Beast. Blood flows in the streets of Israel like a river. The Beast leaves a portion of his force in and about Jerusalem to carry out the extermination of the Jews. He takes the bulk of his army with him to meet the invading armies who are approaching Armageddon.

The invading force continually marches until they get to the valley of Armageddon. Now the Russians and the Oriental Army meet in Armageddon. This great valley is 150 miles long. The armies of the world are gathered here for the final battle. It is a high stakes battle, winner takes all. Each of the armies try to kill every last Jew. It is Satan's plan to kill every last Jew.

The armies of the Beast plan to continue their extermination of the Jews. Now only 1/3 of the Jewish race is left. They will not surrender. Their cry is Masada will not fall again. They went peaceably into Hitler's concentration camps and paid the price for it. If God does not help them, they are determined to die fighting. A portion of the invading forces reaches Jerusalem. They divide the holy city. They slaughter the Israelis. Many of the women are being raped by the evil soldiers. With their army defeated and all hope is gone they begin to pray. Satan laughs with an evil glee. The Beast feels the world is in his grasp. Millions of light years away, the cry of Israel has reached the ears of God. God decides,

IT IS TIME

To put an end to sin and wrong.

IT IS TIME

To end all pain and suffering.

IT IS TIME

FOR NO MORE TIME.

IT IS TIME

FOR THE SECOND COMING OF CHRIST!

Christ prepares for His return. He has on His special white robe that has been dipped in blood. On His head is a magnificent crown, consisting of many tiers of crowns on top. When He mounts His horse, those nearby see that on His thigh is written the same words that are on His robe; KING OF KINGS AND LORD OF LORDS. The saints of the ages are dressed in white robes, and mounted on special white horses. They have been redeemed out of every nation, kindred, and tongue. They mount up, and follow Christ as He prepares to leave heaven. The angels watch with great joy as their fellow servants prepare to follow Christ to the earth. Finally the prayers of all the saints of the ages are being answered. The time has finally come to bring peace on earth.

There is tremendous joy in heaven as everyone prepares to leave. They are all mounted up and ready to leave heaven. Christ rears His horse back and says, "IT IS TIME," and He and His horse take off. The horse starts running on air. Christ leads the way, and the other saints start after Him. Their horses run through the air as if they are running on some invisible road.

God, the Father, is preparing to see them off. He stands at the edge of heaven, and tears open a whole in space. Like He parted the Red Sea, He parts the sky. Everyone on earth looks up at the strange happenings in the sky. The sun, moon, and stars, have all disappeared! It looks neither night nor day. Fear grips everyone on the planet as they wonder what will happen next.

Suddenly, it happens. A great light begins to shine in space. The people of earth look up in the direction of this bright light coming from heaven. It is a hole in space and light is coming out of it. The people of earth watch in awe, and terror. They see the source of the light. They see a rider on a white horse. He is called Faithful and True. Only in righteousness and judgement does He make war. He has a title which He alone can understand. He is called the Word of God.

From a million miles in space, the space warp has opened. Even though Christ is a great distance away, He has grown huge enough so people of earth will see him. He is so gigantic that the people of earth see His fiery red eyes and the look of anger upon His face. A great dread passes over all of them and the people of the earth wail because of Him. He is thousands of miles tall and on His head are many crowns. It is Jesus, the Son of God, riding on a white horse and He seems to be coming with great clouds.

As they approach earth, the people see that they are not clouds at all. They begin to realize they are the troops of heaven clothed in white and riding on white horses. From His mouth comes a sharp sword, with which He can smite the nations. For He shall rule the nations with a rod of iron. It is a magnificent sight to behold Jesus and the saints of God riding through space on their way to earth. Abraham, Isaac, Jacob, Moses, Elijah, and all the other prophets are among them. So too are the disciples, and all the saints throughout time. They bless God and think how unworthy they are to receive such blessings. They are traveling through space on white horses, traveling at near light speed. They ride past the moon, on their way to earth.

Jesus gradually decreases His size as He approaches earth. The saints of the ages are in great joy, appreciating the magnificent view along the way. King David is among them. He remembers when he prophesied, the heavens declare the glory of God and the firmament shows His handiwork. Until today, he never knew how true that statement was. He praises God to be so blessed to be one of the chosen few. Some of the saints riding on the horses smile and look at each other, as they ride to redeem the earth. It is such a glorious sight, these saints of God riding on white horses, wearing their white robes and glowing with the glory of God.

Because Jesus said, "As the lightning comes in the East and shines unto the West, so shall the coming of the Son of man be," He must circle the horizon. As He and His stream of heavenly soldiers approach the earth, they circle the globe so every eye shall see them. In Israel it is day, in America it is night. However, God has covered the world with a strange darkness and gloominess that it looks neither day nor night, it is the Day of the LORD.

Finally, Jesus and the saints arrive outside Jerusalem, riding their white horses in the air. Jesus stops above the Mount of Olives. In mid air, He gets off of His horse and floats down to the mountain. He is the conquering Messiah, returning to earth in great victory. When He lands on the Mount of Olives, He opens His mouth and lets out a roar of triumph. It is the most powerful roar to ever be heard by human ears. The people of earth grab their ears at the deafening roar of the Son of God. Jesus roars so loudly that the very heaven and earth rumbles at the deafening vibration of the voice of the Son of God.

As soon as He lands on the Mount of Olives, He stomps His feet and there is a great earthquake. The earth begins to rumble as the mountain splits in four parts, toward the North, South, East and West.

The mountain range that goes from the Mount of Olives to the valley of Meggido is split in two. It forms a new valley 70 miles long. Jesus rides His horse down in the valley on His way to meet the armies of the Beast and save Israel. The saints of God land behind Him, riding their horses to defeat the armies of the Beast.

When the remaining one-third of Israel see their Messiah, whom they have pierced, they rejoice. God gives everyone of them, even the feeble, and the women, and the children great strength. They fight and begin to overpower their enemies. Most of the Israelis who are left run into the new valley that Christ has created.

Some of the saints of God march forward to save the Jews that are hopelessly outnumbered. This army of saints begins to march forward against the soldiers who are occupying Jerusalem and the surrounding areas. They march straight forward and do not break their ranks. The occupying soldiers begin to fire upon them, but they cannot be killed. Bullets, mortar fire, flame throwers are like the buzzing of a gnat to them.

The occupying soldiers of the Beast are horrified. Nothing they can do, will stop the advance of this irrepressible army. The army of the Lord begins to run to destroy the occupying army of the Beast. The immortal soldiers begin to run with unbelievable speed toward their attackers. Their speed and agility is incredible.

They cannot be injured, much less killed. Some of the soldiers of the Beast run and try to hide in homes and in buildings. The immortals run up walls and climb through the windows like thieves. They exterminate the occupying army of the Beast. However, the Beast and most of his forces are in the valley of Armageddon.

Suddenly, the strange shadow that had covered the sun disappears, and the light of the sun momentarily returns. When people see the light of the sun return, they immediately look up. Now something else blocks the light of the sun. It is a gigantic angel standing in the light of the sun. This angel was once the Prophet Ezekiel. God commands him to prophesy to all the birds on the earth.

He cries with a loud voice to every bird on the planet, "Come and gather yourselves together. It is the supper of the great God. It is time for you to eat the flesh of kings, and the flesh of captains, and the flesh of mighty men, and the flesh of horses, and of them that sit on them, and the flesh of all men, both free and bond, both small and great." The sky begins to grow dark with hundreds of millions of birds. They have come at the command of God, to eat the armies of the Beast.

Zechariah 12:3   And in that day will I make Jerusalem a burdensome stone for all people: all that burden themselves with it shall be cut in pieces, though all the people of the earth be gathered together against it.

The Beast and his armies are enraged along with all the armies in Armageddon. As Jesus and the saints of God come thundering down this valley on their white horses, the Beast and his armies mobilize to meet them. The Oriental Army of 200,000,000 and the forces allied with the Russian Army join forces with the Beast to try to destroy the King of Kings. The armies of Armageddon are like the sand of the sea, numbering hundreds of millions. Both of these armies number in the millions. They charge to try to defeat the King of Kings and Lord of Lords.

Closer and closer these two armies get to each other. Because there are hundreds of millions of soldiers and horses, the very earth rumbles underneath their feet. The howling hordes of hell come charging against the host of heaven. Never has anyone seen the like. As these two armies approach each other, the armies of the Beast are determined to take as many with them as possible. They don't know they will never get the chance.

Suddenly, two angels fly up and grab the Beast and the false prophet. God opens up the ground and they are thrown alive into the lake of fire. God smites every rider and horse with confusion. The armies of the Beast are so disoriented, they begin to fight each other.

While they are fighting, Jesus approaches and He opens His mouth. It looks like a beam of light comes out of His mouth. It is thin and wide like a sword. It cuts like a sword. It reaches out as far as the eye can see. It slices through men, horses, and machines as if they were made of paper. It cuts a path through the army of the Beast, like a sickle cuts through wheat. Even those in tanks are not safe.

When some of the soldiers see the sword cutting a path through the column of soldiers, they begin to dive for cover behind the nearest tank. Like a searchlight, the sword swings toward the first tank. They expect to be safe hiding behind the second tank. The sword hits the first tank right under the gun turret. It is immediately sheared off, and flies spinning through the air. When the soldiers see the turret flying toward them, they scream and try to escape. It falls on the soldiers and crushes them to death.

The sword continues sweeping through the armies of the Beast. When this sword hits other tanks, the beam cuts and burst them apart. The tanks burst easily as if they were children's toys hit by a sledge hammer. The army of the Beast begins to flee like frightened children, but there is no escape. Blood begins to fill the valley of Armageddon.

Jesus continues to slay the remnant of the army of the Beast. Not a one of them escapes. Thousands of soldiers are slain in a heartbeat. Some are cut in half, sheared by the irresistible sword that comes out of the Lord's mouth. Because tens of thousands of soldiers are slain in seconds, the blood has no time to soak in the ground. It is like a flash flood. The blood has risen up to the horses bridle. Jesus slays the rest of the soldiers. None of them escape. Armageddon, the greatest and bloodiest battle in history, is over.

Everyone stops and views this grisly sight. The valley is full of blood and dead bodies. The only movement is from the birds picking the dead flesh off the bodies of the soldiers and their horses. The battlefield is silent except for the squawking of birds. Never has anyone seen so many birds in one place. There are birds as far as the eye can see. It is a macabre sight, watching these birds eat the flesh of once mighty men. The birds are here under the command of God. The birds are feasting, eating the remains of the armies of the Beast.

While Jesus and the host of heaven were saving Israel, the angels were busy with their job. If they were not successful, perhaps all that had been done would have been in vain. The day that men had longed for, the Millennium, has come to pass. The day when peace, finally comes to the earth.

The fallen angels, the devils, have been captured. For centuries, trillions of them roamed the earth, doing their evil work. They have tempted men and helped lead them down the path of destruction. Now every single one of the evil spirits has been captured. The angels have circled the globe and caught every demon and chained them up. The great Dragon, that old serpent himself is caught and chained by an angel. They are all thrown into the bottomless pit. Satan and the other demon spirits will remain there for at least a thousand years.

Jesus turns and leaves the battlefield. As He and His army leave the scene, the birds can still be heard for some distance as they finish eating the remains of the armies.　All those that have taken the mark of the Beast in the palm of their hands, or in their foreheads have been captured and killed.　Their souls are already burning in hell.　They are in torment, and the smoke of their torment ascends up to sky forever and ever.　Because they joined the forces of the Beast and denied God, they are forever doomed.　The immensity of God's love, goodness, and blessings is balanced by His wrath and damnation.　While the evildoers are experiencing judgement, the surviving faithful, are ready to experience His glory and favor.

Chapter 23

The Peace of Jerusalem

by Keith Gino Barr

Oh what joy, to see this day,
When all life's troubles are done away.
Love and joy, are brought to the fore,
When evil, cruelty, and suffering are no more.

Peace and brotherhood, now abound,
For Satan and his minions, have been cast down.
Oh how blessed, to see this day,
When the Peace of Jerusalem comes this way,

Triumphantly He marches, up Mt. Moriah,
For now they know, He's the conquering Messiah,
With open arms, comes Israel's bands
In shock they view, the marks in His hands

But all is forgiven, and at last they know
It was Jesus' blood, that washes white as snow
Now begins the peace, of a thousand years,
When the Lord of Hosts, wipes away all tears

So rejoice ye angels, and everyone,
To earth, has come Jesus, Mary's son
He's the son, and Lord of David, the only begotten One
His kingdom has come, and at long last, His will is done!

Triumphal Entry II

Jesus, the Messiah, the Anointed One, triumphantly, returns to the Holy City. The Eastern Gate, once known as the Golden Gate, has been sealed ever since 1542 A.D. Sultan Suleiman, the Magnificent, sealed this double-arched gate. For more than 500 years, it has been sealed waiting for Christ's return. He rides His horse up the hill up to the Eastern Gate. During Jesus' time, the Golden Gate was the principal entrance from the East. Ezekiel prophesied (Ezek. 44) the wall would be sealed and would remain sealed until the Messiah returns. No man has entered the gate since its enclosure as Ezekiel prophesied.

They that are in the Holy City, see the glory of God of Israel, shinning from the East. His voice is like the sound of many waters. It is a sound unlike anything in the universe. It is refreshing. The sound of His voice is compelling and soothing. It is powerful, irresistible, and melodic. Listening to it is similar to relaxing on a beach, listening to the waves role in. It is all these things and more. As water gives life to thirsty travelers, His voice quenches the thirst in human souls. His voice soothes the mind, body and the soul. This flood of living waters makes you wish you could hear His voice forever.

As Jesus walks up to the Golden Gate, the glory of God fills the earth. The stone wall of the gate begins to crack as a great light shines through. Within seconds the sealed wall dissolves and Jesus triumphantly enters Jerusalem through the Golden Gate. The glory of God radiates from Jesus and fills the temple.

Slowly the Israelis come out of their hiding places. Jesus walks toward them. For many of them it is almost too good to be true. Their Messiah has finally come. Some of the Israelis are afraid, having seen the power of the Messiah. Slowly, reverently, they approach Him. As they approach Him, He opens His hands. There are strange wounds in His hand. Some of them ask, "What are these?"

They have said exactly what the prophet Zechariah prophesied they would (Zech. 13:6). Jesus answers them as Zechariah prophesied. He smiles to them with that special smile of His and says, "This is when I was wounded in the house of My friends."

Now begins the Millennial Reign of Christ. He begins His thousand year rule on earth. All the saints that have come with Him will rule and reign with Him for a thousand years.

Isaiah 2:2-4   And it shall come to pass in the last days, that the mountain of the Lord's house shall be established in the top of the mountains, and shall be exalted above the hills; and all nations shall flow unto it.

{3} And many people shall go and say, Come ye, and let us go up to the mountain of the LORD, to the house of the God

of Jacob; and He will teach us of His ways, and we will walk in His paths: for out of Zion shall go forth the law, and the word of the LORD from Jerusalem.

{4} And He shall judge among the nations, and shall rebuke many people: and they shall beat their swords into plowshares, and their spears into pruninghooks: nation shall not lift up sword against nation, neither shall they learn war any more.

The nations of the world have become the kingdoms of Christ. His kingdom has come, His will is done on earth, as it is in heaven. The lion lays down with the lamb. It is written upon the bells of the horses, holiness unto the LORD. The nations of the world are commanded to come to Jerusalem and worship the Messiah on the Feast of Tabernacles. The Lord instructs the nations if they do not come, there will be no rain in that nation for a year until they come and worship at the next Feast of Tabernacles. This is the plague that He shall smite the nations that do not come to worship.

There is no war. The lion eats grass like an ox. The children who are born during this time are blessed. If a man dies at the age of an hundred, men will say he died prematurely. They will say he was a sinner and was cut off. The wolf and the lamb shall feed together. The Middle East, a seething cauldron of hatred for centuries has become a fountain of love that spreads around the world. There is peace on earth, at last.

After the thousand years are up, God lets Satan out of the bottomless pit. Satan immediately goes to deceive the nations once more. Many of the nations of the earth embrace Satan. They desire to be free from the iron rod of Jesus. They wish to go back to their sinful ways. He goes to gather together the remnants of Gog and Magog, whose number is as the sand of the sea. They come to Jerusalem to make war with the saints. God, the Father, is so angry that He sends fire down from heaven and burns them up.

Judgement Day

God, the Father, has had enough. He decides it is time. He comes on His great white throne to the earth. The invisible God is now visible. He comes in all His glory. He is so large that He dwarfs the planets. He radiates so much power that every celestial body is driven away from Him. From His face, the heaven and earth flee. He enters into our solar system and He draws the planets to Him. He comes to earth and everyone knows that it is the great day.

It is the day that men have dreaded for millennia; the day when the secrets of hearts are made manifest; the day when every secret thing is revealed. It is Judgement Day.

Jesus prepares to shout. It is literally a scream powerful enough to wake up the dead. The dead live again. All that are in their graves get out of their graves. The sea gives its dead. Some have been dead for centuries and no physical trace of their body remains. Some are in hell or Geena. Hell releases them, and God restores their bodies. All that have ever lived, are resurrected. They are all whisked away to the throne of God.

The dead, the small, and the great stand before God. Every man, woman, boy, and girl who has ever lived is there. Kennedy, Hitler, Stalin, Napoleon, Abraham Lincoln, Julius Caesar, Nimrod are all there. You and I will be there. Everyone who has ever lived is there. All the people who have lived throughout time, have been resurrected and are gathered before God's Great White throne. All of earth's masses are like a sea of ants, before the throne of the Almighty. It is time for the judgement to begin.

The Father, Son and Holy Ghost are there, as well as the holy Angels. The Son has prevailed and overcome the world. He has faithfully endured. He submitted Himself to His Father's will and joyfully went to the cross and became obedient unto death. He has shown the universe the blessedness of meekness. He has shown all men and angels the blessedness of submitting themselves to God, for God is a good and just God.

The Father oversees the judging. He will judge no man, but has committed the judgement of men to the Son. Why? Perhaps because the Son was human and He experienced temptation, He is better suited to judge. The Father never was human flesh. The Son became flesh to become mediator between man and God. The Father had Him to become flesh to better understand man and the trials and temptations that they face. Therefore God has committed all judgement to the Son. He, the judge of all the earth, will reward according to their works.

It is time for all to acknowledge the sacrifice of the Messiah. All who have lived are assembled before the throne of the Almighty. Now comes the most awesome moment in history, as all the living stand before God and prepare to bow before the Trinity and confess that Jesus Christ is Lord, to the Glory of God the Father.

The books are opened and the dead are judged out of those things that are written in the books. They must all give an account of every idle word, every deed, and every motive. After the record of each person is read, God, the Father, asks the angel who has the Book of Life, "Does their name appear in the Book of Life?" If their name does not appear in the Book of Life, they are cast into the lake of fire.

Finally, the last person is judged. Satan has been defeated. He is cast into the lake of fire. He has proven himself to be the greatest fool in history, for he dared to rebel against God. All that see him can hardly believe their eyes.

God has humbled him so, people look at him and shake their head and say, "Is this the man that did weaken the nations, that made the world as an wilderness? Is this the man that opened not the house of his prisoners, and made the earth to tremble? Now he is brought down to hell, to the sides of the pit."

God takes hell itself, and death also, and casts them into the lake of fire.

It is time for the former things to pass away. God, the Father, puts His protective power around the saints of God. God is preparing the end of the universe. The heaven and earth will pass away. Jesus, whose power held all solid matter together, causes the binding force of the atom to release.

When this happens, all solid matter dissolves. A gigantic nuclear explosion that fills every corner of the universe begins. The saints of God and the angels beside them are all in awe of this tremendous display of God's power. This display is more impressive than any fireworks display that man could ever conceive. The Apostle Peter, one of the millions watching remembers when he foretold this under the inspiration of the Holy Spirit. The Lord told him, but he had no idea that it would be like this.

As the earth dissolves, there is a great noise and extreme heat. The earth becomes a huge fireball and ceases to exist. Aside from those who are with God and those in the lake of fire, not one particle exist in all the cosmos. Everything is silent as God begins the creation of the new heaven and the new earth.

The New Heaven and The New Earth

Revelation 21:1   And I saw a new heaven and a new earth: for the first heaven and the first earth were passed away; and there was no more sea.

God creates a new universe. It is a heaven that never was touched by the hand of Satan. A new earth free of spiritual and environmental pollution of man and Satan. There will be no remembrance of the former things. This earth is more beautiful than the first. Although there are many beautiful lakes, bountiful rivers, and refreshing streams, there are no more seas or oceans. Everyone is so happy. The saints can hardly wait to come to the new earth. God transports the saints to the new earth. As they begin to look around the new earth, they see a light coming from heaven. They look up and see a gleaming object coming like a bride to the earth. It is New Jerusalem.

The saints are breathless, as they behold this gleaming city. This city is so massive that it is bigger than most of the previous world's nations. It is surrounded by four walls that seem to be made of a material similar to jasper. The walls are 1,500 miles long. Each of the four walls are 1,500 miles, forming a perfect square.

As the city continues to descend, the people see that the walls are 1500 miles high, reaching into space. That is 7 million, 920 thousand feet. A commercial airplane by comparison only flies at 40,000 feet or 7.5 miles. Some of our low orbit satellites today only fly at an orbit of 100 miles. Yet the walls of New Jerusalem reach 1,500 miles above the earth. The walls are 216 feet thick. The streets are made of gold, so pure that it is near transparent.

The city has 12 massive gates, three on each of the four sides of the wall. Each of the gates is named after each of the twelve tribes of Israel. There is an angel stationed at each of the twelve gates. The name of each gate is written over the gate. The gate itself is made of one solid pearl. The wall was made of jasper, while the city itself was made of pure gold, clear and transparent like glass.

As the city descends, the people can see that the wall of the city has twelve foundation stones. The foundations is named after each of the twelve apostles of the Lamb. Each foundation of the city is ornamented with all the precious stones. The first foundation is jasper, and it is green colored. The second is sapphire, which is deep blue. The third is chalcedony or white agate, and is a grayish, milky white in color. The fourth foundation is the color green for it is made of emerald.

The fifth is onyx, the sixth sardius or ruby, is red. The seventh foundation is made of silica, magnesium, and iron, called chrysolite. It is green in color. The eighth foundation is marine green for it is made of beryl. The ninth foundation is topaz which is yellow in color. The tenth foundation is chrysoprase, which is apple-green in color. The eleventh foundation is jacinth, which is reddish-orange in color. The twelfth and final foundation is amethyst which is purple or violet in color.

It is more beautiful than the mind can imagine. This magnificent city roughly the same size as the 48 continuous states of the U.S. When you consider the height of the city, it is much larger. It is large enough to house all the saints of the ages. It was designed and built ' by the greatest architect and builder of all.

As the saints slowly and reverently approach the city, they see that this is no dream, but the city is real. New Jerusalem dwarfs the size and wealth of anything man could ever create. Its splendor and opulence demonstrates the blessings of God. It is a city that befits Him and those who have endured and have their name in the book of life. Whereas man could only pave his streets with asphalt, God paves His with gold as pure and translucent as glass.

There is no temple or church in the city, for the Lord God and the Lamb are its temple. The city has no need of the sun or moon, for the splendor and radiance of God illuminates it, and the Lamb is its lamp. There will be no night there and the gates of the city shall never be closed.

In the middle of city is the throne of God the Father. The Father sits on His throne. The people of earth can freely see Him. The invisible God is now visible. He is not flesh, but spirit. He is not the color of any human flesh. His colors are red as a ruby, and green as jasper. Perhaps the red represents His fiery power and the green for the color of life. About His head, is a rainbow of emerald green (

Rev 4:3). Next to it, is the throne of the Lamb. His servants are there, and they shall serve Him. They have His name on their foreheads.

Flowing from the throne is the river of God, whose waters give life. It sparkles like crystal and it flows through the middle of the broadway of the city. On either side of the river is the tree of life, with its twelve manner of fruits. It blooms each month and the leaves of the tree are for the healing and restoration of the nations. The leaves are packaged and sent around the world. The are the most efficient medicine ever created.

Although it is not possible for anyone to die, it is possible for someone to be injured. If someone is injured, all they need to do is eat the leaves from the tree of life. The leaves of the tree gives the body the ability to instantly heal from any injury. No matter what the damage to their bodies, they are restored. There is no death, and there shall be no more curse.

God restores the water vapor barrier over the earth. It keeps the earth at an even temperature of about 70 degrees. The vapor barrier radiates the light from New Jerusalem to all over the world. There is no night there, but perpetual day. We will never sleep. I know that this may be hard for you to comprehend.

Presently, we spend an average of a third of our lives asleep. It is one of our greatest needs. No one has ever lived more than a week without sleep. The need for sleep, is even greater than our need for food. Because of the curse of death that lurks within our bodies, we must sleep. Have you ever been so excited and full of energy that you could not sleep? This is how it will be in the hereafter. We have an eternity to live our lives to the fullest.

Seven thousand years of striving are over. God's plan has been completed. He has shown that no angel, man, or fallen spirit can prevail against Him. Not all the powers in existence, nor all the minds in the creation can hope to prevail against Him. Through the sacrifice of His Son, He has shown His love for the universe. The Son has shown the blessedness of meekness. By submitting to God, the Son has shown all of creation the blessedness of obedience to God.

What Satan sought to gain through pride, vanity, deceitfulness, corruption, hatred and destruction, the Son received it through humbleness, truth, holiness, peace, and love. Even though He had a free will, He exercised it to serve His Father, as we all should do. He is an example for all of existence, wherefore, God has highly exalted Him and given Him a name that is above every other name. He rules the earth with His FATHER and His servants.

The servants of God shall reign over the earth forever and ever. The meek have inherited the earth. The meek are not the cowardly and fearful, but those who are submitted to God in love. Righteousness has prevailed. The days of evil are over. There is nothing but peace and contentment, and ultimate fulfillment. The people of God have found their *rest* at last.

I wish that there were words I could use to describe how wonderful it will truly be, when this time finally comes. Pain, sickness, evilness, and death will all be things of the past. There will be rest for God and His people. I try to imagine how wonderful this will be and what it will be like. But, I know that this is beyond the range and limits of even my imagination.

But as it is written, Eye hath not seen, nor ear heard, neither have entered into the heart of man, the things which God hath prepared for them that love him.

I Corinthians 2:9

Will You Be There?

The number of people who will have eternal life is a great number. Yet, it is a small portion of those who have lived on the earth. A wise man once said, "Don't put off for tomorrow, what you can do today." If you have not received the Lord's sacrifice, as your Lord and Savior, do so now, before it is too late.

Only one life to live,
It will soon be past,
Only what is done,
For Christ will last

If you wish to make heaven your home and receive Jesus as your Lord and Savior, all you have to do is pray this simple prayer in sincerity and God will save you. You probably have felt His Spirit as you were reading this book. If you don't know Him, you can receive Him right now. He's ready to come into your heart. You can pray this prayer, and the miraculous will happen; you can be born again.

Heavenly Father, I come to You right now in the Name of Jesus, asking for Your forgiveness.

Lord, I am sorry for sinning against You. I know that I am a sinner, and I am sorry for my sins. Please forgive me right now. I give myself to You. Take everything out of me that is not like You. Touch my heart, my mind and my soul. Save me right now.

I surrender my life to You. I open up the door of my heart. Jesus come into my heart and make me a new creature in you. Lord give me wisdom and understanding. Teach me your ways. I thank you for it in advance right now. I ask this in Jesus' name, Amen.

If you prayed this prayer in sincerity, you can rejoice for God has saved you. Jesus promised it.

John 6:37 All that the Father giveth me shall come to me; and him that cometh to me I will in no wise cast out.

If you do not belong to a church or a fellowship of Bible believing Christians, join one. Pray and read your Bible everyday, and if I don't meet you down here, I hope to meet you on the *other side*.

May God bless you and keep you, may His face shine upon you, and I pray the God of Peace, sanctify you wholly, that on that glorious day you may be found without spot or wrinkle, blameless before God, and receive eternal life. Amen.

Ecclesiastes 12:13   Let us hear the conclusion of the whole matter: Fear God, and keep his commandments: for this is the whole duty of man.

Select Bibliography

The Amplified Bible. Grand Rapids, Mi: Zondervan Bible Publishers, 1985

Archer, Gleason. *Encyclopedia of Bible Difficulties*. Grand Rapids,Mi: Zondervan Publishing House, 1982

Barfield, Kenny. *Why the Bible Is Number 1*, Grand Rapids, MI: Baker Book House, 1988

Barr, Keith. *Would God Leave A Record.* Pontiac, MI: Voice of Revival Publications, 1989

Brand, Paul & Philip Yancey. *Fearfully & Wonderfully Made.* Grand Rapids, MI: Zondervan Publishing House, 1987.

The Complete Works of Josephus by Flavius Joshephus. Translated into English by William Whiston Grand Rapids: Kregel Publications, 1981

Durant, Will. *The Age of Faith*. New York: Simon and Schuster, 1950

Hislop, Alexander. *The Two Babylons*. Neptune, New Jersey: Loizeaux Brothers, 1959

Hoekema, Anthony. *The Bible and the Future*. Grand Rapids, MI: Wm. B. Eerdmans Publishing Co, 1979

Huse, Scott M. *The Collapse of Evolution*. Grand Rapids, MI:Baker Book House, 1987.

Jeffrey, Grant. *Armageddon, Appointment with Destiny.* New York: Bantam Books, 1988

The Koran. Translated into English by N.J. Dawood. London: Penguin Books, 1974

Lindsey, Hal. *The Late Great Planet Earth*. Grand Rapids, MI: Zondervan Publishing House, 1977

_____. *Countdown to Armageddon*. New York: Bantam Books, 1982

Morris, Henry M. *The Genesis Record*. Grand Rapids, MI: Baker Book House, 1987.

_____. *The Long War Against God*. Grand Rapids, MI: Baker Book House, 1989.

_____. *The Remarkable Birth Of Planet Earth*. Minneapolis: Bethany House Publishers, 1978.

_____. *The Remarkable Book Of Job*. Grand Rapids, MI: Baker Book House, 1988.

324

_____. *Scientific Creationism*. El Cajon,CA: Master Books,
    1987

_____. *Science And The Bible*. Chicago: Moody Press, 1986

_____. *What Is Creation Science?*. El Cajon, CA: Master
    Books, 1987

McDowell, Josh. *Evidence That Demands A Verdict*. San
    Bernardino,CA: Here's Life Publishers, 1988.

Pentecost, J. Dwight. *Things to Come*. Grand Rapids:
    Zondervan Publishing House, 1964

Rosenthal, Marvin. *The Pre-Wrath Rapture of the Church*.
    Nashville: Thomas Nelson Publishers, 1990

Shorrosh, Anis. *Islam Revealed*. Nashville: Thomas Nelson Publishers,
    1988

Sunderland, Luther D. *Darwin's Enigma*. El Cajon, CA:
    Master Books, 1984

Taylor, Charles. *World War III and the Destiny of America*. Nashville:
    Scepter Books, 1979

Taylor, Paul S. *The Great Dinosaur Mystery And The Bible*,
    El Cajon, CA: Master Books, 1987

Tenney, Merril. *New Testament Times*. Grand Rapids, Mi: William
    B. Eerdmans Publishing Co., 1975

Torrey, R.A. *What the Bible Teaches*. Cambridge, Great Britain:
    University Press, 1986

Vos, Howard. *Beginnings in Church History*. Chicago:
    Moody Press, 1977

Walvoord, John. *The Revelation of Jesus Christ*. Chicago: Moody
    Press, 1966

Whitecomb, John & Morris, Henry. *The Genesis Flood*. Grand
    Rapids, MI: Baker Book House, 1987

Speaking Engagements
or
Teaching Seminars

Rev. Barr is available for seminars, revivals or other speaking engagements throughout the year for churches conferences and colleges.

Subjects included are Prophecy, Apologetics, Creation vs. Evolution and General Bible Teaching.

Please Contact:

Keith Barr Ministries
P.O. Box 431022
Pontiac, MI 48343

Keith G. Barr

Keith G. Barr has preached and taught Bible Prophecy for 18 years. This noted pastor, evangelist and author has preached in churches, auditoriums and college campuses across the country. His Voice of Revival radio broadcast has reached millions across the U.S. and Canada and in over 35 countries.

Get these other books by Keith Barr

Unless You Live Holy,
How To Be Renewed,
How To Be Free From Lust,
Would God Leave A Record,
Baptism Of Power,